Praise for *Our Trespasses*

Our Trespasses is a powerful and provocative witness that compels white congregations and denominational communities to think deeply and confessionally about our past while also summoning us to commit to a much different kind of future. How have our theological language and ministry practices allowed us to participate in and even benefit from urban renewal projects that have decimated Black neighborhoods and congregations? How have we been blind to our neighbors and the systems and structures that hold them in bondage? How can we now use our words, our witness, and our properties to repair the devastations of many generations while also seeking a future that is just? Just as *Our Trespasses* confronts us with haunted urban landscapes around us, it also offers the kind of challenge to be expected as the Holy Spirit convicts, reproves, and summons us to a life worthy of the gospel.

—Paul Baxley, executive coordinator,
Cooperative Baptist Fellowship

Because Greg Jarrell *stands somewhere* (in the physical place of Charlotte, North Carolina), practices *deep neighboring* (tending to joys and sorrows through screen doors and on back porches), and navigates his life by a *theological compass* (mapping to biblical narratives that provide a robust understanding of our place in history), he reads his city's urban social architecture spiritually—demanding both transformative justice and unstrained mercy.

While many have lauded and critiqued urban renewal movements in the US, few have looked deeply into its impact on Southern cities. Fewer still have unpacked the role white Protestant Christianity has played as a driver in city planning, with inevitable race-based schisms. As James Baldwin said in 1963, "Urban renewal means Negro removal."

Jarrell's engaging storytelling, fresh historical research, and commitment to preserving the dignity of all the characters (living and dead) draw readers deep into questions about where we live, who lives around us, and what ghosts of "communities past" are just beyond our sightline.

Jarrell reveals where the religious perspectives of the characters expand or contract in this recovery of the religious history of urban renewal, with a particular focus on white churches in Charlotte. Additionally, he offers fresh scriptural interpretation on Jesus' landowner parables and into the healing encounters that engage spirits that silence and bind. This is a necessary read for city planners, church leaders, real estate developers, social historians, community organizers, and those who believe the Bible speaks urgently to our present condition.

—Rose Marie Berger, senior editor,
Sojourners magazine

Our Trespasses uses a fascinating story about one family, one piece of land, and one church to get us to think about housing inequalities in the US. What if we could point to the people and institutions who are responsible? Would we be brave enough to hold them accountable? Would they be courageous enough to hold themselves accountable? The book is sociological in its conception, historical in its details, and theological in its profoundness. And most impressively, it is deeply personally reflective. To use the words of Charles Mills, Greg Jarrell is a white renegade and a race traitor who has thought a great deal about resisting and refusing the racial contract. *Our Trespasses* is a one-of-a-kind book, an enlightening read.

—Joseph C. Ewoodzie, Vann Associate
Professor of Racial Justice, Department of
Sociology, Davidson College

Urban Renewal—the massive 1960s program of displacement and demolition in US cities—provokes the agonized question "What were they thinking?" By focusing on the actions of churches and their members, this thoughtful book documents the workings of power, both economic and cultural. Greg Jarrell has crafted a "people story" that illuminates the humanity behind public policy decisions.

—Thomas W. Hanchett, historian and
author of *Sorting Out the New South City:
Race, Class, and Urban Development in Charlotte, 1875–1975*

In 1963 Dr. King wrote that it was "necessary to X-ray our history and reveal the full extent of the disease" of racism. Greg Jarrell's brilliant study does just that, demonstrating the revelatory power of rereading the past and present of one's place through lenses of haunted land, race and class genealogies, and traditions of resilience. Having been apprenticed for two decades to one Charlotte neighborhood, Jarrell exhumes stories of struggle against structural racism and poverty entombed beneath parking lots and sanctuaries. He follows white and Black families (and churches) "like ghosts" through epochs of betrayal: from Reconstruction to "Urban Renewal" to contemporary gentrification. The narrative particularities of this book are deeply engaging, laced with (literally) penetrating and achingly honest vignettes of place, people, and spirits. Yet the strategies of development, displacement, and disparity it traces were reproduced in every major American city over the last century, including where I grew up a continent away. I cannot commend more highly the challenging sociological and biblical reflections herein, which take urban theology deeper and offer a personal and political map for how white churches might yet turn to a vocation of penance and restorative justice.

—Ched Myers, coauthor of *Healing Haunted Histories:*
A Settler Discipleship of Decolonization

By doggedly pursuing the history of Charlotte, North Carolina, and particularly the complicity of white churches in its urban renewal, Greg Jarrell makes a striking case for churches in other places to likewise explore the local histories of the people and institutions that have been bulldozed by the racially and economically oppressive forces of such renewal. *Our Trespasses* poignantly reminds us that the histories of our places matter in the formation of who we are and what we hope to become as churches. By wrestling with these painful histories of his place, Jarrell offers a fresh vision for cultivating Christian communities that are attentive to the gospel of healing and liberation that Jesus embodied.

—C. Christopher Smith, senior editor, *The Englewood Review*
of Books, and author of multiple books including
How the Body of Christ Talks: Recovering the
Practice of Conversation in the Church

Our Trespasses

OUR
TRESPASSES

WHITE CHURCHES AND THE TAKING
OF AMERICAN NEIGHBORHOODS

GREG JARRELL

FOREWORD BY
CHANEQUA WALKER-BARNES

FORTRESS PRESS
MINNEAPOLIS

Library of Congress Control Number: 2023942282 (print)

Cover design: Kristin Miller
Cover image: Bulldozer Pushes Over First House In Renewal Area, 1970; and
Charlotte, North Carolina Vector Map, stock photo by lasagnaforone/Getty Images

Print ISBN: 978-1-5064-9492-0
eBook ISBN: 978-1-5064-9493-7

For Helms, John Tyson, and Zeb

All that can save you now is your confrontation with your own history . . .
which is not your past, but your present.

—James Baldwin

The loudest noise in the world is silence.

—Thelonious Monk

Contents

	Acknowledgments	xi
	Foreword	xv
1.	They	1
2.	The Cornerstone	17
3.	The Gleaners	31
4.	Two New Pastors	51
5.	Making Moves	69
6.	Reluctant Destruction	85
7.	Two Visions inside Whiteness	103
8.	Caught Up in a Vision	127
9.	"Churches Can Profit from Urban Renewal"	143
10.	"Our Debts"	155
11.	"The Innocence That Constitutes the Crime"	173
12.	The Ghosts of Christians Present	193
	Appendix	209
	Notes	211
	Bibliography	255
	Index of Subjects and Names	265

Acknowledgments

I first sketched out the idea for a project on white churches and Urban Renewal in 2018, though it had been forming in me well before that. I approached a brilliant Charlotte-based historian about my idea, and his response set me on my way: "This is your project to do. We need this work, and you are the one to do it." He was right. I am situated in such a way personally and professionally that no one else could have done this in the same way. But I did not do any of this work alone. Writing is a communal activity, even though much of it is done in solitude. I worked in a broad community that supported and challenged me and that deserves almost all the credit for this project and whatever fruit it bears.

Charlotte has a small but vibrant community of historians who assisted me from the beginning of the research until the very end of my writing. Tom Hanchett consistently shared research and carefully read drafts and sent insightful comments. Mike Moore is a researcher and storyteller of nearly magical capabilities who took on some of the research as his own and offered helpful comments at every turn. Pamela Grundy was a regular encouragement and provided helpful comments and background along the way. Will Griffin encouraged and offered connections when they were needed. They are all committed to helping Charlotte tell some new stories where the old ones will not suffice, and I am grateful for them.

Where the historians helped me see what happened, it was Ched Myers and Elaine Enns who helped me understand why it happened and how it is still happening. Their work through Bartimaeus Cooperative Ministries and their book *Healing Haunted Histories* provided the interpretive framework for this story, and their influence is woven across every page. I read their work, listened to their podcasts, sourced from their bibliographies, attended their Kayla McClurg Writing Residency, called and texted and emailed them, and spent a recent Thanksgiving in their home with my family. Ched and Elaine have been mentors and friends for quite a while now, and I am grateful beyond what I can express.

Archivists and librarians are quiet heroes. I'm especially grateful to Adreonna Bennett and Dawn Schmitz of the Atkins Library at UNC-Charlotte, Taffey Hall and her staff at the Southern Baptist Historical Library and Archives, the staff at the Rubenstein Rare Book and Manuscript Library at Duke University, Shelia Bumgarner at the Charlotte Mecklenburg Library, Brandon Lunsford at Johnson C. Smith University, and the staff at the North Carolina Baptist Collection at Reynolds Library at Wake Forest University.

Numerous churches provided archival access and resources along the way, including First Baptist Church-West, Friendship Missionary Baptist, Clinton Chapel AME Zion, Myers Park Baptist, Covenant Presbyterian, First Presbyterian, St. John's Baptist, First United Methodist, and Dilworth Methodist. I am grateful to those bodies, their volunteer archivists and historians, and my clergy colleagues. I especially want to offer my thanks to Andrea Betaudier and Brenda Porter-Dewitt at Friendship Baptist.

Several institutions offered support of the work through retreats and residencies. Those groups and their facilitators provided invaluable support, especially in the form of time. They include Louisville Institute, Collegeville Institute (with Jonathan Wilson-Hartgrove and Chanequa Walker-Barnes), Catapult (with Taylor Plimpton), and the Guthrie Scholars program through the Center for Lifelong Learning at Columbia Theological Seminary.

Many friends and colleagues critiqued portions of the work, allowed opportunities to present it in various forums, and assisted with research, including Jemma Suwa, Rodney Sadler, Tim Moore, Gale Kinney, Michael Graff, John Cleghorn, Bill Rogers, Bill Leonard, Lucy Crain, Bob Stillerman, Kelly Roberts, Mike Sellers, Gail Henderson-Belsito, Gerardo Marti, Claude Forehan, Sheldon Shipman, and Tara Dudley. Chanequa Walker-Barnes was generous with her time and expertise in workshops and in conversations in both Atlanta and Charlotte. She offered an incredible foreword for which I am immensely grateful.

The descendants of Brooklyn and other Black Charlotte neighborhoods trusted me with stories. I have done my best to be faithful to them. I want to mention Reynard Wright and Richard Campbell in particular. Both deeply shaped my imagination and understanding. Both died while I was producing the work. May their memory seed the revolution. Tiffany North, Regina North, and Brandi North Williams have offered me hospitality and unusual openness. Their family is a gift to the world. Sandra Caldwell-Williams, Janet Garner-Mullins, and Helen Kirk were inspiring in our time together.

I am grateful to the people of First Baptist Church who offered me time and space and memories, especially former pastor Robert Welch. Without his openness and kindness to me, this project would not have been possible. The team at the Uptown Farmers' Market was also generous in making this work possible, including Jan Johnson, Marvette Monroe, and Gloria Medlock. It is unclear, as I wrap the writing portion of this project, how the work with First Baptist Church proceeds. I am sure it remains incomplete.

Four key friends and colleagues shaped me, and along with me the work, over the course of years of conversation and clarification: Dawn Anthony, Ben Boswell, Piko Ewoodzie, and Brandon Wrencher. They read draft after draft, listened to me talk endlessly about this work, and pushed me to do it deeper at every step. They are some of the best friends I could hope for.

Laura Gifford of Fortress Press has had a deft hand in shaping this text. She saw the potential of this project when a bunch of others had turned it down. Laura has been instrumental in bringing it to completion. I am grateful to be part of Fortress and the work they do in the world.

Lastly, I am grateful to my wife, Helms, who has been an unyielding critic, a patient encourager, and a companion along the way. We've pushed each other toward radical discipleship since 1997. There's more to do and no one better to do it with. Perhaps our most important work is raising John Tyson and Zeb, who are already fierce followers of The Way, in a way that makes sure the silencing spirit does not pass to another generation. It is to Helms, JT, and Z that I dedicate this work.

Charlotte, North Carolina
May 2023

Foreword

This is not just a North Carolina story, even though it was in eastern North Carolina where I remember meeting Greg Jarrell for the first time in 2019. We were at another important site of the state's racial history, the Franklinton Center at Bricks, a former "breaking plantation" where incalcitrant enslaved people were sent to be tortured into submission, later reclaimed by African Americans as a school and now operating as a retreat center and social justice incubator. We were there for the writing retreat that I facilitated together with our mutual friend, Jonathan Wilson-Hartgrove. It was there that Greg shared the story that he had uncovered in Charlotte, how he was tracing the destruction of a Black community through the story of a Black family, the Norths, and the White church, First Baptist Charlotte, that now occupies their historic home.

Reader, it turns out that this is a false memory. Greg has reminded me that we met the next year, via Zoom, when the pandemic forced us to move the retreat online. I know that this is correct now, but there is part of me that refuses to accept it. Maybe it's because I have been waiting with bated breath for this book's publication, often mentioning this work to my students as an exemplar of church-based racial justice work. But my memory still insists that Greg and I were walking around the Franklinton Center, the former site of racial terror that has been reclaimed and redeemed by the descendants of enslaved people, when I told him, "The world needs this book. This is not just a story about Charlotte."

The story of the displacement of Black communities is not unique, not even within North Carolina. The same urban renewal that destroyed Charlotte's Brooklyn community also gutted Hayti, the Durham community once monikered "Black Wall Street," because, as one lifelong Black Durhamite once told me, "Duke [University] wanted a highway." Throughout the United States, White institutional, political, and economic desires have often been met via the destruction of communities built by decades of Black labor and love: Charlottesville's Vinegar Hall, Detroit's Paradise Valley, Minneapolis's Rondo, Tulsa's Greenwood, San Francisco's Western Addition, and so on.[1] The problem is so pervasive that the University of Richmond has developed a digital mapping site to track the impact of these displacements.[2] So this is not just a North Carolina story. It is not even a unique story. But Greg's telling of the story is.

Greg is a careful researcher who puts names and vivid detail to the abstraction we think of as "urban renewal." This is impeccable historical research, the type of church history that needs to be taught in seminaries and congregations. Greg shows us that the work of church historians should not be limited to the timeline between the patristic era and the Reformation. These more proximate historical moments shape the life and theology of the church as much as the ancient councils did.

But what really stands out about *Our Trespasses* is the way that Greg weaves his research together via compassionate storytelling and theological insight. First, he manages to avoid the tragic, and unfortunately all-too common, error that White Christians make when writing about racial issues: centering the stories of White people at the expense of Black people. He does not erase the North family or use them as a convenient object lesson to demonstrate the folly of White political, business, and religious leaders. Instead, he tells the North family story across generations, showing us how racism continues to impact descendants of American chattel slavery, Jim Crow, and urban renewal. And in doing so, he points to the deeper, more complex work that is required for White Christians to truly be antiracist.

The great failure of White Christianity is that it has never reckoned with how it was co-opted by White supremacy and Western imperialism. From Pope Nicholas V's issuance of the Doctrine of Discovery in the fifteenth century, European and US Christians have used religion to justify racial and religious terror, including land theft, genocide, slavery, and apartheid. Greg's narrative of Charlotte's urban renewal project demonstrates that conquest remains the sensibility shaping the White Christian imagination. His careful documentation of the church membership and involvement of the figures in Charlotte's Redevelopment Commission shows us that urban renewal—and its modern counterpart, gentrification—is not just a political and economic phenomenon; it is fundamentally a theological one. Civic and religious leaders in Charlotte utilized the Exodus narrative to justify conquest as God's action, obliterating the traces of the human hands that orchestrated it. Racism so thoroughly shaped how they saw the world that even their perception of God's answers to their prayers was filtered through it. They could not see the beauty and vitality of the families, businesses, and churches that made up the Brooklyn community. They did not care about the economic impact of the loss of homes and businesses, or the emotional impact of the loss of social ties. Their architectural imagination was thoroughly racialized.

It is especially striking that these were not rabid segregationists or even a group of highly conservative congregations. It was an ecumenical effort spearheaded by White Christians who would identify as moderate or even liberal. Ironically, it was their supposed commitment to being a downtown church, and not being sequestered in the suburbs, that led First Baptist to take advantage of the displacement of the Black Brooklyn community. Perhaps it was the fact that even in the 1960s, they had already mastered the new, color-blind racism, talking about racial issues without overtly mentioning race.[3] Or maybe it was that, as my seminary professor and the former president of the Methodist Church of Southern Africa Peter Storey said about White churches in apartheid South Africa, they had learned to let institutions do their sinning for them. They did not have to think about the pain that they were complicit in.

Greg offers an invitation to remember, not just the idea of an abstract Black neighborhood that once existed, but the specific lives of Black families who continue to struggle economically because of the cascading impact of urban renewal. It is an invitation for White Christians, in and beyond Charlotte, to transcend the fear of confronting their pasts, to move beyond silence, and to remember.

White Christians like to speak of reconciliation when it comes to racism, but there can be no reconciliation without truth-telling, even when it is hard, especially when it is hard. Reconciliation is an eschatological journey, but it begins here and now, with one step toward repair. And then another, and another. There are no easy solutions here, and I'm grateful that Greg doesn't pretend to offer any. What he does offer is an example of how to remember.

And somewhere in the memory, there is hope. It is tempting to look at the sin of urban renewal and to throw our hands up in despair, thinking that the sin is too big and the wound too deep to repair. But the story of the Brooklyn community shows us the power of Whiteness to literally move an entire neighborhood. If that can be done in the name of injustice, surely it could be done in the name of justice. As Greg states,

The theological architecture of decades past still stands today. Repairing what can be repaired, and demolishing the rest, presents the greatest and the most daunting work for white churches who wish to enact justice, which is to say, to disavow their whiteness in the pursuit of repair. Only by breaking the silence to tell stories on ourselves, and by identifying the persistent theologies that prop up those stories, can white churches conjure differently and live into a future healed from the hauntings in which we live.

White churches, you do not have to choose the silence. This is your clarion call. It is time to put up or shut up, to move beyond the pretense of racial innocence and feigned helplessness. How will you respond?

Chanequa Walker-Barnes, PhD

CHAPTER ONE

They

Reynard Wright and I are standing in the back parking lot of First Baptist Church of Charlotte, or, as he used to call it, home. His street was Watkins Lane,[1] an alley packed tight with residences from Alexander Street to McDowell. From our resting point, we must imagine everything: houses, streets, yards, churches, people. All of it vanished. The neighborhood is gone. Rey's old yard is now part of a reflecting pool.

Sixty years ago, the city government inundated the area with sledgehammers and bulldozers and after that with water and unchecked ambition. They built a new city hall and a courthouse and a jail and a park with a pond and no people. The city ran off a dozen churches, four of them Baptist. They held an auction with a predestined winner—First Baptist Church, now conjoined across empty sidewalks with the structures of local power. Rey remembers the vibrance of the area. I have only his memories to go on.

Rey and I were in the parking lot of First Baptist Church together after we'd been leading one of our series of tours centered on the development of neighborhoods in Charlotte. "How did our city come to be the way it is?" we asked. Rey—Black, early seventies—would talk in great detail about what the neighborhood was like years ago. My job—I'm white, in my early forties—was to narrate the policy context sweeping across the hundred years from Reconstruction to Urban Renewal that shaped American cities into what they are today. I had memorized the dates and names of far-off decisions as a complement to Rey's intimate memories of the place where we were walking. We talked about disappeared neighborhoods and how they ceased to be. Those stories, we thought, tell us a lot about the cities we live in now, defined as they are by affordable housing crises, hardened segregation, and manifold entrenched social issues. The stories of yesterday describe the cities we have today.

Rey and I made a good team. I would zoom out into a wide-angle shot. Rey would zoom in and capture just the right detail. After doing these tours numerous times, we developed a good rapport. We could select just the right narratives to animate the place.[2]

But we still had gaps. People would raise questions we could not answer. We would notice things that were missing that we could not account for. We would also see things that were present, but we did not know how they got there. The largest of those presences was First Baptist Church, a white congregation now in the center of the place that was central to Black life in Charlotte for many decades. Standing in the First Baptist parking lot with Rey, it was clear to me that there was a story to tell and that I needed to dig below the surface to find it. I could not shake the feeling that its importance extended far beyond the confines of any one church and into the political and theological entanglements that have made the United States. But no one I could locate knew the story in any detail. It was hidden from public view.

Rey's neighborhood was called Brooklyn. It was the chief cultural and economic center of Black life in a fast-growing city that fancied itself part of the "New South." Residents of Brooklyn set out to build what they needed on their own. They lacked the same access to money and resources that the white districts around them had, and yet they persevered in building a vibrant home for themselves. They saw in their neighborhood the promise of a great urban area, and so they named it after the New York town that was one great city next to another.[3]

Many people thrived in Charlotte's Brooklyn. Neighbors there squeezed every ounce of goodness possible from the materials available. And yet their lives were circumscribed by the limitations that white institutions imposed on Black ones. There were hundreds of businesses and associations and well over one thousand families but few landowners. By 1960, fewer than 10 percent of residences were owner-occupied, making the neighborhood susceptible to slumlords who made large profits at the expense of tenants.[4] Like other Black neighborhoods in the city, Brooklyn lacked the same public investments that white neighborhoods received for basic amenities like sidewalks and paved streets, schools and flood-control measures.[5] Yet it was also filled with immense creativity and determination. There were businesspeople who met the needs of neighbors, social reformers, and doctors and lawyers. Alongside them were working-class people who labored long hours to provide for their families, and hustlers whose daily bread depended on their creativity, and desperately poor people for whom consistent employment was a challenge. Brooklyn was a complex village, a city within a city that was at once both self-reliant and deeply interconnected.

A neighborhood like Brooklyn created space for growing culture, for growing businesses, for growing families. Within the friendly blocks there, neighbors maintained a certain order, a way of structuring life that made for the best possible scenario for Black people within the iron frame of the Jim Crow South.

"We had everything we needed right down the street," Rey says, stretching his hands southward from the corner of Second and Davidson. "There was one big grocer but lots of smaller ones as well. There were tailors and barbers and restaurants. On Fridays, everybody fried fish. You could walk up and down the sidewalk and smell salt and grease from every house you passed."

He remembers other smells, especially from the laundromat. "The largest laundry facility in the state employed people from all over the neighborhood, all over the city, really, and when it was running—which was almost all the time—you could smell the clean clothes for several blocks. It was just a block down from here. You know, where the expressway is now."

I see you are not there.[6]

"During the summer, the churches took turns having Vacation Bible School so that we would have a place to go and get out of the house. Dozens of us kids would show up at one church for a week, and then the following week we would go on to the next church. You could do that for basically the whole summer. That's probably how our parents managed to get by."

Charlotte's Brooklyn was a living, breathing example of Black brilliance and resilience in the heat of the Jim Crow South. It was bakers and mechanics and undertakers and musicians, holidays and funeral processions and struggle and triumph. Rey says, "This is what it was like: The preachers lived here, as did architects, and businessmen, and lots of domestic workers, and railroad men, and day laborers. I went to school at Second Ward School. I walked over every morning. My teacher lived just down the block from me and spoke to my mother regularly, so I had to stay on the straight and narrow. Which I didn't."

"It was a real community, and the way you could tell it was this: not many folks had telephones, but if you acted ugly out in the street, your mama would know before you got home, even though there was no phone to call her and tell what you had done."

Each time I hear Rey, he raises a new image. He walks between two worlds, the one of his childhood just as close as the one of today. He speaks, and I can see gray air in winter from the coal-burning fireplaces or visualize workers tromping through muddy, unpaved streets after spring rains.

I can imagine the crowds outside the Savoy Theater on McDowell Street, thrumming with energy as they wait to get into a live show. Little Richard is in town maybe, and the young people are lined up hours early to get in. The fellows without dates are looking around to see who they might ask to dance. An older man with a snack cart stops by a group of young women to hawk cold drinks and popcorn. Word on the street is that the star of the evening is already nearby, getting his famous hair touched up at Ivy Campbell's salon over in First Ward. The rumor flames down the sidewalk and sends a jolt of excitement through the fans as it does. It gets confirmed when Ivy's son Richard comes strutting down the street with a whole twenty-dollar bill in hand, telling them he had just seen Little Richard, who always treated little Richard extra special since they shared a name.[7]

Rey conjures a memory of the trombone and percussion bands that came parading during the annual convocation of the United House of Prayer for All People. The streets would flood with onlookers as the national bishop returned to the church on McDowell Street, the Main Street of Black Charlotte. "Daddy Grace," he was called, and people showed up from all over to hear him preach. Days of parades, nights of revival services. All of it took place around the House of Prayer, a Black church group that owned all of their spaces outright. They had never once taken on a cent of debt.

When we get to one key part of Rey's life—when he went off to Vietnam to fight in a war for a country that never really loved him back—he says that the bulldozers had already started knocking down houses. "You would go to school in the morning," he says, "and when you came home, your house was a pile of rubble. They just came in and took everything."

They.

Unnamed. Mysterious. Violent. All-powerful. Able to make neighborhoods disappear. Never accountable, always hidden, someone else's names on the paperwork. Ever-present but beyond words.

They: demigods, the masters of the universe, the men behind the curtain, too big to fail. *They* look from up high, stories above, the world at their controls.

But *they* are hard to identify. *They* are surrounded by silence that conceals, obscures, shrouds, masks, covers. *They* aren't talking. *They* may not even know who they are.

In a story of the New Testament, Jesus and three of his friends have been atop a mountain, where Jesus is transfigured from ordinary human form into dazzling brightness. The spirits of two ancestors, Elijah and Moses, join him. It is a moment of miraculous clarity. But as Jesus and his friends leave and rejoin their group, they walk into a scene of confusion. The rest of Jesus's friends, the disciples, are arguing with religious leaders over an attempt to heal a boy possessed by a spirit.[8]

The spirit silences the boy. When he tries to talk, the spirit casts him down onto the ground. It thrashes him around. He foams at the mouth. The spirit throws him into fire or tosses him into water.

The boy's father is desperate. "Help us!" he cries, for the silencing spirit does not only destroy the boy; it holds its grip over everyone around him. It moves across generations. The things the boy would say, the spirit wants unknown, wants to drown in the churning sea. The silencing spirit aims to quiet the boy not only now but always. It removes the boy from his community, a loss for both the boy and those around him. "Help *us*," the father cries, making the scene political. At stake is the health not only of one person but also of an entire community.[9] Of a neighborhood, you might say.

Jesus, confronted with the scene of confusion, exorcizes the spirit but not before it nearly kills the boy. Indeed, the child is like a corpse. He is assumed dead, lost to the silence. It appears for a moment that breaking the silence results in death. Only when Jesus lifts him by the hand is the healing complete. Though the story does not mention it, we assume the boy is now ready to speak.

The Gospel does not say what happened to the silencing spirit after Jesus sent it out. Specters do not die nor remain in the spirit world. The silences that follow children and families and communities are revenants, always coming again. "There are always more ghosts to return."[10] Hauntings persist. The silencing specter moves elsewhere. It returns from someone else's future, from another block or neighborhood.

The story I am telling you is a haunted story.

It is haunted by those who were forcibly silenced, whose names and legacies were written out of most—but not all—of the record. It is also haunted by those who kept silent, who would not speak, those for whom power or prestige or opportunism or misplaced faith rendered them unable to act in defense of justice.

As Reynard narrates the story of his childhood home, he tries to name the presences that came in and took it away, but the words escape. Some force, some system of power, has excluded him from its full telling. *They* kept themselves silent. At the same time, he speaks of the place he remembers from sixty years prior. He sees into the invisible rupture and begins speaking in the present tense. For the rest of us, there is a quavering. We see that the specters of the place remain invisible. We intuit that they are real, even as they elude us. We want to know how to speak of them, but no one has taught us. None of our people knows how.[11]

In our walks, Rey and I are telling stories of "exclusions and invisibilities," as sociologist Avery Gordon has written.[12] Ghost stories. Walking the blocks of Second Ward with Rey, I know I am failing to see what is not there. Some lingering remains, something animating this haunted space, a space where the land still does not have rest.[13] I do not speak of ghosts in the Hollywood sense of escapism, of idle entertainment while avoiding the political and theological confrontations that shape the world. Rather, "to write ghost stories implies that ghosts are real, that is to say, that they produce material effects."[14] The hauntings of Brooklyn—those of the silent and of the silenced—have had material and spiritual effects that continue to influence the geography of the city and the descendants of the people on every side of its story. This work will examine how those institutions who hold a stake in the physical, economic, and spiritual present and future of the place might "conjure differently."[15]

To conjure differently. A ghost collapses time. What was past keeps returning from the future. With a haunting, *the time is out of joint.*[16] The thing that the haunting demands to be done might make possible—though not inevitable—a reckoning with the history that created the haunting.[17] Perhaps a confrontation with lingering silences will alter the future from which the specter returns. "Ghosts hate new things," Zora Neale Hurston said. Short of a detailed accounting of the past that describes our present, the future is phantasmagoria.

The spirits who seize tongues, who throw into the fire those who might speak another future, challenge us for the specificity of names and places and details. They demand working with words to tell stories that have been concealed. Without the words, the possession holds. Conjuring differently requires reckoning with the trespasses of the past and naming how those trespasses exist, unseen but nevertheless real, in the present. Only then can a community speak something new to the ghosts that haunt it.

What I want to know, what I have pursued for years, is an answer to the question Reynard left open: who are *They*? What were their names? I want to know where they lived and where they worshipped. I want to understand the stories they told themselves that kept them comfortable amid a landscape of destruction. How did they teach one another to be silent? And how does the silence still operate in them? In me?

DRIVING A BULLDOZER, WEARING A SUIT

The public program that displaced Rey and more than one thousand families from Brooklyn was called Urban Renewal. Beginning in 1949, cities around the country could apply for federal funding to pay two-thirds of the cost of clearing land deemed to be "slums." The powerful people in US cities who wielded the force of government had learned to see territory occupied by nonwhite people, and to some extent by poor white people, as hopelessly decrepit. The result of Urban Renewal projects was the displacement of families, businesses, and institutions without regard for the displaced, without consideration of the political and economic conditions that had created areas of neglect, and without plans to prevent those conditions from recurring.[18]

There is a photograph, well known in Charlotte, that crystallizes Urban Renewal at one key moment (see figure 1.1).[19] In it, a man sits on a bulldozer. He is wearing a suit. He is ceremonially driving the bucket of the dozer into a house. The post supporting the corner of the house buckles under the weight of the machine. A dozen compound fractures form where the house's frame bursts through the siding that had protected its family from storms.

The picture only captures the man's profile. The viewer must reconstruct the look on his face. There may be a hint of a smile, the feeling that comes from having immense power under your fingertips. Perhaps it is not a smile but a grimace of worry as the building begins to give and the dust cloud behind him begins to widen. Maybe there is nothing, just a man doing his job.

Figure 1.1. Redevelopment Commission chair Raymond E. King assists in the first destruction of a home in Charlotte's Greenville neighborhood Urban Renewal project. Originally printed in "Greenville Renewal Begins," *Charlotte News*, July 22, 1970. Used by permission of *Charlotte Observer*.

A photograph is an artifact that raises the possibility of a haunting through the way it remains recognizable and yet distant. The house in the photo had an address, but the viewer knows that to locate the address and walk to it in the present day—were that even possible—could never reconstitute the same scene. The landscape is different now. At the same time, the machinery is familiar, as is the shape of the house, and the man in the suit, and the cloud of dust. From their own places, nearly everyone has known the reality of this photo—some in the operator's chair, others just outside the frame observing.[20] "When photographs appear in contexts of hauntings, they become part of the contest between familiarity and strangeness, between hurting and healing, that the ghost is registering," Avery Gordon says.[21] A photograph alters the boundaries of linear time. It is not only evidence of what happened; it also creates a collision of what is past and what is present, what is personal and what is systemic. The photograph describes the future that is always arriving until we resolve the hauntings.

The picture of the man on the bulldozer implies all kinds of sounds, but the photograph itself is silent.[22] Often its public presentation is as well, a display of immense power without the words that might destabilize that power. One set of words that might provoke: the story of the man in the suit.

His name is Raymond E. King Jr., chairman of the Charlotte Redevelopment Commission. He was the county's most important Democratic operative, a man of enough national importance to be invited to the White House for talks on civil rights by the Kennedy administration and the Democratic National Committee.[23] A good liberal, plowing down houses. King was a deacon at Charlotte's Trinity Presbyterian Church and a popular Sunday School teacher there. The photograph was taken on a Tuesday, two days after King's last Sunday School lesson, five days prior to his next one. A faithful Christian, working in silence.

Many people are excluded from the photo. Perhaps they are just beyond the border of the shot. Maybe the family who belonged to that house is looking on. The photo is an invitation to watch, but it has cropped out those who cannot bear to look. Many of them had questions, surely, about what was happening and why and why then. The photograph leaves those questions open in perpetuity. The house does not look empty or at least not like it had to be emptied. The disrepair seems to have arrived at the same time as the bulldozer, seems to have been imagined by some officials, seems to have been determined unresolvable just before the photographer opened the aperture.

The boundaries of the photograph are arbitrary. The picture leaves space to wonder what happened in the moments before this most unwanted visitor arrived. Reynard Wright remembers that the officials and work crews would come "like a thief in the night." The weighty trauma and the heavy machinery showed up quickly, at once. Perhaps the official plans were documented on a form in a municipal office, but the knowledge of them did not make it to the block. The night prior, one imagines, a family sat on that porch with a pitcher of tea. The children petted the dog and swatted mosquitoes. Mom and Dad's faces were wet with tears, their bodies weak with resignation. A social worker may have come by to give them a new address. The constraints of an empire that had never been concerned with their flourishing surrounded them. The picture captures none of that. It tells the story as though all of the real action were inside the frame, as though the solitary bulldozer operator was the only character to know.

There is the ceremony, and the picture, and the flattening, and that evening Ray King in his suit probably sat on his back porch, a pitcher of tea nearby. "How was your day, honey?" his wife would have asked as she patted the dust off the back of his tailored jacket.

Did he know? Could he imagine the babies who had been weaned on that porch or the family that fried fish in that kitchen? Could he hear in his mind the lonesome chants of hymn choirs echoing out the doors of the church on the corner, or did the rumble of progress drown it all out? Did he, lying in his bed later, hesitate to sleep?

Did he imagine the wound he had made or only the thrill of sitting at the controls to make it?

Who taught him to feel nothing, to imagine nothing, to say nothing, and when he felt, to ignore it, to keep running the big bucket into one cornerstone after another? Who taught him? What were their names? What might break their silences?

PRESENT IN ABSENCE

When Rey and I were leading tours, I stayed busy studying policies and dates from the big picture—the federal agencies that created redlining practices, the New Deal acts with racism baked in, key figures and data from a place that was physically lost. A smaller voice was calling and would not hold back: *what was here is present in its absence.* I was looking in books about the past, but something was happening in the present that wanted to invite me into a new story. I was experiencing a haunting, one "form by which something lost, or barely visible, or seemingly not there to our well-trained eyes, makes itself known or apparent to us."[24]

When the ghost grabbed me, it wanted me first to see one particular parking lot. Reynard kept telling us about the liveliness of the neighborhood, but I saw four acres of pavement that filled up a certain block. Rey invited us to see that the pavement was a slab sealing a vault. It was maintained to keep stories in the ground, stories that might fly out of control if they were to become visible. Stories with names attached. I could learn those names, I thought. Surely some other people already knew them. I could find those people and hear their stories.

The parking lot belonged—and still belongs—to an institution that had not yet become a part of any public accounting of the story of Brooklyn: First Baptist Church. I knew the congregation from a distance. Some of my extended family attended for several decades. My grandmother long admired a former pastor there. When I decided to go into ministry myself, she seemed to hope I would become like him. I grew up in a Baptist church with denominational affiliations with FBC Charlotte. The FBC pastor at the time of our Urban Renewal tours was delving into a career in state politics. He made sure to keep his name in the local paper, the result of which was not so much fame as infamy.[25] None of those connections made much sense of how a big white church wound up occupying a historic Black neighborhood.

The First Baptist building is unusual. It suggests the architectural movement called brutalism. Like many buildings of that movement, it fails to approach the street despite its urban context. It lacks visual cues for how to enter and engage with the space. There are huge volumes of cold white brick at odd and uninviting angles. Driveways and parking are the central pieces of the physical layout. It has a suburban design in the middle of one of the fastest-growing cities in the country. The building does not belong in a cityscape, but its unbelonging is situated in such a way that allows it to go unnoticed rather than to stick out. It was built in the 1970s, just following the time that the City of Charlotte was razing Brooklyn and displacing Reynard and his family. What the haunting was suggesting to me was that the time for not noticing had long been over.

I knew from some historian friends that I could learn the names of some of the people who formerly inhabited the parking lot. I could also learn about the ones who had planned and executed their destruction. With the guidance of those historians, I went to the archives to find answers. Words. Stories. The tools to break the silencing spirit. Among the first records I found was an annual report from the city's Redevelopment Commission, dated 1969, that contained some surprising information (see figure 1.2). The last page had a picture and a brief biographical sketch of each of the five commissioners. The bios noted name, profession, and education and alongside those, church membership.

It was no surprise that powerful people in official positions were also Christians. In the American South, some version of Christianity has been placed on nearly every cause, just or unjust, from the time the first European settlers arrived here. And yet the fact that every official bio included church membership, from across a range of denominational groups, was a significant clue. Urban Renewal had a political theology and a theological politics that informed both the public and the private processes and results. Even the program's name had theological echoes: renewal, revival, regeneration, resurrection, restoration, rebirth. All are common terms in Sunday School rooms and sanctuaries.

With a casual understanding of US history, it is easy enough to guess the contours of the political theology of the 1960s. Guesswork maintains distance, though. It is specificity that might incite and stir up something in the present. The wide-angle shot provides a veneer of innocence for white people, a way of distancing ourselves from the past, of lamenting someone else's misfortune without ever reckoning with how we might still be accumulating wealth off an ill-gotten inheritance. The details—even the details of someone else's

Figure 1.2. From the Charlotte Redevelopment Commission's annual report, 1969. Obtained from Special Collections and University Archives, J. Murrey Atkins Library, University of North Carolina at Charlotte.

story—might pierce the façade of innocence and help us see how we still operate in similar ways when we read the Bible and organize missionary activity and establish public policy and develop—and redevelop—neighborhoods. The details complicate and implicate and force a confrontation with how we live in this story and how it lives in us. The specifics send us running for help to chase the silencing spirit.

The most important detail for me, on the biographical page of that report, was the presence of W. J. Smith Jr., executive vice president of First Union National Bank and member of First Baptist Church, on the Redevelopment Commission. I did not yet know enough to draw any conclusions about his membership on the commission, but the convergence of political and religious power was plain.

Our Trespasses documents my research over several years into the religious history of Urban Renewal, with a particular focus on white churches in Charlotte. I've spent hundreds of hours in archive collections and done dozens of interviews. Along the way, many people in whom the stories of Brooklyn still live, some of them descendants of those people whose houses were replaced with a sanctuary and a huge parking lot, trusted me with memories and dreams and griefs. Many current and former First Baptist members freely offered their time, knowing that we were headed into uncertain territory. As we progressed, the stories raised specters none of us could control. The stories that refuse to be controlled are the ones that might set us free. That is, fundamentally, the Christian story, that even a heavy stone sealing a tomb cannot lock in life snuffed out by empire. There is still something after the bulldozer, after death by administrative terror. Spirits haunt and terrorize. They raise confrontations. They might also comfort and heal and shock us into new ways of being. But never prematurely. And never without the details. And yet, though the Christian story is finally one of fall and redemption, of shortcomings met with grace, white churches, in particular, continue to live in fear of confronting their own pasts. We've chosen the silence.

The silencing spirit, Jesus says in that story from the Gospel according to Mark, can be exorcised for the one who believes. "Help my unbelief!" the boy's father cries. To hold fast to silence is to refuse belief—a strange contradiction for Christian people. In the immaterial realm, we confess to belief. In examining the material consequences of our confessions, we cling to unbelief. Hauntings clarify that distinctions between the immaterial and the material, among the political and the theological and the economic, are necessarily false, are always strategies for holding on to the thing the haunting is calling us to renounce.

What happened in Charlotte maps well onto what happened around the country, and continues to happen, in changing forms that lead to the same results. The minutiae differ from place to place and time to time. It is the work of readers, historians, theologians, church members, activists, and people of goodwill to learn the details of their own places. *Our Trespasses* will introduce some people and circumstances unique to Charlotte who stand in splendidly for how white churches and people racialized as white across the country engaged with Urban Renewal. Their legacy still lives with us. The hauntings that those churches and their members created persist, and they leave us work to be done.

I will write about myself near the end of this work. I am implicated in the political theology built into this story, though I was not alive when these events took place. Yesterday's displacement by Urban Renewal is today's displacement by gentrification. The details are different, but the story arc is the same. I have a complicated place in the current story. I'll do my best to unpack it, with the knowledge that there are always more ghosts than any of us can acknowledge. I cannot see them all. But with what I know and what I can see, I am offering an exegesis of my city's streets and of the culture and the nation where those streets exist.

In the 1950s and '60s, governments, institutions, and individuals at the federal, state, and local levels were embroiled in the struggle for civil rights, or the Southern Freedom Movement, a series of events that would finally grant legal rights for equality to Black communities. At the very same time, public agencies and the individuals who ran them were taking, by force, the land and neighborhoods that helped give material meaning to the rights won during the Southern Freedom Movement. The policy decisions and expenditures that made these contemporaneous moves possible, one cutting the legs out from under the other, were not just public policy decisions.[26] They were also theological decisions made by church members, decisions worked out in city council chambers and church business meetings, choices shrouded in the pseudo-theological term *renewal* and that expressed the theological understandings of those Christians, their congregations, and their denominations. The theological architecture of decades past still stands today. Repairing what can be repaired, and demolishing the rest, presents the greatest and the most daunting work for white churches who wish to enact justice, which is to say, to disavow their whiteness in the pursuit of repair. Only by breaking the silence to tell stories about ourselves, and by identifying the persistent theologies that encourage our silences, can we conjure differently and live into a future healed from the hauntings in which we live.

One important story from Charlotte's past traces the institutional and familial entanglements of two men and their families into the larger context of urban life in the South. It is the story of Abram North and Samuel Smith.

CHAPTER TWO

The Cornerstone

In late 1860, Reverend Milton Kennedy made some big life changes. Kennedy was a fast-advancing Methodist preacher. His first charge, in 1854, was in Walterboro, South Carolina, fifty miles west of Charleston, near some of the state's largest rice plantations.[1] Within a couple of years, he had an enviable pulpit in Charleston, South Carolina.[2] Not long into that pastorate, though, he became engaged to Mary Ledbetter, a daughter of the wealthiest family in Anson County, North Carolina, near the town of Wadesboro.[3] Following their marriage in December 1860, Kennedy was appointed in January 1861 to the Charlotte station of the Methodist Church, fifty miles west of Wadesboro. Kennedy had spent his young career in low-country South Carolina. Charlotte, a small city still of only minor importance, likely seemed like a demotion for him.

The South Carolina Methodist Conference meeting had other business in January 1861 besides the appointment of preachers to their various charges and circuits. War was looming in the country, and the Methodists wanted to state their allegiance clearly in the conflict ahead. The conference publicly declared "that while we deplore the necessity that exists for a separation from the Federal Union, yet in view of all the history of the past, the perils of the present, and the threatened wrongs of the future, we feel bound by honor and duty to move in harmony with the South in resisting Northern domination."[4] Rev. Kennedy, like his church, was committed to the cause of the South, which is to say the cause of slavery. Not long after his arrival in the Charlotte area, he enlisted as a chaplain in the Confederate Army.[5] His interest in maintaining the system of enslavement was not only professional, however. He had personal economic interest in human slavery. When Kennedy loaded his wagons to move to the North Carolina piedmont, he trafficked with him at least seven human captives—Sarah North and her six children, Abram, Eliza, Jacob, Henry, Mary, and Richard.[6] Sarah's husband, Allmond, the children's father, was left behind.

When the Norths and their enslaver arrived in Charlotte, they entered a town growing out of its backwoods status into a hub of regional commerce and transport.[7] Settlers had founded the city in 1768 around an ancient intersection, where Catawba and other Indigenous peoples encountered one another at the junction of two trading paths. In the colonial and antebellum economies, Charlotte was too hard to reach to become large or economically significant. Multiple discoveries of gold from 1799 to 1835 started a swell of activity in the area, but for the most part, Charlotte remained small. It was hard to get goods in and out, and so farms rarely grew into the kind of large-scale plantations seen near coastal North and South Carolina. Even on a smaller scale, though, many Mecklenburg County households relied on the cruelties of slavery. Fully one-quarter of white families claimed title to at least one person in the 1860 census.[8]

Charlotte's economy changed for good with the 1852 opening of the Charlotte and South Carolina Railroad. Rails connected the city to Columbia, South Carolina, and then to the port city of Charleston. Charlotte quickly developed as a commercial hub where farmers could sell their goods to be shipped to the market. More rail lines followed, along with a growing merchant and financial class that specialized as the middlemen between farmers and the buyers at port. The city was still not advantageously located, so as the Civil War raged across the South, Charlotte avoided much damage. The out-of-the-way location, plus the presence of multiple rail connections, even led to Charlotte becoming home to the Confederate Navy Yard, despite being two hundred miles inland and not on a navigable river. Workers built the needed naval equipment in town and then shipped it to the coast by train.

With Charlotte's rail lines mostly intact following the war, the city's economic engines boomed at the dawn of Reconstruction. The city grew rapidly in population and in wealth, and with those changes came a restructuring of local and state politics. The federal government stripped Confederate officers of their rights to participate in political processes until they were formally pardoned. The North Carolina General Assembly rewrote the state constitution, opening voting and the holding of office to all male citizens without regard to race or to their status as property holders. The city government changed as well. During this period, Charlotte had its first Black aldermen. Black participation in elections became the norm. The context of new freedoms, enforced by federal troops as part of Reconstruction, was the context in which Sarah North and her children, including Abram, would spend formative years in their new hometown.[9]

The political and economic climate of cities, including Charlotte, was attractive to many Black people around the South. They were free but lacked economic and political safeguards to help give material form to their freedom. Waves of violence by whites against formerly enslaved people created unsafe conditions, especially in rural places.[10] Emancipation guaranteed neither safety nor material opportunity. General Sherman's famed January 1865 Field Order 15, known popularly as "forty acres and a mule," was short-lived, revoked by President Johnson just eighteen months later, and was only ever locally applicable to portions of coastal Georgia and South Carolina.[11] No level of government made efforts at repaying those formerly enslaved for the theft of their labor and their lives, goals they could have accomplished through reparations and the redistribution of land ownership. In fact, from the early days of Reconstruction, federal troops pursued the goal of reestablishing the plantation economy under a supposedly "free" labor market. Federal leaders felt the quick production of commodity crops, especially cotton, was necessary to revive the Southern economy, dependent as it was on plantations. The Northern economy was also dependent on Southern enslaved labor, given its dominance in the global trade of the commodities produced by enslaved people.[12] To that end, in the spring and summer of 1865, "military commanders issued stringent orders aimed at stemming the influx of freedmen into Southern cities."[13] Emancipated Black citizens, along with no small number of poor white ones, poured into cities and towns looking for the kind of opportunity that life in the countryside lacked. Charlotte, with a growing economy and ease of access through rail travel, became a popular destination. In 1860, the city's Black population was 800; in 1870, it was 1,880; and in the year 1880, it was 3,338, when African Americans comprised 47 percent of Charlotte's population.[14] In just twenty years, the Black population quadrupled.

Charlotte, like the entire country, held contradictions. There was Emancipation, on the one hand, with its new opportunities, the birth of new institutions, and the opportunity for self-determination. On the other hand was the reinvention of the antebellum economy, inside which young Abram North began trying to establish for himself a place in the world. At only fifteen, he was already living outside his mother Sarah's home, she in the Third Ward neighborhood with his siblings and her new husband, William Barringer, and Abram as a domestic servant in the First Ward compound of Samuel Smith. Even during the relatively open times of Reconstruction, North's chances to make a new life were circumscribed by the low status of African Americans in the social systems of the country. While Black men could now vote and hold office, white Americans still used every advantage to deny them full access to society. Lacking money and capital, and with a limited range of employment options available, many Black residents in Charlotte and around the South had little choice but to do the kind of work they had been doing before the Civil War. The economic arrangements were somewhat different, but the resemblances were obvious. For North, a live-in position as butler or maid or gardener was a common job. The work had the advantage of being a source of housing as well as income. Nevertheless, it remained clear that power relations had not fundamentally changed.

With employment and shelter secure, North was free to reach into new interests not available to him on a South Carolina plantation. He could go for a walk or attend a picnic. He could vote and organize his neighbors to vote. And he could pick up a baseball glove and begin learning a sport sweeping across the nation, putting strong shoulders and lean legs to use in the service of his own enjoyment.[15]

SAMUEL SMITH

Like Abram North, Samuel P. Smith was born on a plantation, but he was born heir to it instead of its captive.[16] Smith was born in 1835 but moved to town while he was still "quite young," sometime in his teenage years, rather than maintain the family business.[17] He entered as a young man into a city poised for growth. He was ready to grow his fortunes with it.

When Smith arrived, his prospects were decidedly different than young North's. He had a family of means and prominence whose wealth and name he could draw from in establishing a career. He chose the legal trade, a profession that could help him maintain a position of social power even as he moved away from his father's work as a planter and an enslaver. Samuel earned a law license and began practicing in both Mecklenburg County and its northern neighbor, Cabarrus County. Practicing law was lucrative for young Samuel, and it made other career paths available to him as well. By 1870, at thirty-five years of age, he was also running a business as a shoe merchant.[18] Smith had made a fair amount of money in his relatively young career. He already owned thirty thousand dollars' worth of real estate and twenty thousand dollars of personal property, assets totaling, in 2023 dollars, just over one million dollars. His financial success continued, leading him to be elected the first president of the new Traders' National Bank in Charlotte after its organization. He moved to New York briefly to work on the financial side of the cotton trade, a reinvention of the economy of his parents, and then returned home to Charlotte in his retirement.[19]

Samuel Smith attended church next door to his home at the Beulah Baptist Church, a congregation that would later become First Baptist Church.[20] So did his three brothers, all of whom chose urban rather than rural life.[21] Beulah was the first Baptist Church founded in Mecklenburg County, in 1832. The congregation had struggled to stay viable in its first several decades. They moved from place to place and regularly fell behind on their bills, which made it hard to keep a preacher.[22] Smith was an important enough member, and a wealthy enough one, to be entrusted with locating a new minister in 1869, during another of their regular pastoral vacancies. Indicative of both the church and its city, Beulah often had a hard time locating a preacher. Though they aspired to attract prominent ministers, they were neither a desirable location nor a prominent pulpit yet.[23] Beulah Baptist's reality was that pastorates were generally short and sometimes ended when the church fell so far behind in paying the pastor's salary that he just quit.[24]

Pastoral struggles notwithstanding, the congregation had big dreams. Not only did they desire a strong minister; they also wanted to establish a prominent location that might reflect their upward mobility. Besides his pastoral search responsibilities, Samuel Smith chaired the committee charged, in 1866, with "securing a lot nearer the center of town for a new house of worship."[25] Moving toward the center of town was an attempt by the church to announce that it was entering into the upper crust of Charlotte society. In just over thirty years, the struggling congregation had dissolved and reformed, moved multiple times, and finally settled on the fringe of the city, a full four blocks east of Tryon Street. A move, if Smith and his committee could arrange it, would be a statement of belonging within Charlotte's realms of power and influence.

Smith lived on a compound of several adjoining lots with multiple buildings near the corner of 7th Street and B Street, now Brevard (see figure 2.1).[26] On the corner was First Baptist Church, with buildings of the Smith compound adjacent to it on both the 7th Street side and the B Street side. The Smith household was large, comprising seventeen people in 1870, including Samuel and his wife, Kate; four children; a sixty-one-year-old woman, perhaps Samuel's mother; three adult brothers, two of whom worked in Samuel's shoe store; another shoe clerk; and five Black residents: Molly Manigault, age ninety-nine; Sylvia Meacham, sixty-five, a cook; Frank Capers, thirty-five, the gardener; Anasha Smith, thirteen, a nurse; and Abram North, eighteen, domestic servant.[27] It was on this corner that an entanglement a century long and more began between North and his descendants and the people and institution of First Baptist Church.

Figure 2.1. The home of Samuel Smith on N. Brevard Street near 7th. This picture is from 1968, at which point the house had fallen into some disrepair and was being used as a secondhand shop. The structure has since been demolished. Photo courtesy of Robinson-Spangler Room, Charlotte Mecklenburg Library.

Late in his life, Abram North recalled Beulah Baptist, and his home next door to it, as the starting point of his regular path to school, housed at the city's first Black Baptist congregation. Writing to the editor of the *Observer* in 1926, North traced his route, while still a teen, from home to a memorable stopping point. The first comprehensive, block-by-block map of Charlotte gives an idea of what he might have seen along the way.[28]

Leaving the Samuel Smith home where he lived, North walked to the corner of B Street and proceeded south. The blocks stretching eastward from B Street were still thinly developed, near to the edge of town. Turning west onto 6th Street, North was walking into the more densely developed commercial area. He crossed the railroad that was so essential to Charlotte's growth from backwoods town to bustling city. Just across the tracks was the large home of Zebulon Vance, governor of North Carolina through most of the Civil War. Vance would become governor once more in 1876 and eventually a US senator. He used both posts to frustrate what was left of Reconstruction policy and to pave the way for Jim Crow.[29]

The next intersection was College Street. This busy thoroughfare was the industrial parallel to commercial Tryon Street, one block west. Money was made on Tryon Street, but the work behind the money got done on College. With a left turn, North walked south on College toward 5th Street, and beyond that Trade Street,[30] into the area known as The Wharf. The nearest sizable body of water to center city Charlotte is the Catawba River, about eight miles west. Nonetheless, the name The Wharf became common locally as the cotton trade increased. Residents called it that "for its functional similarity to the waterfront at Charleston."[31] Along its busy sidewalks was a mix of businesses and residences. On one side was the foul odor of a tightly packed livery stable. On the other were the visual feasts of shop windows in buildings owned by local merchants, including Samuel Smith's shoe store. Reporters hustled out of the *Daily Observer* offices, bankers strolled to offices along Trade Street, and laborers hauled goods from warehouses to railroad platforms.

At the center of The Wharf, along College Street near Trade Street, North recalled one point of interest: "There stood an old dilapidated two-story structure, then run as a bakery by a man named Nimo who had only candy made in sticks, and the sticks put in jars. He also had bread to sell. I remember well reading one of his advertisements one morning as I passed his window in the year 1867. It read thus:

> '*O for a thousand tongues to tell*
> *The bread that Nimo has to sell*
> *Also cakes and candies and everything sweet*
> *All on the corner of Trade and College Street.*'"[32]

Among the fascinating bits from North's letter to the editor is how he cites with confidence a verse of advertisement from nearly sixty years prior. North's other letters to newspaper editors indicated a sharp memory for names and places and dates. In this case, his memory is aided by the verse mimicking the hymn "O For a Thousand Tongues to Sing," a standard of European hymnody written by Charles Wesley in 1739. In other words, Abram North was a churchman. He had been in the pews as a young man long enough to learn the hymns of white churches. He likely also came through the hush harbors, the hidden worship gatherings of enslaved people that passed on the freedom songs of Black Christians. It is not hard to imagine him attending Beulah Baptist with the other members of the household where he was working, perhaps at the insistence of Samuel Smith.

Nor is it hard to imagine young North, still a teen, encouraging the Black members of the congregation when they requested a letter of separation to go and start their own body of faith. That is what happened around 1867 at Beulah, when the Black members and the white members agreed to go separate ways. The separation was agreeable to the white leadership at least in part because the Black members outnumbered the white ones. They did not want to be voted out of the leadership of their congregation.[33] The group that left to form a new congregation took the name First Baptist Church. They settled within a few years on South Church Street, where they remained for a century.[34]

The presence of the hymn, and its usefulness for aiding memory, suggests the depths of the entanglements between Black Christians like Abram North and white ones like Samuel Smith. They occupied the same blocks, even the same houses. They sang the same songs. And yet their communion was fractured by white supremacy.[35] The households and institutions they built around their altar tables—sometimes shared but increasingly separate and unequal—would have very different fates in the coming years. The political and theological decisions made from the end of Reconstruction to the beginning of the twentieth century and the inauguration of Jim Crow would set racial groups on very different trajectories. Those decisions put Beulah Baptist

Church on a collision course with North and his heirs. Though they occupied different spaces, it was precisely space, and the racialization of space, that would chart their differing futures.

LAYING THE CORNERSTONE

By 1878, Abram North had moved to a new job working as a butler for Benjamin Rush Smith, brother of Samuel and a cotton merchant who dabbled in politics. That year was the first of Benjamin Smith's lone two-year term as mayor of Charlotte. Over the course of many breakfasts and dinners, North could listen in on the Democratic mayor's conversations regarding Charlotte's intrigue. Smith held public office at a time when Democratic Party officials were trying to undo eight years of Reconstruction, returning the white elite to power and decreasing the influence of Black people. Overhearing key conversations would have helped North in his own work within the Republican Party. He would later become a key local party operative, likely bringing with him insights he picked up from being rendered invisible in important rooms across the city.[36]

Perhaps Abram North had a ballplayer's build—long, lean, quick—that caught Annice Carson's eye.[37] Perhaps North noted the gravitas with which Carson carried herself. Perhaps it was her welcoming spirit, her delight in entertaining a guest who came calling.[38] When they met is unclear, but they surely saw one another across the street while at work and made a connection. Carson worked for the socialite Mrs. Rufus Johnston, who lived catty-corner from Smith's home at 704 North Tryon Street in a grand residence where she loved to entertain Charlotte's elite. One imagines Abram and Annie carrying on a courtship and meeting where they could—certainly at church but perhaps also walking together to the ball field for some afternoon entertainment when Abram and his brother Jacob North were playing a game with the Charlotte Recruits.[39]

On March 28, 1878, North put on his only suit. It was a prized possession that he had purchased while traveling in Boston with Benjamin Smith. Dressed sharply, he walked the short distance to the Johnston residence to marry Carson. It was a fine event, as he recalled to the Charlotte *News*, and even Carson's boss, Mrs. Johnston, contributed. She "furnished all of the dainties of the season for our pleasure," he said.[40] They moved together to

West 2nd Street in Third Ward, a short walk from the institution that would become the most important one in their lives—Clinton AME Zion Chapel, the oldest Black church in Mecklenburg County.[41]

Annice Carson was there from the beginning at Clinton Chapel. The church counts her among its founders, though she was only about five years old at the time of its founding in 1865.[42] Regardless, she, born enslaved, carried within her an important legacy—present in her early moments in the hush harbors and illicit church gatherings outside white control and at the founding of the first formal Black congregation established in Charlotte as a result of those meetings. Organizing churches was the way "freedpeople laid the cornerstone of the postwar Black community," says historian Janette Greenwood. From churches grew "schools, political meetings, and social functions."[43] Faith was not a matter of making one choice among many options. In the North household, as in many Black households of their time, centering their home on church life was a way of showing their devotion to the full life of their community.

FROM EDGE TO CENTER

Just prior to Abram and Annie's wedding, the project of Reconstruction in the South began falling apart. For about nine years following the cessation of the Civil War, federal policies empowered reforms and new representation, resulting in the democratization of power across the South, in part if not in full. There was no straight line to economic power. Some Black citizens found ways of starting businesses of their own, and buying property, and finding a wedge into greater economic security. However, many more wound up having to take jobs roughly parallel to how they had worked when their labor was forced rather than paid. During Reconstruction, Black organizations increased the economic power of their constituents, grew churches and fraternal organizations, and took advantage of the opportunities given to them within a reforming society. They built political power and used it in electoral politics, leading to many firsts in the former Confederacy. North Carolina governor William Holden appointed Charlotte's first Black town officials and named Black businessman John Schenck as a police officer. Schenck would go on to become one of the most important politicians of either race in the era that followed.[44]

But white Americans wiped out the gains of Black ones in the post-Reconstruction era. Convinced of the righteousness of white men's rule, they turned to the theological realm to describe their crusade against Reconstruction. *Redemption*, they called their movement, as they built a world around the fictions of white supremacy. Black political power generally waned for the next quarter century after 1876, despite the work of Black citizens and institutions. Without federal troops tracking—and threatening—them, white politicians quickly reclaimed their place in the political elite. They used their power to re-entrench themselves into seats of authority and at the same time to enforce the marginalization of Black communities.[45]

As the shift in politics from the Civil War to Reconstruction to post-Reconstruction was happening around them, the members at Beulah Baptist were developing their own ambitions about how and where they would be in Charlotte. The question of where was especially important. They had been tenants in various places for their first three decades or so until securing a lot near the Smith property at 7th and B. But just as the power relations of the post-Reconstruction era reestablished white dominance in Charlotte and across the South, so were the members of Beulah Baptist ready to assert their own place within the culture and the cityscape of Charlotte. One important way to do that was to move from the fringe of town to one of the city's most prominent addresses: North Tryon Street, Charlotte's version of Main Street. Tryon Street was notable in that it housed many of the city's wealthiest businesses and merchants at that time, including Benjamin Rush Smith Jr., North's employer. The space there was racialized, clearly marking the hierarchy of who belonged and who did not belong, of who owned and who served. The built environment of the area "served to produce and sustain racial meanings."[46] To move into it was to assert one's place within the racial and economic hierarchy.

As early as 1866, Beulah had charged Samuel Smith and a small committee with securing a location "nearer the center of town."[47] But the dense settlement of Tryon Street, and the occasional economic troubles of the post-Civil War era, kept the congregation from relocating. It did not help that the church's executive committee initially instructed Smith's building team to find a new plot and construct a new building without taking on any debt, even though at the same time the congregation lost several ministers because they kept falling behind in the payment of the pastor's salary.[48] Given the difficulties of the time, the members of Beulah Baptist saved their pennies but also relented

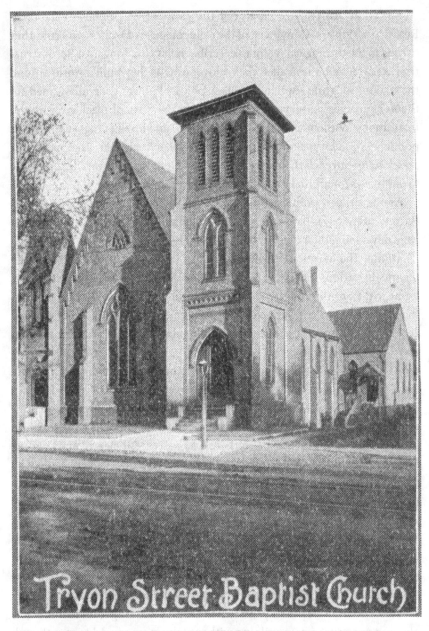

Figure 2.2. Tryon Street Baptist Church, near 7th Street in uptown Charlotte. Picture from 1898. Courtesy of the Robinson-Spangler Carolina Room, Charlotte Mecklenburg Library.

on borrowing. If they were to move to prime real estate in a growing city, they would have to take on some debt.

It took until 1877, a full eleven years, for the church to locate an available lot and to have enough money to buy it. By that time, Reconstruction had ended, and the so-called Redemption movement seeking to reestablish white dominance was in full swing. As that larger social and political movement was happening, so was Beulah Baptist another step closer to the local prominence it desired. The new location on North Tryon Street was just south of 7th Street. Buying a lot was only the first step, though. It took several more years to clear the land of the house that was on it, to prepare the site, and to begin construction. The work moved slowly because workers occasionally walked off the job when there was not enough money to pay them. The congregation finally moved in 1884, nearly two decades after Samuel Smith's committee had started the process (see figure 2.2). They became Tryon Street Baptist Church, a congregation with a proud new name to reflect their social standing and their new location.

CHAPTER THREE

The Gleaners

Following their marriage, Annie and Abram North relocated to 274 W. 2nd Street in Third Ward. The move put them near Clinton AME Zion Chapel and just around the corner from Abram's mother, Sarah North Barringer.[1] Housing segregation had not yet been invented, and the racial environs of the North home were typical of Charlotte households.[2] Their block in Third Ward had several Black families and several white families, most with working-class jobs like laborers, clerks, and porters.[3] Black and white people frequently lived on the same block, in relative proximity to one another. Maps and city directories show that most blocks had some diversity in either class or race and often both. In some cases, a block front would be single-race, but the next block front would be single-race of a different race.[4] Some people did cluster together around common racial or economic interests—Fourth Ward was a bit wealthier and a bit whiter; Second Ward had a narrow majority of Black residents—but the differences from block to block were not stark. There was no Black neighborhood or white neighborhood.

The North family grew quickly. Abram walked to work at a Black grocer on Trade Street near Independence Square. Annie worked at home nurturing babies and establishing their residence. First came Alma, then Allmond, then Bessie, then Hazeline, and eventually eleven total children. The North family did what families do: raise babies, educate children, keep house, attend religious services, care for neighbors. Though there is no record of it, it is not hard to imagine that the young North children played with other nearby kids, including the McAllister kids, Ernest and Lillie, from the white family across the street. They could not go to school together, but the proximity of

Black and white families, sometimes as close as next door to one another, complicated the racial narrative that white politicians and preachers were casting forth during the post-Reconstruction era.

As the family grew, Annie North became one of the mothers of the Clinton AME Zion Chapel, always there for meetings and meals and mission within the community. She had been there since the beginning, in the hush harbors, and would have been a mentor in the faith for many others. Abram North kept working various jobs to support the family and was a trusted member of the religious and political world centered around Clinton Chapel. He became enough of an influence in the local Republican Party that by 1885, he had won a job with the US Post Office. Postal work was a political patronage job. Those positions were given as rewards for work within the party structure—they were the spoils of electoral victory, given to those who demonstrated loyalty and effectiveness. North's was one of only five postal jobs in town, and he made a salary of three hundred dollars, a solid paycheck for his time.[5] He was becoming a man of political activity, using his place in life to influence the well-being of his family and neighborhood during uncertain times.

Church life and political life went hand in hand, as they often do. Black churches were the most significant social and political institutions in Black communities, and the mingling of party issues with organizational and theological debates inside the church was common. One AME minister stated, "A man . . . cannot do his whole duty as a minister except he looks out for the political interests of his people."[6] Black clergy and church leaders tried to negotiate a political world where no established party took their well-being and interests seriously. There were patterns, though, and party alignments in their time were different than in current times. Most Black people were Republicans, "the party of Lincoln and emancipation," while elite whites were mostly Democrats.

Debates within churches on how to align Black votes and voters for the betterment of the community could become heated, as one did at Clinton Chapel. At the center of the disagreement was partisanship inside the Sunday School. Passions spilled onto the pages of the *Charlotte Observer* in 1893. In a fierce letter, J. C. Cunningham wrote to the editor that local Democrats ought to beware of a certain leader of the "Republican-Third Party Sunday School" at Clinton Chapel—one Abram North. Cunningham was one of a significant minority of Black Charlotteans who believed that the best path for the Black community was to stay in the good graces of Charlotte's white Democrats, who had been consistently winning local elections. White Democrats cared little for the fate of their Black neighbors. Black people knew this. Rather, the strategy of those Black Democrats was that by appealing to class solidarity, wealthier Black citizens might capture the favor of the wealthier white citizens, most of them Democratic Party members. Faithfulness to Democratic causes, Cunningham argued, might help Black communities curry some favor in the partisan landscape and at the very least reduce the ongoing harm.[7]

By the time of the Sunday School conflict in 1893, North had already staked his claim with the rising Populist or Third Party "fusion" movement.[8] During his clash with Cunningham, North spoke to those gathered at Clinton Chapel and made the stakes clear: no Democrat could be a friend of the Sunday School. To do so was to stand against one's own people. And with that, Cunningham was "ejected" from the Sunday School, and North was made its superintendent.[9]

North turned out to be right about the strategy that would best help his community. The Republican-Populist cause was building strength in 1893 in Charlotte and across the state. Since the end of Reconstruction in 1876, the Southern white ruling class had eroded the gains toward equality that Reconstruction-era policy had made. Republicans, then the party most likely to appeal to the economic and social interests of Black families, had won some elections but generally faced uphill battles in their electoral efforts in Charlotte and across North Carolina. However, 1893 saw a bit of change coalescing around the common interests of factions that had not generally voted together: white farmers, poor white urban dwellers, and Black citizens in both urban and rural settings. All three groups could see that the election of Republicans and Populists to state and local office meant better results across their constituencies. The election of Democrats effectively entrenched the white elite, whose policies hurt nearly every other constituency.[10]

Common interests did not necessarily result in automatic trust among the groups, but they did start working together. In churches, community halls, and living rooms around the state, they adopted policy proposals and selected candidates. They became powerful enough that the movement gained a name: Fusion. Democratic opposition gave the movement that title pejoratively, but it accurately represented the movement in its ability to bring diverse groups together. The Fusionists were a multiracial coalition, with at least one Charlotte stronghold in the Sunday School of Clinton AME Zion Chapel. Over the course of the next two elections, in 1894 and 1896, the Fusion movement won widespread victory. They elected supermajorities in both houses of the state legislature and won the governorship and a majority of the delegation to the US Congress. They set about making widespread changes to governance in North Carolina.

As the Fusionist trajectory pointed up, so did Abram and Annie North's. In 1893, they did the one thing that established a family for generations to come: bought land. It was a small lot in Second Ward, but they got a piece of the dream, the American Dream. Surely they had longed for a little soil to call their own for years. They had been born enslaved, had worked other people's land, and had managed the homes of the wealthy. By 1896, they had built a new house on the lot at 625 East 2nd Street.[11] Now they had a place to raise their family that they would one day leave to their children. It was a space that would eventually become a site of political and spiritual struggle as Charlotte remade its neighborhoods.

Overlapping personal triumph and political triumph must have created a euphoria for the Norths and other families in similar positions. At the same time the Norths were changing their family's fortunes, the Fusion movement was rearranging the state. Over the four years following the elections of 1894 and 1896, the Fusionists legislated greater fairness in registering voters and counting votes, raised taxes to support education, put local municipalities in charge of electing local officials rather than appointing them at the state level—a move that had maintained white and Democratic control, especially in areas with large Black populations—limited certain interest rates, and featured strong leadership from both Black and white politicians at every level of government.[12]

The accumulated changes of the Fusion movement were "a virtual revolution in North Carolina politics."[13] Mecklenburg County had long been a Democratic stronghold within the state, but even Mecklenburg was participating in the revolution. Such sweeping changes were bound to be met with a backlash as the white ruling class felt its power slipping. Democratic Charlotte mayor J. H. Weddington, one of a few of his party who had managed to hang on to his job during the Fusion revolution, commented that Fusionists "wanted to take the government out of the hands of the men who own the property and put it in the hands of those who are ignorant and own no property."[14] Weddington was not accurate in assessing his political enemies, however. The Fusionists included astute local leaders like the

Norths, pillars of their church and community and now property owners in Second Ward.

Though the Fusion movement united Black and white voters in their electoral interests, racism still plagued the results. The Republicans did not divide the spoils of their wins equally. Following the election of 1896, Republicans had twelve patronage jobs to appoint. Only one went to a Black resident, despite the work of Black leaders to have their community vote overwhelmingly for the Fusion ticket. That job was spittoon cleaner at the mint.[15] "We colored Republicans are getting tired of this," Henry Boulware, one prominent local Black Republican wrote to the *Observer*, "and we don't propose to stand it." Writing again a few weeks later, he said, "There must be a fair division of the fodder or we will cease to pull the plow."[16] When it came to the work of turning out voters, Black Republicans and Populists were putting in maximum effort. But the top leadership of the Republican Party remained white. They were unwilling to confront their ongoing racism. In their intransigence, Republican leaders were helping to hasten their own demise.

Seeing the reforms of the Fusion movement, but also seeing the internecine battles within that movement, the Democratic Party in North Carolina adopted a clear strategy, though it was a diabolical one. The strategy was to divide the Fusionists by race and therefore to make the election of 1898 a battle over white supremacy.

The Young Democrats of Mecklenburg County shut down the City of Charlotte on Friday, November 4, just four days before the crucial election. They escorted 1,500 white children out of school and to the sidewalks, where they had organized a parade. Horses and riders from every township and district in Mecklenburg County stretched the full length of Tryon Street. The marchers carried with them banners reading "White Government" and "White Man's Supremacy." They brought in South Carolina Senator Benjamin Tillman, an especially rabid segregationist, to give a keynote address. The rally whipped up support along the terms on which the Democrats had determined the race would be run, namely, the color line. Unable to beat the Fusion movement on economic merits, they'd spent months inciting the racist passions of white people and threatening violence at ballot boxes and in the streets. Tillman made the closing argument succinctly: "The question is whether white men shall rule." It was the classic racial wedge, a strategy that would continue to be employed at political campaigns and rallies more than 125 years later.[17]

The strategy worked. The local press wrote in favor of the Democrats, filing reports that were effectively white supremacist propaganda.[18] In Charlotte, violence at the polls never materialized, but threats of it kept many Black voters home on Election Day. In Wilmington, then the state's largest city, Election Day violence devolved, two days later, into a massacre. The duly elected town government there was unseated in an open coup d'état, deposing the mayor and town council, leaving dozens of Black people dead and hundreds more on the run for safety and burning key institutions like a Black-owned newspaper.[19]

Democrats swept into power across the state and immediately began undoing Fusion's gains. Following the lead of other former Confederate states, they instituted the set of laws known as Jim Crow. Among other things, those acts tightly limited voting rights, separated public accommodations, and segregated neighborhoods. The effect was stark and immediate. The Norths had lived on a block in Third Ward with a white family across the street. Within a couple of years, no such blocks existed in Charlotte. The city was fully "sorted out" by race, with Black residents living mostly in Second Ward. Those outside Second Ward lived in segregated areas in First and Third Wards.[20] White leaders attempted to make Black people a permanent underclass. But for families in Second Ward, their ambitions remained unlimited. In a society determined to exclude them from prosperity and equality, they would have to create their own opportunities.

Over on North Tryon Street, First Baptist Church was growing quickly. After years of steady membership, the congregation exploded around the turn of the century. Now worshippers sat shoulder to shoulder, straining to hear the preacher while sweating through their Sunday best. The original auditorium, opened in 1884, had space for the congregation for about two decades before they needed to expand the building. A construction program began in the summer of 1906. An addition to the Sunday School building expanded capacity from five hundred to more than one thousand. By the end of that year, the expansion plans grew even larger.[21]

The congregation, at that point called Tryon Street Baptist, drew plans for a new sanctuary to seat a thousand people. Its design was grand, in an unusual Byzantine style with a central dome sweeping across the room to highlight the Baptist principle of the centrality of the people rather than the clergy. On its completion, the church had finally established its commanding presence on Tryon Street (see figure 3.1). To dedicate the building, the congregation

CARNEGIE FREE LIBRARY AND FIRST BAPTIST CHURCH, CHARLOTTE, N. C.

Figure 3.1. Postcard depicting FBC's 1909 building, left, which stood next to the city's Carnegie Free Library. Photo courtesy of Robinson-Spangler Carolina Room, Charlotte Mecklenburg Library.

brought in guest preacher Rev. E. Y. Mullins, the most important Southern Baptist theologian of his time.

On the first Sunday of May 1909, with every seat in the new sanctuary full, Mullins preached a message that would foreshadow the direction of First Baptist Church more than six decades later. He pointed to God's providential guidance that, though their destruction at times seemed sure, had worked to preserve God's people on their hero's journey. God was doing God's work in the world through First Baptist Church, he told them, a self-understanding they would rely on for decades to come. And further, Mullins encouraged them that "the spirit of conquest should come over the place" in light of a new structure that would provide them "so effective a means for fighting the battle with sin."[22] Mullins's words would turn out to be prescient in ways that would influence First Baptist Church (FBC) and the Charlotte cityscape far beyond what anyone that morning could imagine.

THE SIEGE

Inside Annie and Abram North's house at 625 E. 2nd Street, they were surrounded. By kids. Everyone had to get fed, the garden needed tending, the knees in the boys' pants needed patching, the laundry kept piling up, and somehow, in just six rooms, they had to find a space to breathe freely. It took everyone to make things work. Abram was now an insurance agent with North Carolina Mutual, plus a church janitor on the side; Allmond, twenty-one, worked as a deliveryman; Bessie, seventeen, was a cook; Hazeline, fifteen, worked as an insurance agent with her father. The next four in line, Mary, Lavinia, Abram, and Annie, attended Myers Street Graded School in Brooklyn.[23] In the year 1900, there were still three more children at home, pulling at Annie's apron, asking questions, and making messes. Henry and Mabel were four and two, and the youngest, George, was only seven months, a full two decades younger than Allmond.[24]

Inside the house and inside the neighborhood, the North family met the challenges of each day through cooperation. Outside the neighborhood, the forces they faced grew increasingly hostile. The election of 1900 solidified the boundaries between white and Black neighborhoods. After more rallies and yet another parade, the Mecklenburg Democrats had thoroughly beaten the Fusion movement the North family had worked for. Abram had been a political player for much of two decades. Now he was effectively erased from influence.

There was no way for the people of Brooklyn to achieve economic and political equality in a world run by white people determined to withhold it from them. Those people cut off the supply of money, of institutional power, and of needed goods to maintain their racial hierarchy. But the creativity and determination within Brooklyn built up a place of independent exchange and mutual aid. Black citizens could not convince white ones to respect them. With their success in creating community wealth, however, they did incite the imaginations of certain white people about the potential of Second Ward as a part of the growing City of Charlotte. In 1912, the *Charlotte Observer* reported on the importance of the area for the future of the city. "Far-sighted men," an article noted, were sure that "this section, because of its proximity to the center city, must sooner or later be utilized by the white population."[25] It was clear enough only one decade into Jim Crow that an expanding city would eventually become hungry for more land to build on. When it did, it would look to capture the urban area that Brooklyn residents were hard at work building.

Neighbors in Brooklyn spent their days doing what people do: working, singing, playing ball, telling stories, cooking for one another, gossiping, fornicating, celebrating births, mourning deaths, building institutions to outlast themselves. To build those institutions, they had to depend only on themselves and one another. They needed their own money, their own insurers, their own banks, their own teachers and preachers and shopkeepers and short-order cooks and doctors and undertakers. That is not so unusual, though. Every community in every place raises children to fill all those roles. What was particularly trying was having to create a community while the supply lines that served most of the rest of Charlotte bypassed Brooklyn. Many residents had to make the small amount of money they had to circulate inside the neighborhood by working outside it, cleaning buildings or acting as maids or butlers or laboring away at dusty, dirty jobs in poor working conditions, where there was no way to move up the ladder.

The neighborhood was nearly self-contained. You could be born there, go to school there, work there, die there, and have your body prepared for burial there. All the stuff of life was within a few blocks: restaurants, shops, backyard gardens, insurance agents, a YMCA. There were theaters and juke joints for Saturday nights and churches for Sunday mornings.[26] Lamentation and grief poured out from the bands at one moment, joy and laughter the next.

Just like their neighborhood, the Norths walked through low valleys and celebrated achievements and rites of passage. Abram had multiple roles, including as an insurance agent for North Carolina Mutual Life Insurance Agency. His daughter Hazeline, at the young age of fifteen, joined the firm as an agent as well. North Carolina Mutual agents went door to door to collect premiums, giving them an important social role within the community. They knew the ups and downs of life in each household, especially when there were deaths or distressing events. Hazeline was unusual as one of the very few women to hold such a position at that time.[27] Abram continued to hold other jobs to support his household. From 1898 to 1913, he was the sexton at Trinity Methodist Church. He later became an elevator operator at the Belk Brothers department store.[28]

The North home was at its most crowded around the year 1900, with all ten living children in the house, ranging from ages twenty years to seven months.[29] Over the course of the next decade, the family would celebrate children graduating from the Myers Street School. They watched with joy as Hazeline married John Riddick. Within a couple of years, the newlyweds moved into a rented house at 610 E. 2nd Street, across the street from the family home.[30] Their joy was tempered by the loss of their daughter Lavinia.

She married the popular Presbyterian minister Rev. J. A. Thomas-Hazell in June 1909.[31] Only one week later, a brief telegraph arrived with news that she had taken her own life, without explanation.[32] The Norths had earlier lost their oldest daughter, Alma, and appear to have lost daughter Mabel during the first decades of the 1900s as well.

The following decade held similar griefs and triumphs for the North family. Bessie, the third oldest, and her husband, Mervin Springs, bought a house in 1916. She and Mervin ran a cleaner and tailor shop on College Street. They had apparently done a strong business despite all the barriers Jim Crow posed. Their house was in the Washington Heights neighborhood, a streetcar suburb built on the edge of the city for the Black middle class. Bessie and Mervin Springs grabbed one of the first lots to be sold in the new development, in a prominent location right on Beattie's Ford Road. The national AME Zion paper, *Star of Zion*, announced the news in a short note, saying that they had "moved into their newly built and modernly equipped home on Washington Heights."[33] Bessie even bought it in her own name and not her husband's. Her parents had prepared her to fly high, and that is precisely what she was doing. She and Mervin watched as Washington Heights became a retreat for some of the better-known business owners and professionals in Black Charlotte and one of the best real estate investments Black families could make.[34]

But in that same year, Henry North died at home while living with his parents. He was only twenty years old. Triumph and grief commingled, one standing alongside the other at every point in the North household. It was the same way in Brooklyn, where the neighborhood developed but did so unevenly. On the one hand, there were sturdy homes and businesses along Brevard Street, like the home of J. T. Williams and the cream-colored brick of the three-story Mecklenburg Investment Company (MIC). MIC invested in Black businesses, creating space to incubate new firms, especially for a professional class of doctors, lawyers, and dentists.[35] On the same block was Grace AME Zion, a church birthed from a split with Clinton Chapel AME Zion.[36] Its handsome brick sanctuary was one of a dozen churches across the streetscape in Brooklyn. The AME Zion denominational presence was especially strong. Besides Grace Church, the AME Zion national publishing house, which produced the weekly *Star of Zion* paper and other Sunday School and denominational literature, was located inside the neighborhood. Publishing house president Dr. John Moreland was a Brooklyn resident.[37]

But not everything was built sturdily and with care. Maps and photos from the early 1900s show large areas of Brooklyn built without the same quality that the more well-to-do areas of the neighborhood received. Landlords, almost all of them white, built for cheap density and without public investment in the infrastructure needed to maintain that density. As a result, dozens of houses were packed tight into alleys off the primary streets. Many were built as "shotgun" homes, long, narrow buildings with a handful of small rooms. Often, they were built with a shared wall, as duplexes, so as to cram as many into one space as possible, and on pilings, without firm foundations.[38]

The chief motivation for owning such spaces was profit. The economics of low-rent housing created large profit margins, especially when unhindered by even basic oversight. Segregation tightly restricted the supply of housing available to Black people, which meant that demand inside Black neighborhoods remained high, regardless of the conditions. Landlords could charge far higher rents than would have been possible in an integrated society. And with few minimum building code standards until 1945, landlords had little motivation to maintain high-quality conditions in their housing.[39]

Brooklyn was a cross section of Black life in Charlotte. Those who were upwardly mobile and those who were desperately poor all lived within a few blocks of one another. They did business together, went to church together, and sent their children to school together. On the one hand, to live within that space offered cultural and institutional freedom that allowed for the relative flourishing of the people there. On the other hand, to live in that space was to be under siege. The powers on Tryon Street to the west, and the Elizabeth and Myers Park neighborhoods to the east and south, held the reins of capital tightly. In their hands were land ownership and the making of policy, the entire workings of the systems that organize life in every place. Living under siege for sixty years meant that upward mobility had a low ceiling. It meant that the title to land was revocable. It meant, in the inversion of the spiritual that Brooklyn churches sang, that one day the white people on every side would march around the neighborhood for the last time and announce in public their conquering presence, and the walls would come tumbling down.

Abram North lived at 625 E. 2nd Street until his death on May 10, 1929, at seventy-six years old. He was still working just a few weeks before he died. His last job was as the elevator operator at the Belk Brothers department store on Trade Street.

Brother Abram North: ball player, political operative, churchman, father, husband, homeowner, free.

North died, according to his doctor's statement on his certificate of death, of heart disease and of "physiological exhaustion." In his later years, as the papers mentioned him and published his letters, white people regularly called him something like a "good Negro."[40] They made him sound "respectable," having assimilated or made the accommodations necessary to win the affections of the white ruling classes, who don't appreciate their position being challenged.

The archives don't always tell the truth.[41]

There's every reason to think that a clever political operative in his early adulthood was a realistic one—and no less clever later. North family descendants testified to me about the costs of playing polite. It is a kind of survival strategy, they said, that might eventually lead to physiological exhaustion.[42]

As his body was prepared for burial, Annie and his children had the opportunity to demonstrate his faithfulness to his family, to his wife, and to his place. They had him buried in the suit he had bought, years prior, in Boston, while traveling with Benjamin Smith. Fifty-one years before his death, he wore that suit during his wedding to Annie. More than a half century later, his community gathered around him for the final time. He was robed in the righteousness of a life well lived. His family laid him to rest in a plot in Pinewood Cemetery in uptown Charlotte.

SURVEYING THE LANDSCAPE

Annie North lived for more than another decade following Abram's death, which took place just a few months before the beginning of the Great Depression. The Depression shook the economic foundations of the United States. The response to the Depression then created new systems and institutions within the country that would eventually lead to the destructions of Urban Renewal. The New Deal made for uneven recoveries from the Depression, benefiting white families and institutions far more than Black, Indigenous, and other communities of color. There is another way to state that: in public institutions, white citizens enforced tax laws on Black citizens and then used the money they extracted to build institutions that benefited primarily themselves. In private businesses, white bosses hired Black workers while colluding together to pay them significantly less than a fair wage. Those public and private efforts together ensured the existence of a large Black underclass whose economic mobility remained limited. The long-term results of these policies were seemingly contradictory places like Brooklyn: independent, flourishing neighborhoods that at the same time lived under the vulnerability of siege.

One New Deal method of democratizing the country's wealth and broadening the middle class was to encourage home ownership. Prior to the Depression, homeownership was quite expensive for those who were not already wealthy. Bank mortgages typically required 50 percent down, were written for five-to-seven-year terms, had interest-only payments, and required repayment in full at the end of the note.[43] The Roosevelt administration wanted the federal government to help families purchase homes and build wealth through homeownership. "A nation of homeowners, of people who own a real share in their own land, is unconquerable," the president said.[44]

The housing and land policies that developed around the New Deal placed white families at a significant advantage over everyone else.[45] One of the early interventions of the Roosevelt administration in the area of housing was the creation of the Home Owners' Loan Corporation (HOLC) in 1933. In the spring of that year, historian Kenneth Jackson reports, "fully half of all home mortgages in the United States were technically in default, and . . . foreclosures reached the astronomical rate of more than a thousand per day."[46] The HOLC purchased distressed mortgages and then issued new loans with extended repayment schedules and altered terms. Among its important innovations was that those mortgages were amortized so that each payment included both some principal and some interest. The altered mortgages built equity over the course of the term. Homeowners could realize their equity, plus any appreciation, at the point of sale, even if that was prior to the maturation of the mortgage note.[47] The HOLC was signed into law in June 1933; in its first two years of existence, it deployed more than three billion dollars of capital to rescue more than one million mortgages, or one-tenth of all owner-occupied, nonfarm residences in the country.[48]

Any lending program requires an assessment of risk, and the HOLC was no different. To create a consistent guide to assessing risk in its loans in cities around the country,[49] the agency first worked to create a standard system of real estate appraisal, an industry that lacked a uniform code. The HOLC then consulted with local real estate men and bankers around the country to draw maps of their local housing markets that would document the risk associated with lending in each of that city's neighborhoods. Those real estate men evaluated every block of their city based on the HOLC's criteria for creditworthiness. By undervaluing neighborhoods that were "dense, mixed, or aging," the HOLC introduced anti-urban bias into the public funding of housing markets. It began pumping money into the shift toward the suburbs, a change that had begun in some places but now became an overwhelming tide.[50]

HOLC appraisers came to Charlotte in 1937 and met with eleven real estate men.[51] Together they assessed each neighborhood according to its perceived risk-worthiness. They coded maps, as such groups did around the country, with four color-coordinated gradations: Grade A neighborhoods were colored green; Grade B, blue; Grade C, yellow; and Grade D, red. These maps became known as "redlining" maps. The HOLC prioritized mortgages in A- or B-graded areas, the wealthiest ones with the most white-collar workers and established wealth. They deprioritized mortgages in C or D areas. The criteria for building the redlining maps included the suburban bias mentioned above. They also included racial preferences for white people and against people of any other racial or ethnic minority, with Black people at the bottom of the HOLC's hierarchy.[52] The HOLC stated this in coded language by defining D areas as those having the presence of any "undesirable population, or the infiltration of it."[53] Every Black neighborhood in Charlotte was rated D, including Brooklyn. According to Charlotte historian Tom Hanchett, appraisers noted that "African-Americans owned quite handsome residences in some areas" but "emphasized that no exceptions to the racial D ranking would be made."[54] Through the HOLC, federal tax dollars, including those paid by Black people, were stabilizing white neighborhoods and building white wealth while denying those benefits to Black neighborhoods.[55]

Following the creation of the HOLC in 1933, President Roosevelt organized the Federal Housing Administration (FHA) in 1934. Where the HOLC secured troubled mortgages, the FHA created opportunity for first-time home buyers.[56] The primary means for doing this was through insuring new mortgages, thus lowering the risk for banks and other lending agencies by providing a safeguard against large-scale foreclosures. In short, public monies were put to work as an insurance policy against bad loans, which is to say against a private lender's risk. This intervention lowered the chances a mortgage would go into foreclosure or if it did, that the lack of payment would be very costly to lenders. In exchange, banks agreed to amortize the mortgages, to extend the length of notes, and to finance 80 percent of the cost, leaving borrowers to come up with only 20 percent down.[57] By making those changes, homeownership became widely afford-able to middle-class families, who now benefited from needing less cash on hand, having lower monthly payments, and building equity throughout the repayment period.

The democratization of homeownership and its wealth-building oppor-tunities did not reach every neighborhood. While the FHA did not use the HOLC's redlining maps, the requirements to qualify for their subsidized mortgage insurance were similar in quality. The agency's appraisal standards included a whites-only clause, encouraged segregated suburban development, warned against school integration, and looked disparagingly even on white neighborhoods in close proximity to Black ones.[58] Again, the results were the same: the hardening of segregated housing patterns and the subsidization of white wealth-building through homeownership while at the same time actively preventing that wealth-building in Black neighborhoods.

What public policy enabled, private actors reinforced through their actions and policies in the areas of housing and real estate. Segregation in the South was enforced by law. In the rest of the country, it was also upheld by the demands of other institutions that required strict adherence to racist norms. In one glaring example, the National Association of Real Estate Boards (NAREB) insisted that a realtor should never introduce racial integration into any neighborhood. Desegregation, they insisted, would be detrimental to property values, and an agent's chief ethical obligation was to protect property values. One NAREB brochure, dated 1943, tried to exemplify the potential danger of selling to a Black buyer in a white neighborhood by sug-gesting that "the prospective buyer might be a bootlegger who would cause considerable annoyance to his neighbors, a madame who had a number of call girls on her string, a gangster who wants a screen for his activities by living in a better neighborhood, a colored man of means who was giving his children a college education and thought they were entitled to live among whites. No matter what the motive or character of the would-be purchaser, if the deal would institute a form of blight, then certainly the well-meaning broker must work against its consummation."[59]

Black communities were always working against systems that refused them service or opportunity, whether in real estate or in any other area of life.[60] Paradoxically, the same Jim Crow restrictions that had plagued communities like Brooklyn since 1898 and marred both the HOLC and FHA enabled Black communities to provide at least some measure of support to their beleaguered neighbors. Decades prior to the advent of the HOLC and the FHA, Black communities had begun creating parallel institutions to fund and improve their neighborhoods. Black people had been sending their tax dollars to public agencies to finance their own oppression for years. Their only option was to create institutions dedicated to serving Black communities while continuing to fight for fair representation at every level of society. Brooklyn was a study in both the successes and the limitations of doing it yourself.

The creation of parallel systems was a necessary innovation, but it was insufficient to make up for the power differential of policies and institutions that were both separate and unequal. Black banks, however brilliant, would never match the financial heft of the US government nor the economic power of a white-dominated banking system constructed from its origins around the economic engine of slavery.[61] Without high wages, strong labor unions, and widespread municipal investment in equitable spaces—and without reparations to compensate for an economy built on the enslavement of Black people—there was simply no way to close the wealth gap.[62] Public and private policy used thousands of major and minor interventions to keep Black people and Black communities as poor as possible. No Black capitalism, however brilliant, could overcome that.

A few years prior to Abram North's death, Abram and Annie's daughter Hazeline moved back home. She and her husband, John Riddick, had lived just across 2nd Street. Following John's death, Hazeline returned to live with her parents, where she walked to her job as a "domestic" at the Bon Marche department store on Trade and Tryon, right in the heart of Charlotte. Hazeline was the bright young woman who was working with her father as an insurance agent by age fifteen. As she watched the Depression unfold, and saw the policies put in place to remake the country through the 1930s, she surely understood what was happening around her. Money was flowing, and customers were returning to the department store. She knew how the money ran, and why, and which places it left out. Most of it still bypassed her house in Brooklyn. Yet those in her community persevered, doing as much as they could with all that they had in hopes that they would reap a larger harvest.

Hazeline North's mother, Annie, passed into the realm of her ancestors on August 13, 1940.[63] The saints of Clinton Chapel gathered a few days later to celebrate one of their founders, gone to her eternal rest.

Sister Annie Carson North: church mother, hostess, homeowner, mother, grandmother, free. Her community buried her next to her beloved Abram and aside her son Henry and her daughter Mabel in Pinewood Cemetery.

At the death of her mother, Hazeline inherited 625 E. 2nd Street. It was part of Abram and Annie North's legacy in the world. Hazeline had been there when they built the house in 1896. Perhaps she helped paint the walls then. She had certainly swept the floors more times than she could remember. She had mourned the deaths of siblings there, cared for aging parents until their passing, and sat for hours on the porch talking with folks walking down the street. Now it was her place in the world, her inheritance, her refuge.

THE GLEANERS

There is a single artifact remaining from the North house at 625 E. 2nd Street. It is a framed black-and-white print of Jean-Francois Millet's *The Gleaners*, housed in the history room at Clinton Chapel AME Zion Church. In the painting, three women are gathering the leftover grain heads from a field (see figure 3.2). The field has already been cut and the prime of the harvest taken. The three peasants are picking up what was left behind. Behind the women are towers of golden straw in groups of three, a distressing sign of abundance amid poverty. The harvest of the field is plentiful. It is in view. It is not available to the gleaners.

The distance between the gleaners and the rest of the community behind them emphasizes the separation of those who are poor from the rest of their society. In the background, more than twenty figures are building gilded towers on a large farm. An overseer on horseback enforces their separation. The gleaners are far removed from that community, as Millet's composition makes clear, and yet they are the focus of the canvas, painted large and in careful detail.

Gleaning is a traditional practice in agrarian societies of leaving the edges of a field and the leftovers of harvest available for poor people. The political and economic logic of gleaning for poor people is the assurance that they have what they need to survive. For those who are wealthy, it is a practice against greed, a reminder that the abundance of the land is not for the possession or the enrichment of the few but for meeting the needs of all. In the Bible, gleaning has theological purpose as well. The book of Leviticus instructs its

Figure 3.2. *The Gleaners.* Jean-Francois Millet. Musee D'Orsay, Paris.

hearers, "When you reap the harvest of your land, you shall not reap the very edges of your field, or gather the gleanings of your harvest. You shall not strip your vineyard bare, or gather the fallen grapes of your vineyard; you shall leave them for the poor and alien: I am the Lord your God."[64] The last sentence is key. Caring for those who are poor is an expression of faithfulness to God. The greed that harvests all the edges and the leftovers is idolatry.

The best-known Bible story of gleaning is the story of Ruth. The story turns on the encounter between Ruth and her husband-to-be, Boaz, whom she meets while gleaning in Boaz's field. It was through the story of Ruth that artists typically presented the concept of gleaning.[65] Millet had done so himself in his 1853 painting *Harvesters Resting (Ruth and Boaz)*, which portrays a warm scene of Ruth, Boaz, and other workers at rest, playing on the story's comforting theme of redemption. In that painting, the social distance between gleaners and the rest of the community is minimized, even fully collapsed.

The Gleaners portrays no unity between landowner and gleaner, no social divides being bridged during a rest break in the shade. There are three women, hunched. They are exhausted. Their harvest is slim. The sun beats from above. They bend down and then stand. They bend down again. But remarkably, they are the subjects. They have their full measure of dignity, if not of grain. When Millet presented *The Gleaners* at the 1857 salon, it was judged "a political provocation."[66] During that era of French life, poor people and workers were frozen out of land ownership, their opportunities limited in service of greed and power. The challenge of seeing poor people drawn large, placed in the center, the focus of extended meditation, was more than the salon-goers of Second Empire France could handle. Millet fetched a distressingly low price for the painting.[67] In time, it would become one of the best-known pieces of nineteenth-century European art. The reaction of the French ruling class to the painting described Charlotte, where the visibility of those who were poor was an offense to good taste—and still is. Those in the elite do not spend decade after decade moving those who are oppressed from place to place only to have to see them.

Abram and Annie North left no written record of why they purchased the print of *The Gleaners*, or why they carefully framed it, or why they left it to their church as part of their legacy. Perhaps the Norths saw themselves in it. Perhaps they saw themselves freed from it. Perhaps they saw themselves in it, then freed from it, and then placed back in it. The painting certainly described their city, where towers of gold stood in plain sight yet were rendered inaccessible by mounted surveillance or by rules and customs that consigned some people always to the edges. The Norths were not the only Black family who saw something in Millet's work. The childhood home of Martin Luther King Jr. in Atlanta had a print of the painting in the living room. So did the Pittsburgh home of noted Black art collector Vivian Hewitt during her childhood.[68]

There they were, Abram and Annie, part of the city yet kept apart from it, inside the story of Charlotte but held on the outside of it, beloved and respected but always from a distance, always at arm's length, hiding at the edges of the historical record where they might one day be seen, where perhaps some sense of justice might finally come to be, however proximate. They haunt still, as do those who were silenced, who have been silenced, who are silenced. They return, they are returning, they will return, and there are always more with them, holding the future in their hands until the plunder of the past is resolved.

French philosopher Jacques Derrida asks, "What does it mean to follow a ghost? And what if this came down to being followed by it, always, persecuted perhaps by the very chase we are leading?"[69] We have pursued Annie and Abram North across the historical record. We have followed them across the city, from house to house, from job to job, from slavery to freedom, from boisterous activism to the silences of Jim Crow, from mourning to celebration to exhaustion to rest. And yet, one senses, the chase is itself a manner of being pursued by a history we cannot control, a story that presents itself to us making demands that we can neither unhear nor pretend we do not see. Abram and Annie North are yet present. As we follow them in pursuit of justice, they will eventually lead us back to 625 E. 2nd Street.

CHAPTER FOUR

Two New Pastors

Coleman Kerry Jr. was not supposed to be pastor of Friendship Baptist Church. When Friendship's previous pastor, Rev. Dr. John Lewis Powell, left in 1947, the people of Friendship knew who they wanted to fill their empty pulpit: Rev. Coleman Kerry Sr. The elder Kerry was a widower, the father of four sons. He was a powerful figure within the National Baptist Convention, the association of Black Baptist churches in the United States. Kerry Sr., the former president of that body, had stopped pastoring and was making his living as a traveling evangelist.

The church board at Friendship knew that Kerry Sr. was their man, and so they sent correspondence to him. Friendship was calling Rev. Kerry as pastor. Would he come?[1]

But Rev. Kerry Sr. was not interested in pastoring. He was committed to his work as an evangelist. Rather than turn down Friendship, Kerry Sr. sent his son in his place. It was the sort of move that put Friendship in a bind. Kerry Jr. did not fit the profile that Friendship wanted. He was twenty-four years old, single, and still a student in theological school. But Friendship could not insult a man of the elder Kerry's stature. His prominence within the National Baptist Convention and his power among church people around the region were high. To reject Kerry Jr. without giving him a chance would be an insult.

Friendship understood power and stature. The congregation's handsome brick building at the corner of 1st and Brevard Streets signaled Friendship's role within the community (see figure 4.1). Inside the economic hierarchy of the neighborhood, they were closest to downtown and on the highest ground, a statement of their relative power. The church's mailing list from that time

Figure 4.1. Friendship Baptist's Brooklyn sanctuary at the corner of 1st and Brevard Streets. Photo used by permission of Friendship Missionary Baptist Church.

included notable Black Charlotteans like Rev. Dr. H. L. McCrorey, the president of Johnson C. Smith University. On its trustee board were important figures like Fred Alexander, who would become the first Black elected official in Charlotte since the white supremacy campaigns in 1898 and 1900. The Alexander family home was on the same block as Friendship, and they owned multiple Brooklyn-based businesses, including an important funeral home.[2]

Kerry Sr.'s strategy worked. Friendship dared not insult him. The church board had little choice but to agree to a trial pastorate, offering Rev. Kerry Jr. the opportunity to fail or succeed on his own merits. Kerry's trial period began near the end of 1947. His presence, and command of the pulpit, was new enough that a brief item in the *Charlotte Observer* in December 1947 noted that Kerry "would be speaking in both services" that Sunday morning—hardly a noteworthy duty for experienced pastors but at Friendship, an indication of new energy and of handing over the reins.[3]

Kerry Jr. quickly built affection between himself and his new flock. By the second Sunday in January 1948, Friendship formally called him as pastor of the congregation. His "evangelical style of preaching and singing brought the congregation to their feet, shouting in a manner long unseen in Friendship."[4] The young minister lit the fires of zeal in the congregation, which quickly endeared him to the church.

Just as important as the zeal was the treasurer's report. Kerry Jr. had attendees "digging down deep in their pockets," quickly stabilizing the ongoing financial security of a congregation that, despite its stature in its own community, relied on the meager offerings of its many working-class members to sustain its ongoing ministry.[5] With its young minister in place, the congregation was climbing higher and higher in the way of faith.

MENTORING THE FOUR HORSEMEN

Around the time the junior Kerry was moving to Charlotte, C. C. Hope Jr. was returning to the city following his service in the navy during World War II. As he settled back into life in Charlotte, he resumed attending First Baptist Church (FBC). Hope grew up in church and had joined First Baptist while he was in high school after meeting Mae Duckworth, the young woman who would become his wife. FBC was a place he knew and where he was known, a solid base to establish a family and to grow in faith. Soon after his return, Hope was at an evening church meeting when he saw a man on the street with a flat tire. Hope walked over to assist and found himself face to face with Carl McCraw, the president of Union National Bank and a fellow member at First Baptist Church.[6]

A good deed got C. C. a summons to lunch. Lunch won him a job in the bank. McCraw could see Hope's promise as a worker and a leader. McCraw was right—by the end of his career, Hope had worked his way up to vice chairman of First Union National Bank. He served eighteen months as North Carolina's secretary of commerce and received two appointments to the national board of directors of the Federal Deposit Insurance Corporation.[7]

Another figure who quickly seized on Hope's leadership potential was Rev. Dr. Casper Carl Warren, also called C. C., the pastor of First Baptist Church. Warren built his career around creating strong institutions. As Warren saw it, strong institutions required strong leaders, and so he took men with promise under his wing to develop their capacity.[8] His methods got results. After graduating from seminary, Warren moved to a struggling church in Kentucky. He increased the membership there tenfold before receiving a call to pastor Immanuel Baptist in Little Rock, Arkansas. At Immanuel, he helped double the size of a large congregation in just five years. His prowess in evangelism, and the giving and building programs that followed the growth in a church's membership, made Warren a top pastoral prospect for the largest churches in the Southern Baptist Convention.[9]

In 1943, FBC Charlotte wooed him from his pulpit in Little Rock to succeed the most decorated pastor in the church's history, Rev. Luther Little. Warren's pastoral colleagues in Little Rock were sad to see him go, despite his short tenure there of just over five years. They issued a formal resolution on his departure, commending him for his "co-operation and aggressiveness" in his ministry there.[10] He arrived in Charlotte to an eager congregation. In the years following the turn of the century, they had fulfilled their desires—a noteworthy sanctuary, a prominent local voice, and a growing membership in a fast-growing city. Warren was their man to expand their ministry in the heart of Charlotte.

First Baptist members followed willingly and grew in accordance with Warren's ambition. The time was right for such growth as Charlotte was exploding with new people. From 1940 to 1960, the city's population would double, from just over one hundred thousand to more than two hundred thousand.[11] On Warren's first Sunday, the *Observer* reported, several hundred people were turned away at the door because the sanctuary was at capacity. Twenty-five people joined the church that morning, and the transition between pastors appeared to be seamless.[12] Seeing the sanctuary filled to capacity would set the direction for his fifteen years as FBC pastor. Growth in membership required more space, and within only a few months, plans were made to remodel and add seats to the sanctuary. By the end of 1945, the congregation had changed the platform and choir loft to create more room, added two side balconies, and inserted a marble baptistery, where the stream of new members could be immersed into the faith.[13] That same year, the *Biblical Recorder* reported that FBC had the largest Sunday School enrollment in the state, surely a point of pride and a reinforcement of Warren's success.[14]

Warren knew how to design programs that created space for his congregants to grow, to thrive, and most importantly, to belong.[15] His emphasis on programs gave his parishioners a mission within the congregation and around the city. They responded by helping FBC to a sustained period of rising attendance, engagement, and financial support. Warren's focus on administration sometimes took a toll on other parts of his ministry there, including his preaching. Congregation member Nancy Kistler remembered that "some Sundays you knew he had spent little time in study and sermon preparation, but you forgave him because of his unselfish attitude and his caring heart. You knew he had been 'tending his flock.'"[16] With a structure for belonging and a set of exciting programs, lackluster sermons were not a big deal.

During his tenure, Warren identified four young men who would become prominent leaders of the congregation, as well as prominent leaders in civic and political life in Charlotte. They were Allen Bailey, a defense attorney who moved to Charlotte following law school and joined FBC; W. J. Smith, a sharp banker who was working his way up the chain at First Union Bank and had grown up at FBC; Warren's son-in-law Bill Poe, the son of a preacher himself and a high-flying attorney with political ambitions; and C. C. Hope Jr., the bright banker from First Union. Warren thrust these four men into multiple avenues of church leadership. Their growing power within the congregation eventually earned them the nickname "the Four Horsemen," sometimes used in the pejorative but also an indication of their influence in the church and the city.[17] Those four men would steer the growth of FBC for years to come and at the same time would leave their marks on the City of Charlotte through their engagement in various political arenas.

URBAN RENEWAL BEGINS AND ENDS

Like their city, both Friendship and First Baptist were growing. They were doing so during a crucial moment in the story of Charlotte and of the United States. World War II was over, but troops who had fought alongside one another overseas returned home to very different trajectories. For white veterans, the GI Bill and affordable Veterans Administration home loans promised an on-ramp into the booming postwar economy.[18] When white veterans joined First Baptist Church, their publicly financed opportunities for personal advancement could help to contribute to the growth of FBC. Some of their abundant economic opportunities got tithed to their church. For Black veterans coming home to segregation, the Jim Crow South and its cultural equivalents across the country still limited their freedom to participate in the economic and political life of the society for which they had risked their lives. When Black veterans joined Friendship, or another of Charlotte's Black churches, they entered yet another struggle for freedom, where every advancement had to be won against a system of exploitation.

The rapid economic and population growth around the country in the decade following World War II permanently changed the spatial orientation of cities. White families left cities at an increasing rate in search of housing in less dense, quieter neighborhoods. They were aided in their search for suburban idylls by the anti-urban policies of the Federal Housing Administration (FHA) and the Home Owners' Loan Corporation, which created financial advantages for white people moving into suburban spaces. Urban regions were growing at the periphery, with families—especially white families—seeking out the ideal that became so widely associated with the American Dream: no shared walls; no sidewalks; no buses or transit; few, if any, strangers. In the suburbs, you could spread out. There were more bedrooms and larger kitchens. No longer did anyone need a park; everyone had a yard.[19]

White flight from urban cores to suburban settings remade both the spatial orientation and the politics of the country.[20] Private and public investment migrated outside of city boundaries and urban spaces. Local, state, and federal revenue moved toward the construction of the suburbs and their massive, but far less efficient, infrastructure. Cities lost tax bases as wealthier families moved. Aging buildings and public investments in many sections of cities deteriorated. Racism was a driving force in these changes, both in the way that money moved, or did not move, and in the public images and discourse that guided policy and decision-making. Amid the spatial reorientation of American cities and suburbs, segregation hardened and disinvestment in minority neighborhoods increased.[21] The disinvestment from some areas helped set the stage for Urban Renewal in those same places. Cities became, in popular imagery, the sites of ethnic enclaves and teeming masses of suffering poor people; the growing suburbs were Pleasantville.

It was not only federal and local policy that created and maintained a geography built on segregation and inequality. Private actors like banks and real estate agencies helped to keep spaces accessible to some and inaccessible to others inside the systems of white supremacy. Keeanga-Yamahtta Taylor has shown how public and private agencies worked collaboratively to create two separate housing markets that operated under different principles but remained dependent on one another. These segregated markets stood in tension "in the conflict between *exchange value* and *use value*, or more intimately, the difference between real estate and a home."[22] Real estate was a commodity; home, a place of human attachment. Taylor says that "where white housing was seen as an asset developed through inclusion and the accruable possibilities of its surrounding property, Black housing was marked by its distress and isolation, where value was extracted, not imbued."[23]

The divergent trajectories of white and Black neighborhoods formed the backdrop of the actions of white families, investors, and institutions in the postwar period. Black neighborhoods were for maximizing profits; white neighborhoods were for maximizing enjoyment (see figure 4.2). Likewise, white churches played their own role in baptizing a culture that maintained white supremacy. White Christians, including FBC under the leadership of Warren, sometimes directed missionary efforts to Black neighborhoods. However, there was no spoken conflict between the goals of missionary work to relieve suffering, real estate efforts at maximizing profit, and structural designs to create segregated, inaccessible neighborhoods that maximized comfort for white residents. Perhaps those undertaking the missionary efforts saw no conflicts among those goals; perhaps the structures that created racially divergent results in neighborhoods disappeared from view. Probably both of those. In any case, white Christians pursued God's providential leadings into the suburbs to maximize the blessing of their increasing wealth.

While suburbanization was happening around the country, public institutions began developing policy responses to active disinvestment from urban neighborhoods. Among the earliest of those policy responses was the federal Housing Act of 1949, a sweeping piece of legislation that aimed to remake much of the housing policy landscape in the country. President Truman said that act had "the goal of a decent home and a suitable living environment for every American family."[24] The aim was laudable, the means used to achieve

Figure 4.2. An image of Brooklyn's contradictions: center, finely dressed people and sturdy brick building; lower left and right, a crumbling sidewalk, the responsibility of the city. Undated photo of North Carolina Mutual staff and agents in front of their office at 406–408 E. 1st Street in Brooklyn. NC Mutual was the firm for which both Abram and Hazeline North were registered agents. The field office pictured was the local headquarters from 1942 to 1949. Photo obtained in NC Mutual Collection at David M. Rubenstein Rare Book and Manuscript Library, Duke University.

it far less so. The Housing Act of 1949 placed inside the Housing and Home Finance Agency (HHFA) the new Urban Redevelopment Administration, a division charged with administering loans and grants to cities that were engaged in "slum clearance" projects.[25]

Overcrowded slum conditions were part of the popular narrative of distress regarding Black, immigrant, and poor white neighborhoods. To a certain extent, those images were true. As Taylor's work has shown, Black neighborhoods and spaces in particular were valued by the people who held title to them—who were primarily white and relatively wealthy—according to the ability of those titleholders to extract value. Profit motives and few minimum housing codes meant that maintaining low-quality housing was in the best interest of landlords. Hardened segregation practices and laws limited the supply of housing available to Black residents and at the same time created high demand for what supply existed. Consequently, poor people of every race frequently paid too much rent for homes that were too small, or in bad condition, or were built more densely than the infrastructure could support, or all of those. In Black neighborhoods like Charlotte's Brooklyn, the problems were especially acute. The relationships were exploitative by design. That was the framework by which the maximum exchange value could be extracted. The resulting health hazards were significant, and the material suffering in many places was dire. The entire system needed an intervention. The solution proposed by the Urban Renewal Administration for the most distressed areas: slum clearance. Local authorities would use eminent domain to take over entire areas, raze them, erect new public works projects, and auction off the land that was left.

Clearance was not a solution to inequities. It was their reinvention in another form. For one, the authority to define an area as a "slum" was a position of tremendous power, and baked into it was the whole range of American structural and individual prejudices against Black people, against other people of color, and against poor people across races. The URA gave local authorities the power to identify potential projects, assess them, and carry them out. While the federal agency would exercise some oversight from its regional offices, local elected leaders and the elites they would appoint to redevelopment commissions would make the largest portion of decisions.

Further, slumlords, not tenants, create slums, but tenants would experience the most profound effects of Renewal projects. A landlord might lose some potential profits from having eminent domain used on their property. But the results for nonresident property owners were not at all identical to the material effect of the loss of a neighborhood to its inhabitants, with all their entanglements and solidarities, their memories and altars. Tearing down one disinvested area would not remove the economic incentive for landlords to create another one somewhere else; neither would it give residents of those places the substantive opportunities to avoid such conditions in the future by correcting racial inequities in wealth and land ownership.

In fact, one relatively unknown aspect of federal tax policy contributed to the quick reinvention of substandard housing conditions immediately following Urban Renewal. When a property owner received a settlement from a city Redevelopment Authority, that settlement was subject to significant tax liabilities unless it was reinvested in property of like use. For owner-occupants, such a policy was benign—they were moving from one home to another anyway. But for landlords and real estate investors, the policy was an incentive to purchase more units quickly. Thus, the same actors who had created slum conditions in one place were likely to begin creating the same conditions in another place. They had a tax incentive to do so.[26]

Thirdly, the persistence of permanently depressed areas following the Great Depression was simply the most likely effect of New Deal policy. Owner-occupants in areas deemed slums could rarely get financing to improve their properties under New Deal policies, even when those places were rather stable as in neighborhoods like Brooklyn, or like Hayti in Durham, or Jackson Ward and Union Hill in Richmond. Those who wanted to purchase or make improvements were hard-pressed to find money to do so. Redlining and FHA lending, and the private banking policies that mimicked redlining, were clear examples of racism in practice through starving certain neighborhoods of capital along racial lines.[27] Fifteen years later, slum clearance programs began punishing those areas for not having enough money. "Credit blacklisting maps," Jane Jacobs said, "are accurate prophecies because they are self-fulfilling prophecies."[28] Kenneth Jackson notes the results were entirely avoidable: "If the government had invested its funds in maintenance programs for the older housing of the inner city, the poor might have inherited stable neighborhoods."[29]

Like many federal programs, the Urban Renewal program had many rules and regulations that cities had to follow closely. At base, though, the program was simple: a municipality identified a neighborhood or district deemed distressed or derelict. The city government set up a Redevelopment Commission, a group of men appointed with overseeing the program. The commission proved that the target area met a certain threshold of dereliction, typically established by state code.[30] The Redevelopment Authority bought out property owners in the affected area and then razed the properties. The city reserved some land for public facilities or public works projects and sold the rest at auction. The federal government covered between 67 and 75 percent of the cost once all accounts were settled. Urban Renewal became popular with cities around the country. By the time the program came to an end in 1974, more than six hundred municipalities had projects funded, displacing more than one-third of a million families.[31]

As Renewal projects were starting around the country, and as Charlotte leaders were debating whether to participate, the local National Association for the Advancement of Colored People (NAACP) was addressing the problems residents in Brooklyn and other underinvested areas were facing. In January 1950, the local chapter released a ten-point program aimed at improving life for Black Charlotteans. Spokesman Kelly Alexander presented the plan, with the first point calling for "construction in the Brooklyn area of a low-cost housing project for low-income Negroes and the razing of slums there." The fifth point asked for other upgrades like sidewalks and street improvements, including in Brooklyn. The plan also pointed out the separate and unequal facilities available to Black residents and called for the elimination of such segregation. Though the NAACP and Renewal plans had similar language around slum clearance, they represented very different principles. The NAACP posed the problem of blighted conditions as part of an overall set of economic and public policy issues. The request for the "razing of slums" in no way called for the destruction of the entire neighborhood but rather for the city to invest in solving the problem of low-quality housing in a way that would strengthen the area.[32] Alexander got this point across in part by using the passive voice: "Our people," he said, "live in the least desirable areas in the most deteriorated structures; they *are crowded into* these structures and areas often beyond the limits of health, safety, and decency."[33] It was not Black families who were actively choosing the poor conditions where they existed; it was the system of segregation and slumlord ownership that made the conditions unavoidable. Alexander, himself the owner of a funeral parlor based in Brooklyn, knew well the charms and assets of the neighborhood. He wanted the city and the absentee property owners to take responsibility for their part in the neighborhood's blight so that the area could grow beyond the strictures placed on it by a half century of Jim Crow.

Neither the city nor the large landowners, almost all of whom were white, showed any interest in the NAACP plan. They could not see the importance of places like Brooklyn. They could see land. On that land they could visualize a growing city and a growing tax base of a particular racial group. And they could see federal dollars paying for access to that land. Under the leadership of Mayor Victor Shaw (deacon, Myers Park Presbyterian), the city began developing plans for an Urban Renewal application and won initial approval. By August 1951, still fairly early in the program's life, Charlotte already had $750,000 earmarked by the federal government and was on the way to the important step of naming its first Redevelopment Commission. Mayor Shaw had to resort to theological language in describing the importance of this board. "Give prayerful consideration" to whom we appoint to this board, he urged the council: "This is one of the most, if not the most, important boards this council has ever named."[34]

The Redevelopment Commission was the body charged with the authority to make and execute plans for Urban Renewal. It consisted of five white men, all of them known for their success and stature in business and in the politics of business. They were sworn in by the city council and were accountable to that elected body for their work.[35] Under the direction of the city council and the city manager and his planning staff, the commission pushed for two small projects, one on the north side of downtown and the other on the south side of downtown. The initial projects avoided Brooklyn altogether.

Only a year after being sworn in, the commission was presenting plans for the demolition of these two proposed areas, both composed primarily of Black residents. Their report on the Palmer's Alley area in the southern portion of downtown, diagonally across Morehead Street and the railroad tracks from Brooklyn, indicated that more than two-thirds of the area consisted of "blighted" buildings. The commission's report tabulated the significant issues in Palmer's Alley: crowded two-room units with a single bathroom shared among several families, more than 20 percent without a shower or tub, 90 percent with sagging roofs, 86 percent on deficient pillars, 60 percent with fire hazards, and so on. Just three of ninety units were owner-occupied. The commission planned a similar project on North Tryon Street, in an area where conditions were nearly identical to Palmer's Alley.[36] Seeing the preliminary details, the Urban Renewal Administration sent a $25,000 advance of funds to aid Charlotte in setting up offices and hiring consultants.[37]

However, one significant problem stood in the way of approval. When the North Carolina General Assembly passed enabling legislation that allowed municipalities to take property by eminent domain for the purpose of eliminating blight, they created a very strict standard.[38] The state required that to declare an area "blighted," and thus to begin forcing the sale of property by eminent domain, 100 percent of the properties in the area to be reclaimed by the city had to meet the standard of "blighted." If even a single property met minimum building code standards, the city could not force owners to sell.

Many properties in Palmer's Alley met the standard to be called blighted. But not all of them. And not even creative wordsmithing to describe certain properties would help because some were vacant lots. There were no conditions under which an empty lot would meet the state's standard. The

Redevelopment Commissions in Charlotte, Greensboro, Winston-Salem, and Fayetteville began lobbying the state legislature to lower the standard from 100 percent to 67 percent. But the General Assembly refused, sticking firmly with its original language.

The Charlotte Redevelopment Commission was stuck. It knew what it wanted to do. State law stood in the way. For a while, North Carolina municipalities pondered working together to file suit in court challenging the state law.[39] Commissioners dropped the idea after seeing the results of similar suits in a dozen other states. They instead announced that the Redevelopment Commission would disband.[40] The only viable solution was to change the state's enabling legislation, a project they had tried unsuccessfully, and that would take several more years of lobbying to accomplish.

A GREAT OFFENSIVE

While city government worked on how to tap into the major monies of the federal Urban Renewal program, C. C. Warren was applying his abundant energy to the programs at First Baptist. In the state Baptist newspaper, he announced that he was canceling the mundane Wednesday prayer meeting and instituting instead the "Hour of Power." Attendance doubled.[41] The sanctuary was still bursting with people on Sunday mornings, even following the addition of seating. The next construction phase would create more space for Sunday Schools. FBC purchased adjacent structures and plots of land between 1945 and 1949. By 1952, they were erecting an education wing with dozens of classrooms in over forty thousand square feet of space. That building, ostensibly constructed to meet the future needs of the church, was completed in April 1953.[42]

Warren was not only a strong local presence but also part of the national leadership of the Southern Baptist Convention (SBC), including being part of its exclusive executive committee as early as 1944, shortly after he began his pastorate in Charlotte.[43] His strengths in religious programming kept him in the eyes of national leaders. FBC Charlotte was becoming one of the more prominent congregations within the Southern Baptist Convention, which was on its way to becoming the largest Protestant group in the country. Warren had created conditions to maximize growth in each of the three pastorates and had become a trusted national leader along the way. The next step for him was to apply his leadership at the national level, as president of the Southern Baptist Convention. He determined to run for the 1956–57 term and won election.[44] Warren's presidency, and the strengths that gave rise to it, reflected the convention's primary strategy during that period: growth, growth, growth.[45]

Warren's term came amid a divisive moment in SBC life and in American political life. In 1954, the US Supreme Court passed down its important *Brown vs. Board of Education* ruling requiring the desegregation of schools "with all deliberate speed." A young Black Baptist minister in Montgomery, Alabama, was coming to national prominence during a yearlong bus boycott. Southern Baptists in the pews, nearly all white, had little interest in integrating their churches or their schools or their transit or their lives. The convention as a whole had not strayed far from its roots in an 1845 split from the Northern Baptist convention over support of slavery.[46] And yet the convention's institutions, and a small but significant portion of its congregations, contained a diversity of thought on racial relations and desegregation. Some preachers and lay leaders were rabid segregationists, members of White Citizens' Councils and Klan chapters.[47] Others, including some ministers and no small number of seminary professors, were for full integration and were practicing what they preached.[48] Surprisingly, the convention's national meeting in 1954 adopted a statement, with broad support of the meeting's ten thousand voting members, that read, in part, "We recognize the fact that this Supreme Court decision is in harmony with the constitutional guarantee of equal freedom to all citizens, and with the Christian principles of equal justice and love for all men."[49] Reaction to that statement within SBC congregations ranged widely from zealous celebration to recalcitrant defiance.[50]

In the aftermath of the *Brown* statement, convention leadership could see that their coalition of congregations was diverse enough, at least in thought if not in other ways, that they needed a strategy to hold things together. Otherwise, they risked internal factions warring, and eventually splitting, over segregation. A people with a mission and a project to focus on were far less likely to implode over racial politics than a congregation or a convention who tackled the legacy of white supremacy head on or one that gave in to the worst impulses of segregationists and white supremacists. The convention adopted the strategy of keeping the largest portion of leadership in what it deemed to be "the center." Their middle ground was a supposedly apolitical focus on the continued numerical and financial growth of the convention and its congregations. SBC leadership would concentrate on the mission of growing churches and saving souls while adopting a neutral stance on social issues. To satisfy those to the left and the far right of its adopted center, the convention offered seats on commissions and institutional boards but never enough votes to shift the balance of power one way or the other.[51]

Early in the SBC's annual meetings, the president gives an address concluding his service year to the full body of the convention. Warren used his sermon to the thousands in attendance at the 1956 convention meeting in Kansas City to set the strategy of "moderation" and deflection on key social issues that would dominate the SBC at least through the presidency of Warren's successor in Charlotte, Carl Bates, who would serve as convention president in 1971–72 (see figure 4.3).[52]

But moderation is not neutrality. In this case, it was the silent support of broken moral, theological, and ethical practices.

Warren's 1956 presidential address began by appealing to the sense of unity that Southern Baptists felt in their collective numbers and their support of their convention. He cited the SBC's growing membership of more than 8.5 million and its budget of $334 million as one primary evidence that "God's blessings upon Southern Baptists have been phenomenal."[53] Warren then addressed the challenges the convention faced, including the "realm of racial understanding." He counseled careful movement forward. No step should come too quickly. "Extremists and agitators have, and will perhaps continue, to do incalculable harm," he said, in reference to activists pushing for integration. He failed to clarify what "harm" they had done or would do. He cautioned integrationists to remember that "economic and social relationships which have been from one to three hundred years in the making cannot be changed overnight."[54]

Warren also had a word for those who remained resistant to the *Brown v. Board* ruling: "Open defiance of the constitutional principle will endanger our foreign mission work through thirty-five areas of the earth." The problem with resistance to *Brown v. Board* was not its damage to their neighbors but its damage to global mission efforts. By continuing to resist integration at home, he warned, Southern Baptists will "play right into the hands of the Communist who will welcome the privilege of ridiculing, not only our democratic form of government, but the type of Christianity which seeks to win the world."[55]

Warren continued to caution against divisiveness and instead counseled unity so that the SBC would grow by way of missions abroad and expansion at home. SBC leadership thought they could preserve unity in their institutions

Figure 4.3. C. C. Warren addresses the Southern Baptist Convention at its 1956 annual meeting in Kansas City, Missouri. Photo used by permission of Southern Baptist Historical Library and Archives, Nashville, Tennessee.

without addressing a Christian social ethic that encouraged silence on segregation, racial terror, and the destruction of Black neighborhoods. They feared that racism resulted in the ridicule of American churches by the godless communists, without concern for the material effects on the lives of Black and Indigenous people, or on their own souls. The solution to communist ridicule was not destroying a ridiculous social system but instead engaging in more missionary activity. To rally the troops to the cause, Warren offered an exciting new program that he described in military terms. "If we are to accept the challenge of today," he said, "we must launch for Christ the greatest offensive in human history."[56] To that end, he proposed an ambitious program of growth over the next decade by adding five thousand new churches and twenty-five thousand new mission sites—a doubling of the number of Southern Baptist outposts in just ten years.[57]

The cumulative effect of Warren's strategy nationally was to distract SBC churches from pressing social issues that demanded the engagement of the faithful rather than their retreat. Instead of addressing the structures of segregation and white supremacy affecting the daily lives of the Southerners who were the primary SBC constituency, the convention misdirected them with an enormous challenge centered around numerical growth. The work of God, convention leadership was saying, was to build institutions and convert the world. Unity in those twin causes would hold together any divisiveness in the local and national political arenas.

SBC officials put together a plan that would try to steer around the great moral issue of the day and instead focus on an evangelism divorced from material and political realities. Baptist historian Bill Leonard characterized the national strategy as saying, "You can't let either the fundamentalists or the civil rights advocates—either Binkley Baptist [a well-known liberal Chapel Hill, North Carolina, church] or First Baptist Dallas [a hard-right Texas congregation]—inside the Convention enough to control it because that will stop growth."[58]

C. C. Warren's role in this critical moment in US history, and in Southern Baptist history, is profound. As both the executive figure of the most influential Protestant denomination in the country and one of the strategists on the inside of the SBC, he helped to put forward a strategy of quiet acquiescence to the reign of racial domination. He did so, on the surface, to further Christian missionary efforts. Warren not only acted as a national leader in the SBC but also implemented a program to give form to his strategy at the local level in his congregation, First Baptist Charlotte. In Charlotte and around the country, local implementation came in the form of a campaign to erect new buildings.

Leonard says that one of the ways to accomplish the SBC strategy was to "invigorate the church in a new building program. A building program calls for a capital campaign that says, 'We are so successful that we've outgrown the space where we are and now the kingdom of God is not in our old location. It's elsewhere.'"[59] Land, space, and facilities became the primary evidence of church success. Warren's military language was meant metaphorically, but it worked literally as well. The battle the SBC would wage was over territory and the souls that occupied it. The "mighty offensive" aimed at conversions, expansions, and growth was married to Southern Baptist silence in service of white supremacy.

Warren set the stage for FBC Charlotte to become one of the flagship congregations of the SBC for the next two decades. More important than their size were the decisions they made about their facilities and location. It was a curious time for a construction campaign at FBC Charlotte, given the building expansions that opened only a couple of years prior. Nevertheless, in 1957, Warren created a new committee at First Baptist that would give a local expression to the national emphasis on new members and new buildings. The group was called the Future Program Committee. To chair the committee, Warren tapped one of the young leaders he was mentoring: C. C. Hope. He also called on Allen Bailey and Bill Poe to be on the committee, along with Terri Smith, the wife of W. J. Smith. All the families of the Four Horsemen were represented. Warren charged the twelve committee members to assess the programs and facilities of First Baptist Church and to return to the congregation with a recommendation about how the church should plan for a promising future of growth. Though none of them could see it yet, FBC members were preparing to trespass into a space that was not theirs, into a space that would be taken without recompense.

CHAPTER FIVE

Making Moves

C. C. Warren may not have been the best preacher, but he could certainly rally people behind a cause. Southern Baptist Convention leaders grasped his vision. They could see how he was implementing it locally at First Baptist Church (FBC) Charlotte. At Warren's presidential speech during the 1957 convention annual meeting in Chicago, as he was closing out his two-year presidential term, he continued to push on Baptists to "get on the offensive."[1] He reminded them that they had agreed to "providing spiritual leadership for the greatest advance in the history of Christianity."[2] Progress for the first year of their decade-long project was not matching the needed pace for opening thirty thousand pulpits by 1964. Warren appealed to the words of Baptist missionary William Carey: "Attempt great things for God and expect great things from God."[3]

Warren's influence, and his emphasis on buildings and programs as markers of Christian ministry, would persist for years to come at First Baptist Charlotte. But only a few months after the convention meeting in Chicago, Warren resigned from FBC. He concluded his ministry there on the last Sunday of December 1957 and took up a new position as national director of the "30,000 Movement" for the convention (see figure 5.1). The Southern Baptist Convention (SBC) had taken his call to double its number of pulpits so seriously that it organized a new administration around it, with Warren at the helm.

Warren departed FBC Charlotte, but the congregation showed no signs of slowing without him. The leaders he cultivated within the congregation maintained their work, including the Future Program Committee. With a

Figure 5.1. C. C. Warren with Billy Graham in an undated picture. The photo is likely from 1964, when Warren and the Southern Baptist Convention's 30,000 Movement invited Graham to deliver the closing sermon to SBC's national meeting in Atlantic City. Photo used by permission of Southern Baptist Historical Library and Archives, Nashville, Tennessee.

strong, committed congregation, the church could take its time in selecting a new pastor. It took about eighteen months, but in May 1959, they hired Rev. Dr. Carl Bates from a church in Amarillo, Texas. In Bates, they got the opposite of Warren—a man of the pulpit, a poet, a man who spoke from the heart and left the administration to others. Like Warren, Bates had a national profile among Southern Baptists. He was president of the Baptist General Convention of Texas and a highly regarded speaker at SBC events around the country.[4] FBC Charlotte, with its growing influence within the convention, would become the place he raised his profile further.

While he was still a teen, Carl Bates decided to leave the Christian faith. He grew up with the stories of Jesus and the songs of the church as the son of sharecroppers in Liberty, Mississippi. He found no freedom there. His mama and daddy and siblings were a white family beholden to the sharecropping system that captured both Black and white families into its snare. It never gave room for folks to get ahead. Inside that system, you could not own the land that you worked. You barely made the money you needed to survive, never enough to purchase your own land. You were always subject to someone else's decisions, someone else's power. There was no way to hold your ground as a tenant farmer in Liberty, Mississippi, much less to gain enough to be truly free.

Bates grew up reading the Bible with his family around the dinner table, but his youthful imagination told him that he could only find liberty in some other town, writing some other story. So he did what a young man in south Mississippi looking to throw off the constraints of his place might do: he packed up his trumpet and moved a couple of hours south to New Orleans. He chased a dream.

At nineteen years old, Bates was young and alone in a city known for its vivid characters and boisterous parties. One imagines him playing on street corners, perhaps stopping by a rickety bar to try to sit in with the band. Youthful, bohemian. He worked washing dishes in exchange for room and board at the Hotel DeSoto. The grand old hotel was itself struggling through the Great Depression in a part of New Orleans known for former cemeteries and the ghosts that hang around such places.[5] Carl's carefree life could not make him happy. It seemed to be doing the opposite. He recalled reaching a low point one day while standing next to the open window of his room. He contemplated leaping down to join the ghosts under the streets when he noticed the Gideon Bible sitting on the desk near him. He opened it, and the course of his life changed forever.[6]

What his sharecropping parents planted in him through their family Bible readings began to grow intensely in Bates in a way that would continue until the very end of his life. Bates left New Orleans for Mississippi College, a Baptist school, and then Southern Baptist Theological Seminary in Louisville, Kentucky, followed by doctoral studies at Baylor University in Waco, Texas, yet another Baptist school. His commitment to the Bible grew every step of the way. Those who knew him say he was in his study, alone, from 6 to 10 a.m. six days a week, meditating on the Scriptures.[7] Bates took pastorates in Florida, Arkansas, and Texas early in his career, before FBC of Charlotte placed a call on him to succeed C. C. Warren. Though both had grown large churches to even greater size and prominence, the two men were quite different, in ways that worked to Bates's advantage. Bates was the preacher, Warren the administrator. When Bates arrived in Charlotte in July 1959, he already had full attendance, lots of interest groups, and many committees who had continued the work of the church even during the eighteen-month interim period.[8] Among those were the Four Horsemen, who were steering the Future Program Committee even in the absence of a pastor. Bates had the space to shine in his own strengths, while the leadership mentored by Warren carried on the other business of the church.

New to town around the same time as Bates was Vernon Sawyer. Charlotte City Council appointed Sawyer head of the Redevelopment Commission in late 1958, and he was on the job by the beginning of 1959. A North Carolina native, he came to Charlotte from the planning office in Norfolk, Virginia, where he served as assistant executive director for redevelopment in the Norfolk Redevelopment and Housing Authority. Sawyer and his colleagues there were ambitious in their plans to raze neighborhoods adjacent to center city Norfolk. By the time Charlotte hired Sawyer, the city of Norfolk had already cleared 200 acres of neighborhoods and aimed to clear 275 more.[9]

Just like C. C. Warren at First Baptist had cast the growth of his congregation and the Southern Baptist Convention in military terms, so, too, were Sawyer and the project he was leading rendered in militaristic language. The *Observer* described Urban Renewal efforts as "rallying all the forces of the community and states in a broad attack on slum conditions." The 475 acres in progress and in planning for clearing in Norfolk, the paper said, "were under attack." Likewise, a field representative from the Urban Renewal Administration told the Charlotte Chamber of Commerce that the federal program was "an over-all attack on slums and blight."[10]

The overlap of military metaphors among the political and theological leaders of the day as they described their projects is worth consideration. The Southern Baptists were engaged in a "forward program of advance" as part of their "type of Christianity that seeks to win the world," as C. C. Warren had said in his 1956 presidential address. The City of Charlotte was ready to "attack" slums, though not the economic and political conditions that led to the proliferation of substandard housing. The goal of many military actions, of course, is to win control of land. Wars redraw borders. They change how economic power works in a territory and to whom the resources of a place flow. Given the long history of Christian churches and missionaries accompanying and even assisting the conquest of territory around the world for colonial purposes,[11] the consistent use of military language for the programs that would follow conveys the righteous cause that both political bodies and white churches saw themselves engaged in. No wonder, then, that a conquest of the land and its inhabitants followed. For neighborhoods under the siege of Jim Crow for six decades, there was little power to fight off the attack on their territory.

RENEWAL RENEWED

Charlotte City Council lobbied the North Carolina state legislature for new enabling legislation for four years. When they finally won, the council moved quickly in November 1957 to appoint a new Redevelopment Commission.[12] The new threshold of blight needed for cities to take Urban Renewal Administration (URA) funds was 67 percent, an attainable number in comparison with the previous 100 percent. The new commission formed quickly, partly at the behest of the Charlotte Chamber of Commerce.[13] Their sights were no longer on Palmer's Alley, but instead the Brooklyn neighborhood.

The Redevelopment Commission did one year of preparatory work. Sawyer and his staff did another. Written reports formalized the processes, but the city had already reached its desired conclusions before writing down a single word. In the official Brooklyn "Blight Report," the commissioners stated that "if an interior inspection of structures had been included in the survey, there is little doubt that additional evidence of dilapidation and deterioration would have come to light." Commission staff did not even go inside the buildings to inspect them.[14] The commission used cursory judgments to submit reports, make future plans, and estimate costs in service of their desired outcome.[15] North Carolina's enabling legislation required that at least two-thirds of properties be dilapidated and/or deteriorated in order for 100 percent of the neighborhood to be taken. The commission's blight report assessed exactly 67.7 percent of structures to be in such condition.[16]

By January 1960, Sawyer, the commission, and the city council reached a critical point in their planning. After two years of preparation, they sought a formal resolution from the city council to the URA, the adoption of which indicated the city's intention to move forward on the program. The resolution was a point of no return, and, importantly, its approval by the URA would begin the flow of money. On January 18, 1960, the council adopted a resolution, on a vote of 5–2, stating plainly that the Brooklyn neighborhood was a "slum, blighted, deteriorated, or deteriorating area appropriate for an urban renewal project."[17] Councilmen Randolph Babcock (elder, Myers Park

Presbyterian) and Brevard Myers (vestryman, Christ Episcopal) voted against the resolution and took pains to enter a formal disagreement into the record the following week.[18]

Several speakers rose to speak during the January 18 meeting, both for and against the plans. Speaking in favor was Stan Brookshire (member, Myers Park Methodist), then the president of the Charlotte Chamber of Commerce and, beginning in 1961, the mayor of the city—though many might argue that this was a distinction without a difference. Brookshire pointed out that the chamber had endorsed Urban Renewal in Charlotte since April 1957. The business and political leaders of the city saw in the program an opportunity to remake an entire district while expending mostly federal monies. If there was one thing that would trump Charlotte's small-government predilections, it was the opportunity to build The Next Big Thing.

Martin Waters of Waters Insurance and Realty (elder, Myers Park Presbyterian) summarized the arguments against renewal that kept returning in public forums. These were the arguments of the white propertied class, and they found resonance with councilmembers Babcock and Myers, along with others who spoke before the city council and wrote letters to the editor at the *Charlotte Observer*. Addressing the council, Waters first disagreed on the matter of government using eminent domain to take private property. Second, he and other opponents were concerned that the deal was not as sweet as the advocates of Renewal wished them to believe. When all the accounts were settled, they thought the city would be out far more money than the rosy projections the Redevelopment Commission was making. Third, Waters said, "many widows, whose sole income comes from property within the area, will be deprived of this income and will be unable to reinvest funds for the property to obtain a like yield."[19] Landlording was profitable, especially so in segregated areas where conditions were allowed to deteriorate with few consequences. Waters warned that the effect of so-called "slum clearance" would be to clear out derelict housing to the detriment of those who owned and profited from it. Waters was not speaking on behalf of widows, though, or not only them. He was himself in real estate and echoed years of opposition by landlords who wanted to keep their large profit margins.[20]

The arguments put forward in public by white Charlotteans—most of whom, like Waters, were also Christians—were grounded in notions of how to remake the city in ways that benefited the white propertied class. Concerns over the welfare of African Americans remained secondary, at best, to arguments for property rights and return on investment. But the effort to remake center city Charlotte into a place that would look friendlier to white businesspeople and customers was taking place during exactly the moment when white residents were fleeing downtown for the rapidly growing suburbs. Indeed, among the primary projects that governmental bodies would produce from Urban Renewal efforts were the superhighways that made traveling into and out of center cities much faster.[21] As the racial geography began changing in Charlotte, white residents mostly went south and east, often down Providence and Park Roads, while Black residents began to be pushed west and northwest, setting off a pattern of segregation that remains evident some sixty years later.[22]

The spatial rearrangement of the city was of secondary concern to those in power, though they heard protest voiced loudly and repeatedly by Black leaders. In January 1960, the local National Association for the Advancement of Colored People (NAACP) chapter filed a lengthy report and inquiry with the Charlotte Redevelopment Commission. The report was loaded with incisive analysis of the cause of slum conditions and the national statistics documenting how Urban Renewal projects were destroying housing stock without replacing it. Leaders Mrs. U. S. Brooks and Kelly Alexander went on to name three ways that the projects were likely to strengthen white supremacy rather than to change the character of the city: by reinforcing segregation through the failure to utilize a democratic framework, by "uprooting" Black families and moving them out of "the community of their choice," and by having white leadership whose internalized "bigotry and prejudice" would move against the small progress already made in integration, especially in schools.[23]

The NAACP's report went on to list several dozen questions and recommendations that would create real improvement in Brooklyn and in other Black neighborhoods. Their concerns went unheeded, despite their public presentation in numerous forums.[24] The NAACP's concerns turned out to be correct. Black families continued to face both low supply of available housing and high demand for what was available. This led to artificially high prices and overcrowded conditions.[25] Planners were determined that Brooklyn could not be fixed without starting over. As to new housing options, city officials explained, the private market would fix the problem, and the construction of new public housing would be avoided unless absolutely necessary. At a 1961 city council meeting, then-mayor Brookshire tried to reassure the NAACP that the Redevelopment Commission was working to ensure that every family would have an affordable place to live and that they were relying on privately owned housing to do so. Alexander was incensed. "This is a dream. This is a farce," he said.[26]

Alexander was right. The private market would not, in fact, fix the problem.[27]

FIRST BAPTIST ON THE MOVE

City officials and Redevelopment Commission members claimed they were going to remake downtown, but other institutions saw clearly the spatial trends taking over American cities. At FBC, members were already making plans to respond to white flight and suburbanization and to do so in ways that would focus on growth in order to distract from "divisive" moral issues around the civil rights movement and Urban Renewal. The Future Program Committee had been studying the trends within the congregation and the city to make recommendations about how and where the church needed to grow. The committee issued a brief report in late 1958 under the title "Forward Program of Advance."[28] That report primarily cited the need for more space, including an auditorium, dining and recreational facilities, and off-street parking. Three methods for getting that additional space were expanding the existing building, moving elsewhere, or combining with Pritchard Memorial Baptist, the nearest white Baptist church. By April 1960, the Future Program Committee had studied these options and was ready to recommend a relocation.

The committee at FBC gave its recommendation at a crucial time in the city. The Redevelopment Commission was awaiting confirmation of the plans submitted by the city council in January of that year. Federal approval meant federal dollars to act on their years-long planning. The timing of the separate processes at FBC and in the city government converged in public on April 26. Atop the local section of the *Observer* was a large headline: "Brooklyn Plan Approved by Federal Government." The Redevelopment Commission had finally won approval of the first $1.4 million in federal money to fund its Brooklyn plans. The article detailing that milestone in the process explained what had happened and what would come next.

Nestled under the "Brooklyn Plan" headline was a smaller headline reading "First Baptist to Relocate?" The adjoining article was about the

Future Program Committee at FBC. Chairman C. C. Hope told the paper that an upcoming church business meeting would determine the right step forward from among three choices: do nothing, expand the present site, or move. It also included one short paragraph that made a connection that would go unrealized for some time at FBC, though it would eventually come to define the future of the congregation and, to some extent, of the entire city: "Several sites are being considered for a new First Baptist. Among them is a location in Brooklyn, the midtown slum section soon to be cleared through urban redevelopment. However, neither it nor any other has been chosen by Hope's committee."[29] Brooklyn land was a possibility for FBC, but there was not yet any agreement on whether it would become their new site.

Hope and Bates scheduled a congregational meeting for Sunday, May 8, for the committee to present its recommendation. The cover of the church newsletter sent out the week prior to May 8 featured big block letters on the front. "WE MUST PROVIDE," it proclaimed. Next to the block letters was a sketch of a suburban church campus, surrounded by parking, with a baseball field in the back corner. The committee, it seemed, already had a desired option. It used the imagery of the church newsletter to plant into the imaginations of members the kind of move it anticipated would come next—the suburbs, with ample parking.[30]

The May 8, 1960, meeting replaced the morning worship service. The sanctuary, with seats for 1,000, was no match for the crowd, which overflowed into a nearby small auditorium and was connected by a sound system. This was a monumental moment in the life of the church, which had met around downtown Charlotte for 128 years. They now looked ready to abandon their geographical prominence and to take their social and political heft elsewhere, though exactly where remained unclear.

Members of the committee offered personal testimony to the conclusion they had reached, as well as their reading of the facts that led to their decision. Congregation members asked questions and attempted to understand the decision they were being asked to make. Finally, the question was called. Pastor Bates rose to ask for the vote, first restating the issue at hand: "Based on the recommendation of the Future Program Committee, First Baptist Church will begin planning to relocate." The method of voting for such an important decision was to be fully open and to involve physical buy-in. Members would stand. "All in favor, signify by standing," Bates intoned. Around the auditorium, an "overwhelming majority" rose to their feet, ready to step forward in faith into new and unknown territory.[31]

The congregation was clear that there was no decision about where this move would take them. But within just a few months, the Future Program Committee was making its case to the deacon board. A majority of the committee wanted to move to a sixteen-acre lot about five miles south of town, the former home of North Carolina governor Cameron Morrison.[32] Their peer churches were making similar moves. St. Mark's Lutheran, one block north on Tryon Street, had already moved three miles south. Second Presbyterian, one block south on Tryon Street, had moved two miles south.[33]

The deacons rejected the proposed move, though it is not clear why. Pastor Bates, just a year into his ministry, thought the move was exactly the right one. However, he felt that he was too new to the congregation at the time to take a strong stance on the topic.[34] He would need a few years to build the necessary clout to make his opinion on the matter clear. A few blocks away, however, the Redevelopment Commission was not waiting to make its move.

A CHOSEN PEOPLE

On Sunday, November 6, 1960, Redevelopment Commission Director Vernon Sawyer walked up to the doors of Friendship Baptist Church. The brick sanctuary sat at the corner of South Brevard and East 1st Street, only ten blocks from FBC on North Tryon. Since 1892, the congregation had grown steadily into probably the most prominent Black church in Charlotte. Its roots could be traced back to the founding of Beulah Baptist in 1832, at a time when Black members were enslaved and not afforded actual membership in the church.

Walking up the steps, Sawyer and the *Charlotte Observer* reporter who accompanied him would surely have been greeted the way visitors at Friendship Baptist are greeted even today. A deacon opened the door. He was wearing a black suit, a crisp white shirt, a thin black tie, and a small nameplate marking him, in capital letters, as "DEACON." He was trained to contain his surprise at the sight of two white men entering for Sunday School and quick enough on his feet to transform his surprise into a look of hospitality. "Welcome to Friendship," he was expected to say, extending his cotton-gloved hand.

Sawyer moved through the door to locate Pastor Coleman Kerry. Sawyer brought an announcement this Sunday. In an act of presumption and conceit, he asked the pastor for access to the pulpit to deliver it (see figure 5.2).

Taking a place in front of the congregation, he delivered the message he brought for the day. The content of the message was plain: The City of Charlotte has determined that your neighborhood is blighted beyond repair. We are beginning a process of buying all 238 acres in the Brooklyn area. By fall of

Figure 5.2. Vernon Sawyer delivers his message to Friendship Baptist on November 6, 1960. Note the looks on the faces of Pastor Coleman Kerry Jr., to the rear of Sawyer, and the unnamed deacon or minister to Sawyer's left. Even with only a profile, the unnamed man displays clear shock and grief. Photo used by permission of *Charlotte Observer*.

1963, we will tear down the first of five sections we have created in Brooklyn, including this property. You will be responsible for locating another place to establish your church and for moving yourself there. "The time is getting late to make plans to rebuild your church," Sawyer said.[35]

And then, having asserted his political power over Friendship, he framed his speech to them in vaguely theological terms: "Without trying to sermonize, I'd like to point out one thing. Somewhere in the span of endless time, it was *you who were chosen* to lead in solving this problem in this crucial hour. . . . The challenge is before you."[36] God's work in history, he claimed, was to elect Friendship's torment. The congregation was to rise to the challenge of their divinely appointed suffering. What animated Sawyer's words, as well as the moves of the city council, the Redevelopment Commission, and the institutions who would profit from Friendship's misfortune, was the belief that the conquest of Black people and places by white people was providential. It was the work of God in the world, and it would soon be carved into the earth as a new streetscape and new sacred symbols.

The scene that Sawyer created shows the continuity of Urban Renewal with slavery and Jim Crow, earlier forms of racial domination. Reflecting on those earlier movements, Saidiya Hartman points to the telling example of minstrelsy, where "violence directed toward the [B]lack figure came to be identified as *its* pleasure and danger."[37] The photo above shows Sawyer's conceit—he is smiling, anticipating that his audience will enjoy their coming agony. But behind him, Rev. Kerry's face shows what Sawyer always had his back to: terror, rage, helplessness. When Sawyer pronounced the coming destruction of Friendship, he framed it as working for their benefit. It was Friendship who was *chosen*—a theological term that might indicate some sort of favor. But Hartman says that in the terms set forth by white supremacy, built from slavery, "injury and punishment defined the personhood of these characters. . . . Whether venerated as an opportunity for Christian endurance or legitimated by darky pretensions and trespasses, violence engendered [B]lackness."[38] Sawyer staged a drama that reinforced the absolute hegemony of the city's power structure over its Black citizens. His performance in the pulpit recreated a sort of minstrel theater, where he anticipated the congregation would show their gratitude for the violence to be enacted on them. They were chosen, gifted, elected, appointed, the happy recipients, in their agony, of divine favor. Sawyer, for his part, was the oracle, the angelic voice to announce the gift. The photo captures the theological world of Urban

Renewal: the redemptive suffering of an elect brought about entirely by the preferential option of those recreating white supremacy. Inside that world, white planners and councilmen and commissioners were little gods acting out their Christian faith and its long legacy of domination.

Sawyer's message came as a surprise to Friendship.[39] Though the plans for Urban Renewal in Charlotte had been publicized and argued over for several years, the reality of "erasing" the entire neighborhood and all of its institutions, not just its homes, was not yet clear.[40] During a Charlotte City Council meeting in January of that same year, two councilmembers filed a formal written objection to the renewal program. Among the reasons they cited for their opposition was that the program "assumes that the schools and churches which are left standing will continue to be attended after the people's homes have been bulldozed away."[41] Apparently, even city council members thought that only homes would be demolished. Besides, the target of the program was blight, and Friendship's condition was certainly not "blighted." Quite the opposite. Even so, Sawyer's visit was the first wrecking ball to tear through the sanctuary. The others would come later.

Pastor Kerry called for a congregational meeting that afternoon, following Sawyer's departure. He did his best to rally his stunned congregation.

"How many of you would like to do the impossible?" he asked. "How many of you, within the time limit, would like to see us have enough money to build and to operate and to meet the challenge of the future?"[42]

The entire congregation rose to their feet in response to his call. They declared their intent to move forward, even though their feet were rooted in that particular ground. Even though there was nowhere to go.

THE FIRST SALES

Since its institution in 1957, the Redevelopment Commission had developed extensive plans to be reviewed by Charlotte City Council. The plans were subject to official debate and public comment before the city council approved them. Sawyer and his staff then filed stacks of papers with the Housing and Home Finance Agency regional office in Atlanta. Sawyer and several commissioners would travel to Atlanta to defend their proposals to a board of government planners. The newspapers reported the various debates and hiccups in the process.

Eventually, with all the formalities checked off, the commission could begin acquiring property. Initial offers from the commission to homeowners were based on an appraisal, but lurking behind those offers was a threat: taking the property by force. If necessary, the city would claim title by eminent domain, the legal doctrine whereby a government can assert its right to a property when there is a compelling public interest. In mid-1961, Sawyer's staff began contacting individual owners to let them know of the coming transactions.

The first sale closed in August 1961, when real estate agent Lee Kinney (member, First Church of Christ, Scientist) signed over the deed to 616 E. 4th Street, which he had purchased in 1952. His case shows how housing economics from the New Deal through Urban Renewal worked to enrich white landowners during Jim Crow. Kinney was white. He had been in the real estate business for several decades. When Home Owners' Loan Corporation workers arrived in Charlotte in 1937 to draw the redlining maps of the city, Kinney had been one of the real estate men they employed for their local expertise. He had been purchasing properties in Brooklyn at least as early as 1926.[43] He redlined his own property.

Kinney was a large landowner with easy access to capital. Redlining had little effect on his personal stake in the property or the hundreds of others he owned. A 1960 *Observer* article made the math clear on the profits available. The paper cited one unnamed owner with a portfolio of forty-one homes valued in the tax records at about $1,000 each, a figure far below their replacement value, and noted in the city records to be of "very cheap" construction. Those homes together produced income of about $21,000 in a year, with less than $1,000 due annually in taxes.[44] When Martin Waters had argued to the city council that the incomes of many widows were at stake with Urban Renewal, these are the figures he was seeking to protect.

Kinney and the Redevelopment Commission invited the press to the transfer of the first deed of Charlotte's Urban Renewal project (see figure 5.3). Vernon Sawyer and the Redevelopment Commission lawyer joined Kinney and his attorney for the ceremonial signing, and Kinney left with a check for $18,000 (in 2023 dollars, about $180,000). Kinney's was the first transaction of 238 acres' worth of lots that would be claimed by the city over the coming decade.[45]

Exactly how the news broke to Hazeline North Anderson is unclear. Perhaps she received a letter. Maybe someone visited her house. At some point,

Figure 5.3. Vernon Sawyer (left) looks on while Lee Kinney, next to Sawyer, signs over 616 E. 4th Street, the first transaction in Charlotte's Urban Renewal projects. Photo use by permission of *Charlotte Observer*.

she received a notice. The Redevelopment Commission would purchase 625 E. 2nd Street. It was the house that Abram and Annie North built, the one Anderson spent most of her first years in, the one where she cared for her dying parents, the house where she had spent the last three decades. It was part of her parents' legacy, part of her own legacy, a place to be left to nieces and nephews. The Redevelopment Commission assessed that legacy at $6,300 (in 2023 dollars, about $63,000). Lee Kinney, on a lot of similar size, got three times the money for a structure about twice as large.[46]

It was an offer Anderson and her husband, Sam, could not refuse. With the force of eminent domain close behind, rejecting the city's offer would only risk not receiving any payment at all. They could hold out while watching their neighborhood mowed down around them, or they could move.[47] The Andersons had no leverage for negotiating with the Redevelopment Commission, which was empowered by the combined force of the City of Charlotte, the State of North Carolina, and the US government.[48]

Hazeline North Anderson herself was part of the work of God in history, attached as she was to the church her mother had helped to found and to a home her formerly enslaved parents had built, one she helped to maintain from the time of its construction. But for those holding the power and the planning documents, the providence of God looked otherwise. It was accompanied by a bulldozer and paperwork. Taking a place was a legacy as old as the Doctrine of Discovery, a manifest destiny to benefit a chosen nation. Hazeline North Anderson would become the first homeowner forced out by yet another chapter of serial displacement. In the place of her family's heritage there, the city was newly constructing an old vision. For Black Charlotteans, it was a terrible dream. It was a farce. But for white Charlotteans, it looked more and more like the hand of God.

CHAPTER SIX

Reluctant Destruction

In 1961, Stan Brookshire won election as Charlotte's mayor. He had previously been executive of the local Chamber of Commerce. In a town run by its booster class, one might wonder whether his new post was a step up or a step down. Among the issues facing Brookshire from his first moments in office was the city's Urban Renewal program, which stood on shaky ground in terms of public support. Black leaders, often working through the National Association for the Advancement of Colored People (NAACP), continued raising objections over the destruction of their neighborhoods and the lack of reasonable options for those displaced by the projects. White conservatives continued calling the program "socialism" and "government overreach" while seeking to protect high rates of return on their real estate investments.

The reworking of federal housing policy in the Housing Act of 1954 had made several demands on cities wishing to pursue Urban Renewal programs. If the US government was going to cover two-thirds or more of the costs of a massive project, then federal administrators wanted their local counterparts to meet numerous criteria that would ensure the overall success and acceptance of the projects. The Urban Renewal Administration required each municipality to create "a 'workable program' for utilizing appropriate private and public sources to eliminate and prevent the development or spread of slums and urban blight, to encourage needed urban rehabilitation, to provide for the redevelopment of blighted, deteriorated, or slum areas." Other requirements included considerations of new or existing housing for those to be displaced, proper accounting of the conditions of the areas targeted for clearance, and citizen participation to demonstrate the general support of the city where the project was to take place.[1] Charlotte's program was failing to meet the terms of the required "workable program." There was no plan for providing new housing. Multiple factions of the city raised persistent withering criticisms. Citizens were only engaged in opposition. Urban Renewal in Charlotte was in jeopardy in 1961.[2]

Mayor Brookshire needed allies in the push to maintain the program. He called on white liberals to support the city's efforts and rescue the "workable program." Among Brookshire's first acts was appointing a new Citizens' Committee on Urban Renewal (CCUR), a group that existed on paper but in practice had never produced any work. CCUR took up the task of winning over the city at large in the cause of the Redevelopment Commission. Their efforts became the most consequential for developing public support for the program. Two members in particular—one a member of the most liberal white church in Charlotte, the other a white Presbyterian minister who styled himself as something of a radical—helped to build that support. In the process, they paved the way for four more phases of destruction in Brooklyn and then four more Urban Renewal projects in other Black Charlotte neighborhoods.

THE CITIZENS' COMMITTEE

Brookshire's challenges came not only from the citizenry around him. They also came directly from federal regulators who noted the shortcomings of Charlotte's program. There were multiple issues, including the lack of a Citizens' Committee that would help to drive public engagement with the program. Brookshire appointed committee members and set them to work. CCUR's task was to study and transform the public narratives around the Redevelopment Commission's work. The initial group was led by real estate man Harry Brown. Other white members, by profession, included two more real estate agents, an architect, a mortgage banker, a representative of local women's clubs, a sanitation engineer, and a doctor. There were two Black members on the committee: Fred Alexander (member, University Park Baptist), brother of NAACP leader Kelly, who worked as a property manager; and funeral-home director Arthur Grier (member, Grier Heights United Presbyterian), who was one of the larger landowners in Brooklyn.[3]

Brookshire may have thought he could satisfy the Urban Redevelopment Administration (URA) office in Atlanta with those appointments, but federal regulators sent notice within a week that simply appointing a committee was insufficient. Program requirements included a specific subcommittee of CCUR that would study "minority group housing problems." The group should include "representative members of the principal minority groups [on] the committee."[4] Ongoing certification of the Brooklyn project required the subcommittee, the letter stated. No subcommittee to study housing problems, no funding. Another letter three weeks later demanded immediate rectification of the issue, at which time Brookshire appointed Alexander and Grier to a subcommittee alongside sanitary engineer Tom Bivins and Realtor Harry Brown.[5] Despite the dustup with regulators, though, there is no documentation that the Citizens' Committee held any meetings or otherwise did any work until midyear 1962. At that point, perhaps seeing his need for better public relations, perhaps feeling the heat from the URA office again, Brookshire appointed new leadership. The new appointees turned the Citizens' Committee into one of the most significant groups in Charlotte's Urban Renewal projects. They used their energy, skill, and connections to change the public perception of the program.

The new chair of CCUR was Zeb C. Strawn, an active member of Dilworth Methodist Church and the president of Citizens Bank, one of the elites in Charlotte's large banking industry. He was noted for his work in housing and urban development, having served terms on various city and regional boards.[6] Strawn publicly connected his work to his faith, as when he told an assembly of Black clergy that it was "God's will" to build a better life for everyone, including by providing better housing. His statement, like Vernon Sawyer's earlier statement to Friendship Baptist, was another example of the vague theological language used to justify the destruction of Black communities without altering the systemic conditions that created unsuitable living environments in many Black neighborhoods.[7]

Another appointment was George W. Crisler, a member of Providence Methodist Church and a retired loan officer. Crisler chaired the Relocation Resources Subcommittee, which took over the federally mandated function of studying the housing shortages created by Urban Renewal. Crisler reported back to Strawn that there were around four thousand families facing displacement by Renewal projects and that public housing would be necessary for some of them, especially elderly citizens and those with larger families. Mayor Brookshire and the Redevelopment Commission had long insisted that the housing market would absorb those displaced without the construction of any public housing. There were no publicly backed plans for new housing.

Crisler's subcommittee was not the only one to note the growing problem of displacement, though. In October 1962, the URA cut off Charlotte's Urban Renewal funding for lack of adequate housing plans. Only following the embarrassment of public consequences did Charlotte begin preparing to build more housing for Black citizens facing displacement. The general public learned of the federal suspension of Charlotte's program on a Monday in October 1962. The following Monday, the mayor approached the city council with a proposal for building hundreds of units of new public housing.[8]

The most important of the new appointments to the Citizens' Committee was Medd F. McNeill. His work, which he carefully documented, shifted the public view of Urban Renewal from one of skepticism to one of relative acceptance and support. McNeill, a member of the prestigious Myers Park Baptist Church (MPBC), used all his energy and all his connections in support of the city's efforts. Charlotte's "workable program" was not working. McNeill and his subcommittee became the crucial figures in turning it around.

BEAUTIFYING FAULTY FOUNDATIONS

McNeill joined the Citizens' Advisory Committee for his first meeting in August 1962.[9] It was a crucial moment for the entire Urban Renewal plan in Charlotte. Mayor Brookshire, Vernon Sawyer, and the city council had pushed against opposition for several years, but their most strident critics continued to speak against the program while it went through its various phases of administrative approval from Washington. Brookshire was concerned with the public relations problems posed by the opposition rather than with the nature of the plans themselves. He, the Redevelopment Commission, and the city council were fully convinced that Urban Renewal was the best—even the only—option for Charlotte. But without wider buy-in from the city at large, Brookshire could not keep his critics at bay and risked losing the program altogether. To keep moving forward, Brookshire needed to be able to demonstrate the active support of his citizenry.

In McNeill, Brookshire found the right man to help craft a new narrative. Brookshire and new Citizens' Committee chair Zeb Strawn assigned McNeill to chair the Community Improvement Subcommittee, and McNeill applied his ample energy to the task. He was eager to develop public buy-in and to help to build a new image of the Urban Renewal program. The Redevelopment Commission wanted the public to see the program as "a way of turning slums into places where children may play and grow up safely and where business may flourish . . . a way of making Charlotte a better place in which to live," though the actual plans were simply the displacement of people and the redistribution of land.[10] The members of the Citizens' Committee would "enlist the cooperation and service of the local newspapers, radio, and television stations . . . in presenting facts about the Urban Renewal program." They would further engage a bureau of speakers, who were also members of the Citizens' Committee, to give speeches about the program's origins and vision. The speeches, as they attempted to reset the image of the program, were to be "approved by the executive committee to be sure that they are factual."[11] In other words, the committee was engaged in a public relations campaign, with approved talking points and a cohesive strategy. To move forward, Mayor Brookshire, McNeill, and the committee would need to control the narrative.

McNeill worked his position with zeal. Whereas other subcommittee chairs left little documentation and made few reports, McNeill used the time opened by his recent retirement to maintain a full schedule with CCUR, which he documented at nearly every step. He began his tenure with a flurry of meetings with stakeholders in many sectors of Charlotte.[12] The federal workable program requirement demanded engagement across a city, not only in the areas subject to clearance. So McNeill proposed the establishment of neighborhood organizations "in every depressed area," modeling them after the Improvement Association of Charlotte's Belmont-Cordelia neighborhood. That organization, he reported, had more than one hundred members who went about "cleaning up the grounds surrounding every home, beautifying them through planting of grass, shrubbery, repairing many homes, [and] removing some of them that are beyond 'reasonable cost of repairs.'"[13] McNeill was going to build grassroots support for Urban Renewal by engaging people in beautification projects.

Neighborhood leaders around the city began replicating the kinds of efforts McNeill was encouraging. In the Greenville neighborhood, a Black district north of downtown, several ministers and leaders conferred with him in late 1962. He offered the group his method of "cleaning up around each and every house, business establishment, inside and out, planting shrubbery and making the place look attractive. Clean up every street, sidewalk, all rubbish to be hauled away . . . by city trucks." Once all the cleaning was done, he instructed, "then, we propose to ask ALL property owners to give immediate consideration to making repairs, looking toward bringing every house . . . up to the minimum City of Charlotte Building Code requirements."[14] McNeill's energy was contagious, at least within some segments of the population, but his goal was never going to have any long-term effect. As late as 1966, he was still organizing neighborhood cleanups in Brooklyn, after the city was more than halfway through the effort to raze 238 acres to the ground.[15]

At the end of 1962, McNeill provided a comprehensive summary of his aims with the Community Improvement Subcommittee. He outlined his goals and the results he thought they would produce in a speech at the Dilworth Rotary Club in December. Dilworth was primarily a well-to-do neighborhood that developed as the city's earliest streetcar suburb.[16] Its Rotary Club membership consisted of businessmen, church deacons, local political and social leaders, and significant numbers of landowners and real estate men, all of them white.[17] McNeill appealed to them in several ways, beginning with their purse strings. Bringing all properties up to the city code would cut fire losses, reduce police spending, and raise tax values, he offered.[18] The program would offer not only economic benefit, McNeill proposed, but also spiritual and moral uplift. He suggested to his audience that morality in poor neighborhoods was lacking, a prejudice they already held: "There are too many of our people who do not care for anything except themselves, what they want and get is a bottle, a woman, and a place to be together." He went further, saying, "[There is] another group with little or no ambition, education, or foresight for the future [who] are living, or just existing, five or ten or more in these 2- or 3-room shacks." McNeill recruited the Rotary Club into the scenario as well, saying, "It's taken us 100 years to get into this fix. We are guilty of gross negligence, every one of us."[19]

McNeill posed the problem as primarily one of individual guilt, on behalf of individuals from every side. In this way he was consistent with the dominant theological strains of his day, especially among the Southern Baptists to whom he belonged. Sin was an individual problem; salvation was the individual's solution; holiness, as the outward evidence of individual salvation, was the individual's attempts to resolve social problems through self-improvement or by charitable acts for those impoverished. McNeill proposed to the Dilworth Rotarians that they could voluntarily make efforts at improving conditions. People could move private resources to address housing deficiencies, for instance. "BUT," he said, "if we are not willing, cannot, or will not do so, bring our living standards up to minimum requirements, then a way must be found."[20] The way, of course, was already underway in 1962. It was the razing of certain Black neighborhoods, beginning with Brooklyn. That move had significantly different results on those whose neighborhoods were taken, though, than on those whose high-return investments were lost. Nevertheless, McNeill was convinced that there was some cohesive "we" who must grapple with the problem. "If every civic group, every church, and every employer . . . would organize and face this problem squarely, then— WE—all of us, could get on with the job," he said.[21] McNeill never named that the "solution" of Urban Renewal and the burden it brought did not fall evenly on those it affected—landlord, tenant, homeowner, church member, business owner. Whoever he thought "all of us" was, it did not include the people losing homes, businesses, churches, and institutions. Or at least it did not include them in such a way that would have meaningful effects on the end results of Renewal projects.

McNeill made the passive statement "a way must be found." Passive voice is grammatical reticence. McNeill's statement concealed who was acting and whom was being acted on. It hid the nature of the decisions that powerful people had already made. Passive voice is one of the ways the silencing specter slips in, where it may trespass on yet another system, another place, another family, another soul. Passive constructions create mystery—"how did this come to be?"—and render issues too difficult to solve. It helps white people make the silent pact among ourselves to uphold white supremacy. As with the disciples in Mark 9, the silencing spirits become nearly impossible to cast out even as they wreak destruction across generations.

McNeill's passive statement acknowledged—perhaps even threatened—that if those with the power of land ownership could not find enough goodwill, then the government would apply force to coerce a change of behavior. Either people would alter their landlording practices or the government would do it for them. There was, of course, no solid evidence that the preponderance of white citizens would change their racial ideology or their business practices. Nor was there any reason to think that public institutions would alter policies that encouraged and rewarded absentee landlording. When governmental intervention came, it was an expression of power. It would not harm those who hoarded land and with it political and economic control. The harm would fall squarely on the shoulders of those who had spent their lives maneuvering through a system designed to render them powerless. In fact, as noted in chapter 5, IRS policies requiring that payouts be reinvested for like purposes had the likely effect of reinventing exploitative landlord relationships in other neighborhoods.

McNeill was not unconcerned with the plight of those who stood to lose their neighborhoods. However, he characterized them as spiritually weak rather than politically oppressed, as deficient in morality rather than over-burdened by the accumulated effects of white supremacy. To the Rotarians, he suggested, "There must be organized many groups: to look after the moral questions! To look after the spiritual side! Where are all of our Christian citizens and what are they doing?"[22] One of the answers to that question is that one Christian citizen was the mayor. Five other Christian citizens were Redevelopment Commissioners. What they were doing was making the material conditions in Brooklyn worse without providing even basic housing opportunities in other neighborhoods for those displaced. There was a "spiritual side" of those white Christians that needed attention and care. So far as the record shows, their pastors or Sunday School teachers also found themselves in the hold of the silencing spirit.

McNeill's beautification program saved no neighborhoods, but it did comport with the logic of Christian practice in his time, especially in white churches. So he wrote to churches and ministers for support. He assumed that in churches he could find volunteers for charity work. McNeill asked pastors to form small groups to help in neighborhoods across Charlotte. He wanted them to "promote better health and living conditions for ALL our people through 'clean-up,' 'wash-up' and 'paint-up' programs as a means of developing pride in cleanliness, orderliness, and the beauty of one's surroundings." Following that, churches might also help to "create a sense of MORAL, SPIRITUAL, AND MATERIAL values."[23]

McNeill's notes and correspondence lack any consciousness of the historical forces that established material deprivation. For liberal Christians like McNeill, the conditions in poor neighborhoods reflected malformed souls. Cleanup projects made sense, as though they might at the same time polish the economic and spiritual conditions of poor people. Not far below that belief was the self-justification of Christians who worshipped in progressive places like Myers Park Baptist Church and who saw their own wealth as evidence of blessing, of God's benevolent work for them in the course of history. McNeill turned to churches for assistance in addressing the façades of neighborhoods without asking them to examine the foundations of the issue. Churches were a ready-made audience, and white churches in particular, conditioned as they were by decades of teaching and preaching that rarely, if ever, challenged white supremacy.

Around them, white Christians could have heard Black people, including Black Christians and Black ministers, calling for a deeper excavation of the faith practiced in white churches. Such calls were happening locally through the NAACP. They were also happening nationally. On April 16, 1963, one day after McNeill's letter to churches, Rev. Dr. Martin Luther King Jr. penned a letter to white clergy in Birmingham, written inside a jail and published nationally a month later. In it, King criticized the white moderate, about whom he said, "In the midst of blatant injustices inflicted upon the Negro, I have watched white churchmen stand on the sideline and mouth pious irrelevancies and sanctimonious trivialities." King was not writing directly about Urban Renewal, but it was going on around him. He and other Black leaders lived inside a reality that well-meaning white leaders could not, or would not, see: underneath the visible looks of a neighborhood was a theological and political project that was about power and control over land and space, justified by a commitment, sometimes overt and sometimes unstated, to white domination. Beautification projects left domination unchallenged while providing "a negative peace which is the absence of tension" rather than "a positive peace which is the presence of justice."[24]

Robert McClernon, one of McNeill's pastors at Myers Park Baptist, had been thinking about the moral concerns that Urban Renewal projects raised. In November 1962, he wrote to Redevelopment Commission chair Elmer Rouzer, inviting him to present at a Myers Park Baptist Men's Club meeting in January 1963. In his invitation, McClernon asked Rouzer to give direction to the men of MPBC and offered his own take. "We are desirous of having the facts presented to us no matter how disconcerting these might be and of hearing from you what you believe the church ought to be doing in this area. For my own part I sense that in the main Christians have been looking at urban renewal as property owners rather than as exponents of ethical values," he wrote.[25]

McClernon was informed in his perspective by an opinion piece published in *Christian Century*, the leading journal among white liberal Christians, in June 1962.[26] In that piece, church strategist and urban planner Rev. Lyle Schaller called into question the goals and practices of the Urban Renewal program across the nation. He pointed out that the goals of cities to increase their tax base and developers to increase their profits stood in contrast to the stated goal of the program for relieving slum conditions. He questioned the matter of citizen participation—the very work McNeill was engaged in—because it was limited largely to support of conservation and rehabilitation projects and was "of practically no relevance to the far more important matter of selecting clearance projects and assigning priorities among the many renewal possibilities." Schaller pointed out how the punitive measure of destroying urban dwellers' neighborhoods stood in contrast to the strategy of federal assistance to farmers. In one program, those who were poor were punished for their poverty; in the other, "the whole nation . . . was held responsible and taxed . . . for a 'rehabilitation and conservation' program ranging from soil conservation to price supports and the farmer [was] considered a victim rather than a creator of the problem." Though he did not mention race directly, the contrasting examples of farmers and poor urbanites certainly suggested the common images of how those two categories were racialized. Schaller was clear-eyed in assessing how greed and racism were primary inputs into Renewal and that white churches were failing to speak or act in accordance with their faith. He concluded, "Both urban renewal and the general public are suffering from neglect of the moral questions implicit in such a far-reaching program so full of temptations to sinful man."

Schaller, and McClernon in echoing him, took a position consistent with a small movement among liberal Protestants at the time. The Renewal movement, whose name overlapped with Urban Renewal, tried to connect the physical decline of American cities with the institutional decline of liberal Protestantism. Historian Mark Wild says "the concept of renewal—understood by secular planners as the physical and, consequently, social reconstruction of the urban environment and by liberal Protestants as a perpetual process of self-reflection, repentance, and revitalization, both personal and institutional—promised a solution to both problems."[27] One report from a Renewalist, dated 1957, showed how that movement viewed the overlapping possibilities of renewing both church and city: "The goal of urban renewal and the goal of the church focus on the human individual, his welfare, his chance of happiness, and his fulfillment of a meaningful existence."[28] By the time of Schaller's *Christian Century* piece in 1962, though, most Renewalists had soured on Urban Renewal because of the injustices of both the conceptions and the results of the program. The federal program, and its local administration, was making life worse, not better, especially in Black neighborhoods. Renewalists shifted their strategies for dealing with federal Urban Renewal, at times by trying to influence and reform the program and at other times standing in outright defiance.

The Renewalists never had much presence in Charlotte. McClernon's meeting suggested some coming resistance from liberal Protestants like those at MPBC, but none ever materialized. Indeed, the opposite seemed to be the case. McNeill's note from the January 1963 meeting at MPBC said that of more than one hundred men in attendance, many got involved "in various phases of our voluntary efforts in more than ten areas of the city."[29] Rev. Carlyle Marney, the senior pastor at MPBC and the most recognizable white liberal Protestant in Charlotte, invited McNeill to present to more than two hundred ministers at the Charlotte Ministers' Association meeting in February 1963. Marney joined the cause further by volunteering for multiple local television appearances arranged by McNeill, where he and other prominent public figures spoke on behalf of the program.[30]

FACELIFTS AND FOUNDATIONS

Over the course of the next several years, McNeill pushed hard for citizen involvement in beautification projects. His 1963 reports alone noted no less than twenty different neighborhood and civic groups whose participation in various cleanup efforts he had helped to coordinate.[31] He continued to use mass media to spread word of his efforts, reaching thousands upon thousands in the process. The media provided him with good coverage. The *Observer* highlighted his efforts at least a dozen times in the five years he served on CCUR.[32] So did the *Charlotte News*, which cast the work as salvific: "Residents Pitch In to Save Some Fine Old Neighborhoods," it proclaimed.[33] Adding to the ongoing echoes of theological language around Urban Renewal, the full page spread prominently featured a preacher taking the lead in the clean-up efforts, Rev. Richard Hildebrandt. He would become McNeill's most important ally within the Citizens' Committee.

McNeill naively believed that beautification efforts would alter a trajectory that had been set by a system of racialized land ownership and its resultant profits, not by individual acts of dropping or picking up litter. Embedded in the landscape of white Christianity was—and still is—the concern for spiritual good over material benefit. As with McNeill and the theological world he inhabited, white Christians tend to consider wealth, land ownership, and social and political power as evidence of God's work on their behalf. The silent assumption implicit in their/our belief is that material poverty is accompanied by spiritual poverty. When McNeill organized a beautification project in the west Charlotte neighborhood called Hoskins, he noted the spiritual results. "Without exception, in every committee that has organized clean-up campaigns, there has been an increase in church attendance," he said.[34] Perhaps that was true. But it would not stop the bulldozers from running through Greenville, or Third Ward, or First Ward, and tearing down those churches with their increased attendance.

And it certainly was not true that church attendance was on the rise in Brooklyn. McNeill was organizing cleanups there at least as late as 1966, half a decade into the razing of the neighborhood.[35] Even as neighbors tossed out old furniture and filled up refuse bins, the City of Charlotte was continuing to tear down the sanctuaries where those neighbors had spent several generations worshipping. The irony, for McNeill and others, is that while he thought that his cleanups were enriching the spiritual care of poor people in their neighborhoods, they were more likely laundering the souls of white folks in churches like Myers Park Baptist, the sorts of places where powerful people and groups quietly resided. And even as the cleanups continued, the destruction of churches and homes—centers for spiritual care—proceeded in Brooklyn and began to be planned for other neighborhoods.

Neither beautification nor any prescribed act of "citizen participation" was going to prevent the trespass of the bulldozers into Charlotte's Black neighborhoods. Charity cannot be the answer to justice claims; façade repairs will not solve foundation issues. McNeill had asked the Dilworth Rotary Club, "Where are all of our Christian citizens and what are they doing?" He posed the question in a generalized way when it had a racialized answer. Black Christians were picking up the pieces of their lives and trying to preserve their institutions under attack. They were fighting for the right to vote, and for equal access to education and transportation and public accommodations, and for the geographical space they needed to help give their rights material meaning. They were inviting white Christians to break their silence and work together for something like liberation. It was a call that would go unheeded, even by the most progressive of the white preachers in Charlotte.

RELUCTANT DESTRUCTION

"The church has failed, very definitely, to be responsible in some areas of the city." So said Rev. Richard Hildebrandt in a 1964 public meeting sponsored by the Citizens' Committee.[36]

His tendency for straight talk and his sense of joining together ministry and activism had won Hildebrandt an invitation as a clergy representative on the committee in 1963. He was then relatively new to Charlotte, a young minister on the move from a church in rural Elkin, North Carolina, to the state's largest city. Hildebrandt served at Wilmore Presbyterian Church. The church's neighborhood was adjacent to Dilworth, both of them just south of the center city. Whereas Dilworth was mostly a well-to-do district, Wilmore was a bit more working class. Both neighborhoods were primarily white, though certain blocks within them had Black residents. Both Dilworth and Wilmore had some areas that had faced long enough periods of disinvestment to have landed them in conditions of disrepair.

In response, Hildebrandt helped in 1963 to start the Dilworth-Wilmore Community Improvement Association, one of Medd McNeill's growing number of neighborhood organizations. Shortly after starting that, Hildebrandt landed himself a seat on the CCUR. He became one of the committee's favorite speakers to send out for public addresses on Urban Renewal. Hildebrandt had a fiery spirit and was not afraid to stir up controversy with his words.[37] Among the white members of CCUR, he was the most vocal about how public and private policies governing land use and housing were at the source of oppressive conditions in Black neighborhoods.

In a July 1963 meeting of the Dilworth-Wilmore Association, held at Dilworth Methodist Church, Hildebrandt gave a speech about Urban Renewal where he addressed the economic issues that had created persistent substandard housing problems. "There are a whole lot of people making a living off of the kind of substandard property [the housing] code is designed to stop," he said.[38] Hildebrandt correctly identified that one significant factor keeping substandard housing in place—perhaps the primary factor—was its high profit margins. For those facing tight housing supply because of racial discrimination, low wages due to racist labor practices, and the difficulty of buying due to the policies of both banks and the federal government, there was often no other choice than to overpay for substandard housing. Renting what was available, regardless of its condition, was not a moral failure on behalf of Black residents. It was the result of the greed of landlords and the structure of the housing market.[39]

At a later speech for the Dilworth Rotary Club, in December 1963, Hildebrandt was even more forceful. "We are never going to see the end of slums until we have broken the back of the high profits that are available to those who own and operate them," he said.[40] That comment caught the ire of some listeners, including one J. J. Pierce, who wrote Hildebrandt in response. Pierce, an owner of low-rent properties, told Hildebrandt to mind his own business and to remember who was paying his salary. "Did you ever stop to think that your bread and butter—even the clothes on your back, your salary and the building of our churches, and the upkeep of [the] same all come from profits?" he asked. "Are you opposed to our form of government? I would not dare call you a Communist, but your thinking and your teaching is right down the Russian line."[41]

Hildebrandt was unimpressed. He kept speaking in other venues on behalf of the CCUR, and he kept the pressure on his own constituency as it related to facing the problems of entrenched and racialized poverty in Charlotte. To one CCUR-sponsored public meeting in March 1964, Hildebrandt proclaimed, "The church has failed, very definitely, to be responsible in some areas of the city." He described the problem as a class problem, though that economic designation appeared to be doing double duty as a marker for race also. "We want to get away from our problems, we want to get away from being poor, we want to get away from poor people, all of them," he said. In Hildebrandt's mind, isolation from the poor classes was a lack of faith.[42] McNeill took up the same theme in that meeting, saying that "the city's churches were falling short of their responsibilities to help out several thousand forgotten people."[43]

Hildebrandt turned his overt attacks away from those who were poor in his community and toward his own people. He pointed out to them their neglect of their neighbors and their preference for profit over the good of their fellow citizens. Strangely, Hildebrandt remained a favored member of the CCUR, regularly called on to speak in support of the city and the Redevelopment Commission.[44] Hildebrandt's colleagues in the Citizens' Committee, as well as other city officials, thought that their support of the Redevelopment Commission was solidarity with those who were poor, but in practice, it was hegemony over them. It was a critical contradiction that allowed them to perceive of a trespass of enormous magnitude as a public good.

Despite his public testimony that verged on radical, Hildebrandt's imagination remained captive to the logic of Urban Renewal. He gave speeches regarding the problem of predatory landlords but still could not help but take aim at those who were poor. In the 1963 Dilworth-Wilmore Association meeting at Dilworth Methodist Church, Hildebrandt said, "Our problem is that we have some sadly neglected neighborhoods. We see this neglect all about us. We see it in our schools. . . . We see it in our churches. . . . We see it in people. Neglect is particularly noted among that 'front-porch sitting,' undershirt clad, beer drinking, dirty element that has moved in as purposelessly as they will move out."[45] The temptation to blame poor people for their poverty was too great, the spectacle of the bulldozer too alluring.

In that speech, Hildebrandt identified the three steps to come for redressing blight. First, he said, the association would conserve and preserve every block that had not yet given in to blight. Second, the neighborhood would rehabilitate those properties that could be repaired. They would do so by pressuring landowners to bring their housing up to code. And thirdly, the association would employ the help of the Redevelopment Commission to raze those areas that could not be rehabilitated. "It is the extremity with which we hope we will not have to deal," he said. "But if we must, we will."[46]

In his public statements, printed to tens of thousands of *Observer* readers, Hildebrandt had pushed for Christians to side with poor people. Finally, though, his language betrayed him. His *we* was not the *we* of solidarity with those oppressed but the *we* of an appointed member of a city bureaucracy, of a proponent of a program of widespread displacement, of those wielding the sledgehammers and planning the devastation.

When Stan Brookshire reactivated the Citizens' Committee in 1962, he knew that the city's project was in jeopardy on multiple fronts. The city's missteps with the federal government, plus the faltering public relations for the program, threatened to undercut the work of the city council and the Redevelopment Commission, as well as the young administration of Mayor Brookshire. Above any others, McNeill, Hildebrandt, and Strawn turned the tide. Not only did they shift the public narrative regarding the Brooklyn project, but they also helped to expand the work further into the city. Poor people, almost all of them Black, on every side of the center city would soon find themselves being displaced from the spaces they called home.

When CCUR chair Zeb Strawn filed his annual report with the mayor in January 1964, he was effusive in his praise of McNeill and this subcommittee, including Hildebrandt. "The work done by this committee is astounding and the good accomplished is beyond comprehension," Strawn said. "Mayor Brookshire, I am happy to report to you that the disturbing and discouraging criticism of a year or more ago has all but vanished. I have every reason to believe that the good people of this city now have a better understanding of our Urban Renewal program and the activities of the Citizens Advisory Committee and are willing and anxious to support it in its entirety."[47] The "workable program" was working.

The *Observer* agreed. Columnist Dorothy Knox wrote that CCUR's efforts had fulfilled its task. "It seems to me the Mayor's Citizens' Committee on Urban Renewal, which is so largely a matter of educating the public in various ways," she wrote, "would be a wonderful, constructive interest for Charlotte's large number of outstanding, retired business leaders, civic and professional men."[48] She cited two men who were significantly responsible for the committee's success—McNeill and Hildebrandt. McNeill, she reported, had recently concluded yet another cleanup, one that ultimately got landlords to make repairs to several dozen homes. And regarding Hildebrandt, she recommended him to a religious friend who was complaining that her pastor did not seem to make the Bible applicable to real life. She wrote, "Maybe she should attend a few sermons by the Reverend R. E. Hildebrandt, pastor of the Wilmore Presbyterian Church and president of the Dilworth-Wilmore Community Improvement Association. His fight against filth and ugliness to halt the physical and moral decline of this city has all us gals and guys of the press cheering."[49]

At the same time, Rev. Carlyle Marney was still speaking up for Renewal efforts. From the pulpit at Myers Park Baptist, he encouraged his members to "get to work in the same manner as that young Presbyterian minister over at Wilmore, and [Medd] McNeill, who is doing an outstanding piece of work among many of our Charlotte people, bringing to the attention the poverty, shamefull [sic] living conditions of all of our people through the NEWS MEDIA. [I]t's time we take inventory, do something to help McNeill and his associates."[50] Marney at the same time praised Brookshire for his leadership. He used the paternalistic language of a Southern Baptist missionary—a "piece of work among many of our Charlotte people"—combined with the guilt-reducing language preferred by his wealthy congregants—"bringing attention to poverty"—all at once, from the city's leading white civil rights advocate. When Marney spoke to his congregation, he stood in an ornate pulpit, carved of walnut, capped by a ciborium, and raised eight feet above the main floor. His congregants sprawled out below him on pews made from the same walnut. The wooden furnishings supporting them had been harvested from a grove of walnut trees in Philadelphia, uprooted for one of that city's Urban Renewal projects.[51]

For his part, Hildebrandt lived in a state of reluctance, being of a divided mind. He could see and articulate the economic and material issues that kept some people and some neighborhoods poor. He could issue words with enough force to rile up his opposition, getting himself branded a "communist" along the way. And yet the capitalist logic practiced in white Protestant space still ran through his speeches and his ability to envision the world. Though perhaps he did not want to, he still blamed poor people for their poverty. He characterized them as lazy and drunk. Ultimately, his *we* that he sided with was not the poor to whom Jesus came preaching good news[52] but the *we* who would finally raze the neighborhood if that choice seemed prudent. That was the same *we* that was running his fellow ministers out of the Brooklyn neighborhood, but he was unable to show a solidarity formed by common vocation and religious identity.

Brookshire ultimately won the narrative battle. Beautification worked in the effort to change the public discourse around Urban Renewal. Telling a better story did not change the results that Brooklyn and other neighborhoods faced. It enabled them. White churches were present and active. Their members pushed for the program in their official work capacities.

Progressives and conservatives, like those at Myers Park and at First Baptist, disagreed over the advances of the civil rights movement. But they were joined by their common conviction of white sovereignty over the land they had learned to call "Charlotte" and the country they called the United States of America. The civil rights movement won rights to the ballot and to desegregated public accommodations, often with the aid of white progressives. At the same time, white society reasserted its domination of title to land and space.

And so white liberal Christians played their parts, following the leadership of civic leaders and clergy who called for their support. When Charlotte's Urban Renewal program was struggling, the Citizens' Committee and its white Christian leadership put its influence to work in rehabilitating and expanding the program. They succeeded in keeping the bulldozers running through Brooklyn, so they next turned their eyes to other neighborhoods. Surveying the city in 1965, the Citizens' Committee reflected on their work. They then issued a resolution to City Council:

> Whereas the Committee has been most gratified with many phases of the total urban renewal effort . . . and the Urban Redevelopment program which to date has been confined to the clearance and redevelopment of the Brooklyn section of the city . . . ; Now, therefore, be it resolved that the Executive Committee of the Citizens' Advisory Committee on Urban Renewal recommends that the City Council expand at the earliest possible time the city's Urban Redevelopment program into the First Ward, Greenville, Third Ward, portions of old Dilworth, and the downtown sections of the City which the City Council has already suggested that the Charlotte-Mecklenburg Planning Commission study.[53]

More and more bulldozers would begin to run. In an ever-reaching quest for territory, more and more Christians would join these trespasses of the holy.

CHAPTER SEVEN

Two Visions inside Whiteness

Bill and Jenna Poe loaded their children into the family car in the fall of 1963.[1] A northward turn out of their driveway at the top edge of Myers Park would point them toward downtown. They made that drive multiple times each week as they headed to First Baptist. Sunday morning, Sunday evening, Wednesday night, and whenever else the door was open, the Poes were fixtures. Jenna had spent years there as the daughter of former pastor C. C. Warren. Bill was from Oxford, North Carolina, a small town near Durham. He was a preacher's kid who married a preacher's kid. He quickly fit right into the ministries at the First Baptist Church (FBC). The building was a second home for each of them.

One typical path the Poes took to FBC went through the Brooklyn neighborhood. The kids' favorite landmark along the way was the brightly colored tile on the steps and the portico of the United House of Prayer for All People. Among the faces on the sidewalks in Brooklyn might be Ms. Love. She lived in the neighborhood and came to Myers Park to work in the Poe household. She lived differently in their imaginations than the other people of Brooklyn. She was like a part of the family, they told themselves. And to some extent, they acted that way by treating her with honor and kindness for decades after her employment with them ceased. The characterization of her as "family" never collapsed the differences, though, between Brooklyn and Myers Park. Their affection had political and economic limitations defined by race and geography, limitations they might exceed for an individual but not for the larger group.

On this fall day, though, the Poes headed south, away from downtown and toward the southern edge of Myers Park. They were quickly onto Charlotte's grandest boulevard, Queens Road West, lined with mansion after mansion. Below soaring oak trees, homeowners mixed several architectural movements: Windsor, Tudor, Edwardian, Ostentatious. They pulled to a stop at a wooded lot just beyond the southern tip of Myers Park Country Club, near Sharon Road and Runnymede Lane. This, Bill Poe told the family, was the new place the church might be moving. He encouraged them to imagine a new sanctuary, a playground, a cafeteria. Perhaps a gym or a ball field. There would be plenty of Sunday School space and a wide yard for massive dinners on the grounds.

Charlotte's suburbs were spilling over into the countryside. Runnymede Lane was to be part of a new loop road, a wide path that circled five miles out from downtown. It attached to Tryon Street on either end. In true Charlotte form, it carried four different names along the way. The city planned the loop road to move a high volume of cars. The FBC leaders were betting that the road would make it easy for hundreds of people to descend on a new campus Sunday morning, Sunday evening, and Wednesday night, and at other key times during the week. There would be plenty of parking available when they arrived.

Along the loop road, and moving farther southward from it, developers were building thousands of homes as fast as possible and along with them new shopping centers. The Federal Housing Administration (FHA) mortgage insurance program was an accelerant for the construction industry, and builders were churning out houses as fast as they could clear land. The federal FHA program was rife with racism, a problem exacerbated by the influence of local policies from the obvious—Jim Crow laws—to the seemingly benign—zoning regulations like minimum lot sizes. But purely from a numerical sense, the FHA programs aimed at increasing homeownership were wildly successful.[2] The cumulative effect of federal and local housing policies had cities across the country exploding into their adjacent countrysides. Charlotte was keeping pace in the race to build outward. There was no shortage of land or redevelopment opportunities available within the already developed areas of the city, but repair was not the course that development took. The policies of the day made fixing old cities expensive. By comparison, new subdivisions and strip malls were cheap.[3] Federal tax laws incentivized building new subdivisions and shopping centers rather than renovating old neighborhoods and commercial centers. The outward stretch of cities and suburbs was on.

Leaders at FBC were strategizing their future based on the trends they saw. Their people were moving farther from town, mostly to the south. The church's pool of likely new members was growing as the city itself grew, and real estate agents were steering them toward the southern suburbs.[4] For six years, the Future Program Committee had gone round about debating locations, until finally settling on these sixteen acres. A majority of the committee could see where much of Charlotte's future development was headed, even if some did not like it. They were not unanimous, but it was time to move forward. In October 1963, the committee was ready to make a bid on the land, with the congregation's approval.

Poe told his children nothing of the debates and disagreements inside the congregation. He shielded them from the church's politics and taught them to love the institution, regardless of what happened with the move or with any other decision. That is how he operated, both personally and professionally. Silently standing at the edge of the woods, near the corner of Sharon and Runnymede, Bill Poe remained convinced that the future of his church was not in the southern suburbs. He had lost in the committee, and he was preparing his children for the change he anticipated. But he was not yet ready to be silent. Poe did not lose arguments easily, and until the defeat was final, he would not concede.[5] The debate was set to move into a public forum. Attorney Poe was ready to press his case.

THE TERMS OF THE DEBATE

The week leading up to FBC's October 27, 1963, business meeting was charged with anxiety for First Baptist families. They were set to make perhaps the most consequential decision in the history of the congregation. There was a spirit of unsettledness with their ranks, though. Tangible evidence of dissent within the church arrived in the mail that week. The church office sent a large packet containing three letters to every church household. One letter came from C. C. Hope, chair of the Future Program Committee. Over four pages, he presented the evidence for a move and outlined the basic facts and figures the committee had considered in the process. A second letter was signed by Pastor Bates, stating his case for making the move over two pages. A third letter, also four pages long, came from the members of the Future Program Committee who opposed the committee's decision to move to the new South Park area.[6]

Sending such a packet is an unusual strategy for church governance. Baptists often appeal to their long history as dissenters in public affairs, but

Baptist pride in dissent typically comes from churches seeking the exercise of religious liberty against a state actor, not from differing factions inside a congregation. The leadership choosing to make public the terms of an unresolved debate indicates what a difficult spot they had arrived at. They were stuck. Six years into the work of the Future Program Committee, the group could not build a consensus among themselves, so they resorted to making their disagreement public in hopes that their fellowship would hold together in the face of intense conflict. In a fashion often spoken of in Baptist churches, but rarely put to such a test, they decided to trust that God would guide the congregation in making a decision. "We earnestly ask every member to be in prayer over this momentous decision," C. C. Hope wrote. Likewise, Bates said, "It is my conviction that the Holy Spirit is giving this church the opportunity to move on and upward for God. I do not ask you to join me in this conviction. I simply plead with you to let the Holy Spirit speak to YOUR heart."[7]

Hope's letter outlined the process of the previous six years, including the adoption, in 1958, of the church's "Forward Program of Advance." Since that time, Hope said, they received instructions to "select a site on which to build a new First Baptist Church." In looking for such a site and making their recommendation, they had sought to keep in mind the need to provide "for the total life of our children and young people, including an inspiring church facility as well as a recreational area." They also accounted for the desire to "maintain a pace of growth commensurate not only with the growth of our city but also with the needs of our city." The committee had considered the congregation's aspirations and projections for growth while "realistically appraising our land needs, our building needs, and our financial resources," he said.[8]

For the first time, Hope's letter made public a list of fourteen properties that the committee had investigated. Those included several downtown properties adjacent to the First Baptist site. They also included the opportunity to purchase property from the Redevelopment Commission, namely, the land that was being cleared in Brooklyn. First Baptist's move was associated with Brooklyn as early as 1960, but as the debate in 1963 unfolded, the Brooklyn land did not seem to have gotten serious consideration from the committee. The two sides were focused on moving to the suburbs or expanding the then-current footprint.

Hope closed his letter with a series of financial statements and projections. He sought to make the case that the church could take on an enormous building project without risking any financial distress. The numbers worked, according to Hope and W. J. Smith Jr., two of the most prominent bankers in town. They were well able to make this move. Thus, Hope closed his appeal while asking members to prayerfully consider such a "momentous decision."[9] He summarized the facts and figures. The other two letters in the packet would ratchet up the stakes of the debate as FBC hurtled toward the coming business meeting.

You could see in the relentless focus on growth the imprints of the previous pastor, Dr. C. C. Warren. It was numerical and financial growth that, even within a congregation of well over three thousand members and a long record of planting new churches, provided an ostensible distraction from the key social context happening in the late 1950s and early 1960s, namely, the civil rights movement. The church, and especially its leadership, had gained significant wealth following World War II and was ready to exercise it to their advantage. One way of employing that wealth was to change their location to reinforce the comforts of their racial privilege, which would best be exercised in the white suburbs. Hope's letter set the context of suburbanization inside a Christianity built around whiteness. Bates's letter would make the racial bias more explicit and frame it in theological terms.

THE MIDDLE-CLASS MOSES

Bates wasted no words in his pastoral epistle. He quickly made his position plain: "I am writing this letter to say to you that I am convinced with all my heart and soul that we ought to take this awesome and wonderful step."[10] Though Bates told his members to test their own hearts and vote their own consciences, the position of the top leadership was unequivocal. The recommended relocation was the right move at the right time.

Before he pushed his case, Bates made an apology. In 1960, he said, the Future Program Committee made this same recommendation to the deacons. Bates supported the plan then as well, but the deacons rejected it. Bates, being only a year into his pastorate at FBC, did not push the recommendation any further.[11] In his letter, he apologized for not bringing the issue to the full congregation at that time. He attributed that step to "the Providence of God," for the congregation needed the "extra time so that many facets of our situation might be . . . clarified."[12]

In his letter to FBC, Bates pointed to God's providence[13] leading to this moment of the congregation occupying a land that was destined to be theirs. He wrote,

> It is my belief—my whole-hearted belief—that God has saved the 16 acres on Runnymede Lane for First Baptist church to build on to his glory. It is a real miracle that in all these years, Mr. and Mrs. Harris have refused to sell that beautiful piece of property. And here it is, offered to us at the only reasonable price we can afford—on a wonderful location to be proud of—a part of the estate of the former Governor of North Carolina.[14]

As Carl Bates understood the work of God in history in Charlotte, North Carolina, God had saved a particular plot near Sharon and Runnymede, for reasons that were only then becoming clear, to open a new space in the world for First Baptist Church. As he developed his argument, Bates assumed the pastoral role of Moses, shepherd of the people. He had led his flock to the edge of a new promised land. Like the biblical Moses, he had already accompanied them to the border of the land once, only to be forced to wait to cross over. But now, if they would just look over and peek at the land's riches, they would see a place flowing with abundance.[15] Only through the providence of God was this possible, Bates was telling his people. They had weathered years of wilderness wandering with the Future Program Committee. They had already been at the border of this property once. But now, in October 1963, the time had arrived. God had chosen First Baptist to fulfill its destiny and the destiny of the land.

By reading his congregation's story through the "hermeneutic of Providence," Bates showed his formation inside a Christian vision "idolatrously calibrated to a racialized vision of humanity."[16] He tied himself to a long tradition of reading the Scriptures and the events of one's own day in a manner that reinforced existing power and that sacralized the taking of lands and places as divine gift.[17] As it relates to land and space, the doctrine of providence has echoes early in the Bible. In Genesis 15, God promises to give Abram and his descendants the land of Canaan, a promise later fulfilled by the conquest of the Israelites in the book of Joshua. Among the problems, though, is that God's supposed provision of land does not solve the problem of displacement but merely passes it to someone else to deal with. Using the rhetoric of providence, especially with its racialized history of justifying conquest since the Doctrine of Discovery, Bates stood in concert with ages of "white

Christians who explicitly and self-consciously invoked divine Providence as the lens through which to render their actions theologically intelligible and claim them as righteous."[18] Bates would soon find the elasticity of providence useful as he advocated that the hand of God was working to secure a move that was not going to happen. He was a deft enough theologian to later turn the claim of God's providence to a new place, building on the same logic to justify a different conclusion.

Following his appeal to providence, Bates then painted an image of the idyllic setting of the new church site at Runnymede and Sharon. Surveying the plot in his imagination, he foresaw "a place where our young families may bring their little children to Sunday School and Church without fear of dangerous streets where traffic threatens by day and uncertainty lurks at night. I see a place where our children and grandchildren may receive kindergarten training and enjoy their playtime among green leaves and shady trees. I envision a program for our young people where the church may be the center of not only their spiritual life but their social and recreational life as well."[19]

The land on Runnymede Lane was flowing with milk and honey. The people needed only to cross its border. They would no longer need to battle the wild city streets nor to confront the shady characters who prowled at night. Their children would receive every opportunity, and no one would be afraid.

Bates's vision of a renewed FBC ministry sounded as much like the television program *Ozzie and Harriet* as it did any compelling vision of the church engaged in the world.[20] His theological imagination was captive to the political norm of white flight to the suburbs. Bates's own denomination had helped to plant this vision in him, including his predecessor at FBC.[21] Those dangers and "uncertainties" that "lurked at night" were racially coded language. Readers knew what he meant without him having to say it.[22] The notion of a church in the suburbs that is the center of spiritual, social, and recreational life was a strategy of white dominance. Out on Runnymede Lane, physical distance would entrench the geography of segregation. In the suburbs, they would primarily hear from other white people, helping to create a psychic and spiritual distance between themselves and the problem of segregation. They could protect children and families from having to engage in the moral crisis happening around them and inside them. The problem would forever be elsewhere, in someone else's neighborhood, in someone else's church.[23]

In his letter, Carl Bates positioned himself as Moses for his people. He was ready to lead them away from the wilderness of downtown into the miraculous, verdant suburbs. It was a freedom meant only for themselves. Bates's contemporary Gibson Winter called it "the suburban captivity of the church"—a strange liberation.[24] Near the end of his appeal, Bates echoed the words of an old Baptist missionary, the same words his predecessor C. C. Warren often quoted—the move would be "expecting great things from God as we attempt great things for him."[25] And with that, Bates staked out his claim.

BENEVOLENT CONQUEST

The letter of dissent from Bill Poe and his group outlined their reasons for wanting to remain in the downtown area.[26] But first, it tried to address the process, stating that their aim was merely to "stimulate serious deliberation" in advance of the vote and not to foment dissension. However, Poe noted, "this identical recommendation was made by a majority of the same committee to the deacons of First Baptist Church with request for its approval prior to its presentation to the church." The deacons engaged in a lengthy debate, Poe said, and then "a substantial majority of the deacons rejected this recommendation by the Future Program Committee."[27] Poe, ever the attorney, started by questioning the process before turning to the substance of the arguments. He started building his case by making public that the same motion had been denied before. It was time for the opposing counsel to move on.

When it came to the substance of the arguments, Poe and his group found the reasoning for moving to the suburbs lacking in economic, theological, and practical terms. They began with a call back to the May 1960 vote to relocate the congregation, which used broad language to state that First Baptist would make preparations to move, without specifying any location or type of setting. Poe's group claimed that the 1960 resolution was built on the "assumption that the church would be relocated in the inner-city or down-town area and that it would not become a suburban or neighborhood church."[28] Their argument sounds geographical, but it was more than that. The FBC of the 1960s had developed a culture, according to its members, of inclusion across classes. While there was no racial diversity, FBC members spoke often of their common ground as a community of faith comprised of people from many different walks of life.[29] Members who were youths in the 1960s noted this broad economic inclusion by identifying that their youth group or Sunday School classes had members from every white high school in Mecklenburg County.[30] Church directories from the time list addresses from wealthy neighborhoods like Myers Park and Eastover and also from mostly working-class white neighborhoods like Enderly Park and Belmont. Poe and his group addressed the economic diversity of the congregation in their letter, stating that "First Baptist should always remain a people's church, drawing its membership from all classes and all walks of life." Further, they stated, moving to South Park would "inevitably change the character of [FBC] from a 'people's' church into a neighborhood or area church, with its membership drawn from relatively narrow social and economic strata."[31] Poe's appeal to inclusion around class connected with large portions of the FBC membership. Allen Bailey, of the Four Horsemen, had moved to Charlotte from a desperately poor background. Carl Bates grew up in a sharecropping family. Everyone above thirty years old remembered the Great Depression.[32]

Poe's volunteer work in other Charlotte institutions demonstrated his commitment to offering support to poor people and why he and others in the congregation thought that support to be significant for Christian ministry. A 1960 feature in the *Observer* highlighted his role as president of the Charlotte Rescue Mission. The mission did outstanding work in saving souls, Poe had argued. In fact, the mission's efforts were far better than even his own church. "At First Baptist Church," he said, "we put considerable emphasis on saving souls. Last year we had 150 additions—which we considered pretty good. But at the mission last year there were ten times as many decisions for Christ. And First Baptist's budget is more than six times that of the Mission's."[33] Moving to the suburbs would damage what Poe thought to be the chief mission of the Baptist church: evangelism. In the 1963 letter to the congregation, Poe and his cohort framed the shifting demographics of the city, saying, "The rapid expansion of hotel and motel accommodations and apartment houses in the downtown area has given increasing emphasis to the need for a downtown church."[34] Remaining in the center city was essential if FBC was to be engaged in vital ministry in Charlotte. On the downtown sidewalks, members would be able to meet the human needs around them. Poe's vision of Christian ministry was urban rather than suburban.

Poe and Bates were making variations on the same argument, simply with differing emphases. For Poe, poverty was a problem that called Baptist churches to a certain kind of ministry where they would be present with those who were poor. As he would make clear, the geographical location of the church plant would be significant precisely because of how it made the congregation accessible to lower classes and how it made the congregation's interactions with poor people inevitable. But as would have been common for a person from Poe's social location, such an understanding of ministry was framed in highly individualistic terms. Those who were wealthy, like Poe, were personally responsible for creating places of welcome where a poor person might make an individual decision to follow Jesus. Following Jesus was assumed to be an economically rational decision that led to financial stability, the life of Jesus notwithstanding. Such a conception is loaded with the class and economic assumptions built into white Christianity—that wealth is a blessing or sign of favor from God, that poverty is a sign of moral failing, that poor people do not already have active faith practices. Poe's benevolence toward poor people—which was like most white evangelism—would draw them into the middle-class life of mainstream white America.

Bates was putting forward the flip side of the same argument, in his case by stating that First Baptist should spend their wealth on the miraculous deal made available to them in a prominent location. Wealth was a blessing to be used in the pursuit of a social and ideological purity embodied in white suburban life. Neither saw the structural issues around them, even as they ventured through the growing piles of rubble in the Brooklyn neighborhood on their ways home from church. Wealth and poverty were signs of virtue to them, and the lack of wealth was, at least in part, a sign of the lack of virtue. Poverty could then be redressed by individual interventions like religious conversion, not by larger-scale social change. In Bates's words, "Sin is the problem."[35] Sin was individual, and individual sin problems had individual solutions through salvation in Jesus.

As their rebuttal continued, Poe and his group pointed out the large number of available parking spaces and the availability of land adjacent to FBC's downtown location. The consistent appeal to the need of congregants for off-street parking on a church-owned lot was overblown, they thought, and could be easily resolved without moving.

Finally, the group made one more claim that offers some insight into the fractured vision of white Christians trying to wrestle theologically with this moment in US history. They stated that "the down-town area needs a strong Baptist witness, as is true in the case of other major denominations in this city, and the move to the proposed location would constitute the abandonment of the area by the Baptist people."[36] But there were at least six Baptist churches in close proximity to both the bank headquarters and the government institutions that formed the city's core of power. They were Friendship Baptist, St. Paul Baptist, Shiloh Baptist, and Ebenezer Baptist in Second Ward, Greater Mt. Sinai Baptist in First Ward, and First Baptist Church-West in Third Ward.[37] All were Baptist churches. One of them carried the name "First Baptist Church," a name it held forty years longer than the white congregation. Poe and his dissenters built part of their argument on the racist assumption that Black Baptists were insufficiently Baptist. This is an offshoot of the racist idea, prominent from the origins of American society, that Black humans are insufficiently human. Racist ideas are not incidental, the inadvertent remnants of old ways of life. They are active ideas with purpose, namely, the purpose of supporting power within institutions and systems.[38]

Members of FBC knew Black people. They knew Black institutions. Black Charlotte was not invisible to them, especially not amid the civil rights movement that was being organized, in part, by Black Baptist churches and their ministers. But those Baptist bodies were not aligned with the interests of the Baptists at FBC, where they wanted a Baptist presence downtown that would continue to maintain the racial and political hegemony of the day.

With that summary, all sides had made their cases. The lines were clearly drawn in preparation for the coming Sunday, which was sure to be the most important business meeting in the congregation's history.

CLOSING UP FRIENDSHIP

While FBC was debating their move, Friendship Baptist grappled with an impending move that they hadn't had the freedom to debate. The initial warning came in November 1960 when Vernon Sawyer arrived to tell the congregation that they would be moving. The timeline of demolition and construction got delayed, but eventually the word came from the Redevelopment Commission that the city would take possession of the building beginning October 1, 1963.

During the intervening time, members set about raising money and locating a property (figure 7.1). Back in 1960, Pastor Kerry had asked the membership to stand on their feet if they wanted to rise to the occasion and take on building a new home for the congregation. The people did so, despite the grief and anger they must have felt at their displacement. Over the next

Figure 7.1. Friendship Baptist Sunday School classes in front of their building, ca. 1963. Photo used by permission of Friendship Missionary Baptist Church.

several years, Friendship quickly made progress in creating a new vision for themselves. By May 1961, they had purchased a 2.5-acre lot about four miles north of their Brooklyn home. The land was owned by the Charles Ervin Construction Company, one of the largest homebuilders on the East Coast. Ervin included a $6,000 gift in the sale, and Friendship brought $12,000 they had raised or saved to complete the purchase. The *Charlotte Observer* characterized this quick movement as Friendship "carrying their own weight" in the entire process.[39] Those 2.5 acres were on the very edge of the city's development at that time, as suburbanization pushed northward up Beattie's Ford Road.

As was typical of Kerry, he did not dispute the characterization that Friendship was "pulling their own weight" in an interview with the *Observer* later that year. In public statements, Kerry remained relentlessly optimistic about the situation and about the congregation's mood. "The general consensus is that the move will be good for us," he said. Sixty-eight percent of the congregation already lived in the vicinity of that site, one indication of how segregationist policy was reshaping the city as the exodus began from Brooklyn.[40] Between May and September, Friendship had raised another $6,000 and was beginning a pledge campaign for further funding. The developing problem, though, was the cost of constructing a new building. Kerry anticipated they needed about $250,000 for construction. They expected about $18,000 from the year's fundraisers. The payment from the Redevelopment Commission for their old property would not generate anywhere close to what they needed.

The City of Charlotte forced Friendship to sell their facility at an assessed valuation that was far below its replacement cost. Vernon Sawyer had already made clear to the congregation that the burden of Urban Renewal, unchosen, unwanted, and unnecessary, was theirs to bear. Mayor Brookshire understood this sequence of events to be a bit inconvenient, so he sent a letter to the congregation: "As you face the challenge of relocating your Church after 75 years of Christian service in the community, I wish for you much success. As a token of my good wishes, I am enclosing a small check for your new building fund, and only wish it could be more. The churches of our community face a real challenge in the development of character and citizenship that will make Charlotte an even greater city than it presently is."[41]

The Redevelopment Commission issued a date for Friendship to abandon its facility—September 30. The congregation decided to fill the rafters with their praises and laments in their final days in Brooklyn. The month of September was to have thirty consecutive nights of worship services, culminating in a lengthy service on the last night of the month. The saints of Friendship would pray and preach and sing until the final moments when their sacred building was taken from them (see figure 7.2).

The loss of their building and the razing of their neighborhood was enough grief for one congregation. But the United States in September 1963 was in no way calm. The civil rights movement continued to raise the pressure on city and town councils around the country as people agitated for freedom and equality. Churches were the home base for organizing that movement. On September 15 of that month, the evening worship service would have included special prayers for 16th Street Baptist Church in Birmingham, Alabama, which was that morning shaken by a bombing. The saints at Friendship voiced moans for their kindred several hundred miles away. They knew the feeling of the foundations of the building shaking—in Birmingham by extrajudicial terrorism, in Charlotte by a committee that filed paperwork and ran public relations campaigns.

TAKING A STAND

First Baptist was crowded and bursting with nervous energy on Sunday, October 27, 1963. Nothing was normal. The early worship service was canceled,

Figure 7.2. Women of the L. L. Walker Missionary Circle inside the sanctuary at Friendship Baptist, ca. 1963. Photo reprinted by permission of Friendship Missionary Baptist Church.

Sunday School was moved to an earlier slot, and then everyone piled into the sanctuary for the meeting.[42] Whereas a Baptist church business meeting generally only brings out the most dedicated members, this Sunday was different. One thousand and one members, plus children and youths, filled every available pew and spilled over into another room. With more than three thousand members in 1963, fully one-third of those on the rolls came to the meeting. Part of the strategy for hosting the meeting on a Sunday morning was to attract as many attendees as possible. It worked.

Having the sanctuary filled beyond capacity helped to illustrate the importance of a move to everyone assembled. The heat generated by a thousand bodies in suits or pantyhose was an object lesson that the facility at 318 N. Tryon was no longer capable of meeting the congregation's needs. In just eighty years at their location, the church had built two sanctuaries, had renovated and expanded the second one only a decade earlier, and still needed more seats. This autumn day was to decide the fate of the buildings and the future of the congregation.

The meeting went on for three hours. Babies got hungry, ate, napped, and woke up hungry again with the meeting still going on. Children were restless, mothers grabbing them by the ear and whispering threats. Passions were high all around.

At the podium, what was taking place was a theological debate. The speeches sometimes seemed to be about process and real estate and budgets and methods of voting, but under every presenting issue was a theological question about the meaning of being the people of God, as Christians often speak of themselves, situated in a particular place.

When the basic reporting was done, Hope used his position as Future Program Committee chair to be the first to stake out his claim. "With respect to the ministry of our church," he said, "[it] is what we make it." The downtown location was not necessary, in other words, and the opportunity in South Park was both accessible and too good to pass up. As to the potential difficulty of travel to the site, Hope reminded attendees that there was a new belt road planned and public bus service to the area.[43] The land was in a neighborhood site rather than the current plant in a business district. Such a shift would open the congregation to the rush of new residents moving to Charlotte.

"We have picked a location we think is in the center of the population," he said. With his case made, Hope formally presented the committee's recommendation for a vote.

Bill Poe was characteristically vocal about his disagreement. Ever the lawyer, he first made a motion to extend the time of the discussion, lest Hope or Bates try to call for a vote prematurely.[44] With time to make his case, he then proceeded.

FBC belonged in the city, not in the suburbs, Poe claimed. This was a church, and churches exist for ministry. Moving to suburbia would be running away from their call: "Drunks, unclean people, people without the 'right' clothes—these all come to First Baptist. They're just as welcome as anybody. The downtown church is a mixing class of all types."[45] Such ministry was not the type of work that could be sustained in a neighborhood church: "It cannot be maintained in any church except a downtown church. We come to the downtown First Baptist Church because we believe in and want to support its downtown ministry."[46]

Committee member Rod Alexander sided with Poe: "If we vote to leave the downtown area, it will leave Main Street without a Baptist voice."[47]

W. J. Smith spoke up for Hope's side of the debate, attempting to play a trump card. The banker reminded the congregation that the church had lost members in recent years and that giving was down. Failing to move would likely result in "continued decline," he said.[48]

Poe could not abide by such a power play. The church is not in decline, the attorney retorted. "We are today the most powerful church in the Mecklenburg Baptist Association," he said.[49]

Round and round they went, battling for the future of the church and the meaning of their ministry. Two hours into the debate, Pastor Bates stood to interrupt it.[50] The majority of the committee had taken fifty minutes to present their recommendation, he said. The dissenting group had taken fifty-five minutes. As the moderator of the meeting, he would no longer recognize any of the leadership to speak unless the congregation explicitly instructed him to do so.[51]

Another hour of debate followed. Ed Linsmier brought a map showing that the vicinity of downtown was still far more populated than the South Park area. Mrs. Rovy Branon raised the cause of missionary activity, stating that "moving from the downtown area would be the equivalent of closing the door on [the] mission program." Mr. Gene Bobo, likely trying to manage anxiety more than anything else, reminded members to listen closely to the leading of the Holy Spirit as they cast their vote.[52]

Near the end of the third hour, the body deliberated the method of taking this important vote. Some members had floated the idea of a secret ballot, but that was struck down. Instead, they decided to vote precisely as Bates had instructed in the end of his midweek letter to them: "Whichever way you vote—Stand Up For Jesus!"[53] Bates gave the instructions: "All in favor of the motion to relocate to Runnymede Lane, please stand." Three hundred seventy-two men, women, and children stood. "All opposed, please stand." Six hundred and twenty-nine stood. The plan to move, years in the making, once denied, resuscitated, and championed again, was formally rejected.

Pastor Bates was livid. C. C. Hope was crushed. He had pioneered the efforts to study a move and make a recommendation over the course of more than six years. When the crucial moment of adopting the decision arrived, the congregation voted him down by a margin of almost two to one. But Hope saw in that moment a crisis in the making. These were the sorts of decisions that split churches. Having 37 percent of the congregation fiercely upset over the decision would not portend well for the future. Hope loved his church home too much to allow that to happen.

Surveying the crowd, Hope knew he had lost the day. But he could not lose his beloved church. So he breathed and approached the microphone once more in one of the most humbling moments of his life. "It is not right," he said, "that we make such a momentous decision outside of the spirit of Christian unity. The majority has made themselves known here. I would call for a vote on the question once more and ask that every member stand in support of the majority to make it clear that we move ahead together, in unanimity."[54] Bates once more posed the question on whether to adopt the committee's resolution to move. "All in favor, respond by saying 'aye,'" he commanded.

Silence.

"All opposed, please stand."

Together, 1,001 members rose and firmly planted their feet in the soil of downtown Charlotte.

Allen Bailey had worked alongside C. C. Hope all those years to craft the plan for the move. When he and his wife, Ebbie, and their children got home that afternoon, she called out to him. Allen was an attorney, and Ebbie knew him to be cheerful and ready to keep moving even after a big defeat in court.

"There's something you're not feeling good about today," she said.

Allen, head hanging low, responded, "I let my church down today." And he walked away and never spoke of the meeting again.[55]

Hope acted as a statesman, though he must have felt like Allen Bailey felt. But Bates had something to say. Preachers always do. He would not go quietly. Bates had been brought to the church, at least in part, to help facilitate growth. He and his denomination had chosen suburbanization and new buildings and new mortgages as a way to keep the numbers rising and to avoid the thornier social issues of their day, namely, the civil rights movement. From everything Bates could see, the congregation had rejected the direction he was offering. They might very well, at the same time, have rejected him.

For many public figures, such a significant public defeat, the rejection of years of work, would result in a resignation and a new career. Bates chose a different path, though he must have been tempted to pack his office up. C. C. Hope set the tone at the end of the meeting to avoid a messy church split. Bates followed Hope's resolve, but he would not hold his tongue about it. He took his anger to the church newsletter the following week. Though he tried to keep his words pastoral, his disagreement, verging on the tone of a disappointed parent, came through anyway. "It may take some time before the full implication of our action dawns upon our people," he wrote. He called into question the commitment of some of those who voted to remain:

Did you know that we have people who hold official positions in our church who have attended prayer meeting less than a dozen times in the past three years? Many of you who come down here on Wednesday nights, bring your children, eat a good meal provided by the church, and as soon thereafter as possible sweep through the exits for home without pausing to pray with our church and for our church. . . . Of the "one thousand and one" who voted yesterday, I wonder how long it shall be before I see them in worship again?

All was not lost, though. Bates could see through his anger to some hope. The church may yet prosper, he said, building on the "golden heritage" left by its ancestors, even though they lacked the needed land to continue expanding: "Who knows, it may even turn out that God has saved us in our blindness."[56]

Despite his protest of the decision, Bates was resigned to moving along in faithfulness as best he could. It was all he knew to do. But he also understood that the future of the church would be determined by its property—where and how much it owned. The forebears of First Baptist had left a "golden heritage," but they had not foreseen the coming suburbanization of the country when they purchased the lot at 7th and Tryon in 1877.[57] "They left us no property upon which to meet the demands of this automobile age," Bates reminded his congregation.[58] Auto culture required space for storing automobiles, which were quickly becoming the sole mode of transport for the FBC membership driving in from the suburbs. Americans were headed into the "crabgrass frontier,"[59] which required ever-growing swaths of land, much of it reserved for roads and parking lots, each new development pushing further and further. Prime real estate was defined not only by an address but by acreage, a place to spread out. A place to park cars.[60]

TWO VISIONS INSIDE WHITENESS

The debate under the great Byzantine dome of First Baptist that morning was not about real estate—or at least it was not only about real estate. It was a theological debate about providence—their discernment of the work of God in history. It was a debate about how geography and culture determined their congregation's response to God's work. Their theological reasoning was formed inside one important category of their existence that went unstated and unexamined: whiteness. The Christian faith on display in their debate, and in the century of practice that led up to it, was fused with whiteness. So thorough was the fusion that, to this day, disentangling the two can still be difficult.

"We have picked a location we think is in the center of the population," Hope said during the Sunday morning business meeting. But his committee's conception of how to account for the population was built on a racist idea: that the city as a whole was defined only by its white citizens. The place where Hope identified the gravitational pull of central Charlotte betrayed his racial, political, and theological assumptions. The center for them was located around a nexus of whiteness, surrounded by old-money Myers Park and adjacent to Myers Park Country Club on one side and within easy reach of the expanding wealthy suburbs on the other side.

Hope and Smith knew that Charlotte was much larger. The city stretched for multiple miles from the downtown core in every direction. What they meant by "center," they defined not by numbers of people but by the political and economic power unevenly spread across the landscape. Attempting such a move fit with the overarching story of the congregation, who for years tried to get Beulah Baptist from the edge of downtown onto prestigious Tryon Street. Here they were again, looking for a new space that would mark their place in the city's structure of power.

Hope, Bates, and others saw that white flight was ultimately about the relocation of power within the city. That power was not neutral, nor did it come about by democratic means. As local, state, and federal governments began subsidizing the suburbs, white people moved to them.[61] They were lured by policies that made segregation possible in practice once it was no longer dictated by law. As white citizens moved, so did the geographic center of power shift away from the density of downtown to the more diffuse suburbs, with their car-dependent strip malls and their reliance on mass media for entertainment. Hope and Bates put forward the argument that FBC belonged at the center of the changing racial geography of Charlotte. By occupying a prominent corner in the new "center of town," they guaranteed themselves ongoing relevance among those who set policy, who made decisions, and who wielded the authority of large public and private institutions. Beyond that, they would also be out of sight of poverty and out of range of accountability.

At FBC's sister congregations around the country, in the Southern Baptist Convention, and in many other white-dominant denominations, churches were engaging in the same sort of debate about whether to remain in historic downtown areas or to move to the suburbs. In Charlotte, though, FBC's eventual solution would carry with it an extra step that asserted their position in the politics of racial domination while expressing their decision as the providence of God.

Bill Poe stood to speak for those who thought FBC should remain downtown. Poe thought it important for the congregation to remain proximate to those who suffered in poverty so that congregants might offer some sort of personal aid to relieve that suffering. Moving away from downtown would make it harder for the congregation to connect directly with those who were poor. Poe's vision for such interactions was crafted inside the domination system of whiteness, though. Poe and his dissenting committee members were not attempting to challenge the structural or systemic nature of poverty, nor its racialization in the United States, in pursuit of upending poverty as a social phenomenon. The common result of evangelical missionary work at FBC and around the country was to offer poor people a place to learn their way into middle-class lifestyles, or in Poe's words, the ability to portray a certain image through "cleanliness and the right clothes." The sort of evangelism he imagined gave space for personal transformation that might land poor people a house and a yard in the south Charlotte suburbs. The desired result of missionary efforts would entrench and justify their commitment to Christianity entangled with whiteness. The theological, the architectural, and the political were working together to reinforce one another.

The culture inside which FBC members were debating the future of their church was not isolated to First Baptist Church. It was common across white evangelicalism.[62] Among the characteristics of that faith was individualistic theology, coupled with an insistence on colorblindness that reinforced the norms of white supremacy. Such a faith was bound to produce an architecture that looked like its theology. Builders constructed more and more suburban spaces, dominated by detached single-family houses, generally on larger lots, in neighborhoods that were fully car-dependent. Architecture and city planning reinforced tendencies to individualism, with every space fenced off and every place tucked into the realm of the private.[63] Mass transit became too inefficient to be useful, given the large distances it needed to cover. The family room with the television became the primary setting of entertainment. By 1976, American households spent nearly three hours a day watching television, longer than they spent on any other leisure pursuit.[64] Especially during the rapid expansion of the suburbs in the 1950s and 1960s, the content of entertainment reinforced the suburban ideal with shows like *Leave It to*

Beaver and *The Brady Bunch.*[65] Popular and influential images of the good life began to look suburban. In the verdant suburbs, the theological and the architectural were reinforcing one another. The architectural move of the period had theological backing from white churches, which, whether they moved to the suburbs or not, preached a gospel of individualized salvation by a Jesus known to them as "personal Lord and Savior."[66] The privatized virtues they practiced inside the culture of whiteness made the "good life" available to them but failed to transform the society or to offer a vision beyond whiteness.

Within white churches, the creation of a "good life" that looked like the emerging suburban norm had a theological character. The material abundance made possible by favorable economic and political policy looked providential. Congregations had a ready foil to stand in contrast to their self-understanding: those who did not profit from racist policy, namely, Black people. White people trained one another to see in Black spaces only poverty and struggle because of personal failings rather than as the consequence of the political and economic landscape. Therefore, Pastor Bates could quote a friend in Birmingham, Alabama, who told him, "Segregation is not right, but sin is the problem and the alcohol curse is as damning ultimately as anything else."[67] Segregation—a social issue devised and upheld by whites—did not fall inside the category of "sin," but alcohol consumption, an individualized choice, did. A longtime member of FBC held a similar view years after the fact. In a 2020 interview, he said that "the city did a great service [through Urban Renewal] because they cleaned up downtown. . . . There was a lot of alcohol consumed, and it was kind of a sad situation."[68] White Christians were disregarding the systemic factors that made slum conditions both possible and profitable. Likewise, they failed to recognize that their own economic success was aided by structural factors not available to Black communities. Instead, Bates taught them to attribute their success to the work of God in history—it was providence. Their understanding, reinforced by their clergy, persisted for decades. Indeed, it may be a permanent feature of the faith in white churches.

The spiritual, the architectural, and the political all worked together to reinforce one another. Systematized political and economic interventions, especially those following the Great Depression, made possible the rapid and contagious growth of the suburbs. The construction of the suburbs gave material form to a political system that had always privileged white people. New construction patterns, reliance on personal vehicles, and the full privatization of home spaces away from front porches and sidewalks to backyards and entertainment rooms provided ample, self-reinforcing evidence that the systemic interventions were working and could create what looked like a flourishing life for a large swath of American households. Pastors offered theological blessing for the architectural and the political. The language and practice of mission as charity, and the privatization of sin as a set of personal moral shortcomings, reinforced the American dream as the blessing of God. Together, these factors held one another up, creating a theological architecture that would both form and adapt to the coming changes in US society.

ANESTHETIZING SECURITY

The national context of the debate at First Baptist Charlotte heightens the significance of the debate within the congregation, not only for what was said but for what was left unsaid. It was the fall of 1963, the height of the civil rights movement. Though Charlotte leaders had mostly kept the national media away by proactively desegregating public accommodations in May and June 1963,[69] the nation was still roiled by the conditions across the South and the refusal of activists to settle for the injustice of segregation.[70] But even as they integrated restaurants, the white power structure of Charlotte was plowing down Black neighborhoods. In that context, Bill Poe's characterization of who FBC welcomed in their downtown ministry said as much for whom it left out as whom it included. Poe appealed to a caricatured idea of poor people being dirty or addicted or unkempt, ideas that have persisted across a society that sees wealth as a blessing from God and poverty as moral decrepitude. He claimed that all were welcome, their unsightliness notwithstanding. "You are welcome, though you look ungainly and smell funny" does not seem like the warmest invitation, but Poe's heart seemed to be charitable. In the categories he mentions, however, he avoids one unavoidable social stratification: race. In white churches all across Charlotte, it was clear that the sanctuaries would remain all white.[71]

Further, some on Poe's side contended that FBC's physical presence downtown would make their voice on public affairs more important. But the idea that First Baptist actively engaged local and national public policy is missing from the written record. The weekly church newsletter, one of the primary extant sources available for understanding the issues of importance within the congregation from 1955 to 1975, contains only a handful of references to issues that might be called "political." One reference from the election of 1960 questioned whether a Catholic—in this case, John F. Kennedy—could be an appropriate president of the country.[72] Another newsletter took aim at President Kennedy for attempting to lower the maximum amount eligible for tax-deductible charitable contributions.[73] Another commended Lyndon Johnson as president immediately following Kennedy's assassination.[74] Only one took a direct approach to the civil rights movement. During the summer of 1963, as the movement was at a crescendo, Bates chose to reprint an editorial he found instructive while on vacation in Prince Edward Island. It cited the historic injustice of slavery as a direct predecessor to the racial injustices that led to the demonstrations for civil rights. But it warned, "The Negro in his struggle for human rights should not begin acting with a chip on his shoulder. The oppressed should not attempt to become the oppressor. Unfortunately, he is beginning to show that, where he has the power, he is not averse to using it wrongfully."[75] Given the lack of national legislation at that point, halting victories in local policy, and the ongoing segregation of nearly every institution across the South, it is hard to see what power the author was referring to or why Bates found the statement so compelling. Apparently, the civil rights movement was having enough success that white Christians were feeling some discomfort about the future of white supremacy in the country.

First Baptist elected to avoid the difficulties of confronting white supremacy in themselves and in their city. Pastor C. C. Warren had led the congregation on a path of avoiding discussion of racism, even as the church made decisions inside a world where race and racism affected every facet of their lives. Pastor Bates willingly followed Warren's strategy. As he did, his congregation gained all the economic benefit of being white inside a system of white supremacy but never developed the capacity to understand the harm their silence was doing to themselves or to their Black neighbors.

Bates's words had a lasting impact. His congregants knew him as a preacher and saw his ministry focused on sermons and writing. "Preaching was the heartbeat of his life and ministry," said one FBC member who knew him well. "He did not give much time to administration," but he was a "strong pulpiteer."[76] Because his public speech was the primary expression of his ministry at FBC, as opposed to other common pastoral duties like visitation or administration, his words were even more significant in shaping his people. So was what he did not say in failing to challenge his congregants in the ruling ideology of the day.

Bates's failure to challenge the ideology of white supremacy effectively provided the silent "scaffolding of segregation."[77] And not only of segregation but of the taking of Black neighborhoods, even the very churches of his Black colleagues only a few blocks away. Carl Bates was the son of sharecroppers. If anyone could have known the importance of having a stake in a piece of land, it was him. He lacked the courage to break the silence. Baptist historian Bill Leonard was a colleague of Bates when the two were teaching at Southern Baptist Theological Seminary in Louisville, Kentucky. "Bates thought of himself as a liberal on race," Leonard said, "but he would have been in that group [of ministers] that Rev. Dr. Martin Luther King Jr. wrote the 'Letter from a Birmingham Jail' to."[78] King wrote of white ministers during the Montgomery bus boycott, "I felt that the white ministers, priests and rabbis of the South would be some of our strongest allies. Instead, some have been outright opponents . . . ; all too many others have been more cautious than courageous and have remained silent behind the anesthetizing security of the stained-glass windows."[79]

In October 1963, the clergy and laypeople of FBC were carrying on a substantive theological disagreement about the meaning of a church body as a physical plant, as an institution, and as a social community. Their debate never touched on race. But as with all social and political discourse in the United States, their ideas grew within the stifling context of racial domination. At FBC, the visions of who to become and where to become it were crafted precisely inside a racial context that had captured and formed their theological imaginations and had stunted their ability to be in communion with their neighbors. They were performing Christianity "inside whiteness."[80] To be performing their Christianity inside whiteness meant that their theological imaginations had been compromised by a principality[81] that narrowed their ability to live or even conceive of the story that they held to be most deeply true.

CHAPTER EIGHT

Caught Up in a Vision

C. C. Hope and his Future Program Committee needed a few weeks to tend to their wounds. All the public communication prior to the big business meeting in fall 1963 indicated that the plan to move would go forward. Generally, a recommendation from a committee of trusted leaders would win a large share of support in a church business meeting. Little in their process had gone smoothly. Some time away from church work to observe the holiday season in quiet must have been welcome.

Beginning in 1964, the committee had a new charge. The congregation had voted in April 1960 to move to a new facility. They were bound by that directive from the people of First Baptist Church (FBC). But the collective voice in the October 1963 meeting had been clear that the people wanted to remain downtown. That decision left but one feasible option: Brooklyn. To expand their plant, the church would need to buy Urban Renewal land left vacant by the project underway to clear the neighborhood and redevelop it.

The Urban Renewal enabling legislation passed in North Carolina in 1951 provided for cities, under the guidance of a locally appointed Redevelopment Commission, to clear certain neighborhoods that met the state's conditions of "blight."[1] Once a blighted area was cleared, the city held title to it and could use vacant land as it saw fit. The priority for cleared land, according to the state, was public use, including government buildings and public works projects. When no compelling public use was identified, the cities could auction off the land under all applicable state and local regulations for sale to private parties.

The press and some members of First Baptist had speculated about a move of FBC to Brooklyn since 1960, when the plan to relocate the congregation first developed. Four years later, following a long flirtation with the suburbs and a tense meeting that could have resulted in a church split if not for Hope's statesmanship, Brooklyn was back on the table. The bulldozers were running constantly. Crews were churning up the ground and hauling off the rubble. Displaced people were searching for places to reestablish a home and the institutions they needed to support themselves. In February 1964, Friendship Baptist came tumbling down. The *Observer* printed a picture of the demolition. In it, a door frame is the only thing standing, a pile of bricks tumbling through it. Vernon Sawyer's pronouncement from Friendship's pulpit had been realized. "Lonely," said the *Observer's* caption.[2]

The piles of dirt and rubble seemed to charge the imagination at FBC. As the city kept plowing away, and as the people kept moving away, it became easier and easier for members to see themselves comfortably in Second Ward. In June 1964, Hope's committee was making serious visits to the area, especially to a site one block east of the former Friendship building, now only a memory, and one block west of Second Ward High School, where a shrinking student body was headed to a similar fate within a few years. But as FBC leadership began to ask their members to imagine themselves in that place, the school board announced its intention to claim the plot the church was interested in. School administrators wanted to expand the district's offices, they said, as well as to leave room, mysteriously, for expanding the high school, despite its declining enrollment and its neighborhood emptying around it. So First Baptist waited.[3]

The clearing continued. Hazeline North Anderson had already moved her belongings to Oaklawn Avenue in west Charlotte. Now dump trucks were hauling away the house that Abram and Annie North had built near 2nd and Alexander Streets, along with the homes of their former neighbors. They were hauling away Alexander Street altogether—the street itself was removed from the city grid there. The Redevelopment Commission then decided to bundle full city blocks, previously divided into dozens of small lots, into large, multi-acre parcels. Only a few years prior, dozens of houses stood together with a meeting hall and a collection of small businesses. The commission wanted something large and striking in place of the old mixed-use, fine-grained neighborhood (see figure 8.1).

The city prepared those large parcels for auction at an opportune time for FBC. C. C. Hope called the Future Program Committee together in January 1965, and they voted unanimously to pursue the new tract the city would be

Figure 8.1. Illustration from "A Better Charlotte through Urban Renewal," an undated booklet published by the Charlotte Redevelopment Commission in the 1960s. This rendering of a new government plaza came pre-populated with specters. Photo courtesy of J. Murrey Atkins Library Special Collections and University Archives, University of North Carolina at Charlotte. Available online at https://tinyurl.com/3wdfcvn6.

auctioning off. On January 31, Hope and W. J. Smith invited the deacon board to the headquarters of their employer, First Union National Bank. A few stories above the street, they might get a perspective on the site. Perhaps they could see the cleared acreage only a few blocks away. They could invite the deacons to imagine a steeple soaring above the bare trees, looking upon the climbing skyline, speaking hope and a future to their beloved city. The two full blocks straddling Davidson Street between 1st and 3rd: their ministry frontier.[4]

They did not see the ghosts. In the pews at FBC and in white churches like them around the country, Christians had prepared their imaginations over so many generations that they could only see the destiny they had established with their past, not the hauntings they were creating into the future. They now had the opportunity to bring a forlorn city block to maturity,[5] an opportunity the city elite had awaited for half a century since the newspaper had

Figure 8.2. Redevelopment Commission workers destroy a house in Brooklyn. Undated photo in records of Charlotte Redevelopment Commission, Special Collections, J. Murrey Atkins Library, University of North Carolina at Charlotte.

observed that "far-sighted men were sure this section, because of its proximity to the center city, must sooner or later be utilized by the white population."[6] The story of the political origins and destiny of the land had fused with the theological Doctrine of Discovery, which had fused with the myth of white innocence, which had fused with a structure that used individual virtue to conceal overwhelming collective power. To a Black pastor, or a Brooklyn entrepreneur, or a Black child watching the bulldozers complete the takeover of their Brooklyn homes and institutions, the destruction was as overwhelming as another Babylonian army. Their people were left to weep, while their tormentors smiled at their own good fortune.[7] For the leadership of FBC, it looked like those bulldozers were fueled by the power of God (see figure 8.2).

PREPARING THE PEOPLE

By January 1965, C. C. Hope and Carl Bates had become far more adept at the craft of steering church decisions. Their October 1963 disaster could have split the congregation. They could not afford an error this time. Their first target in Brooklyn did not work out, but the visit of the deacons to the First Union Bank boardroom sealed the deal on the second potential parcel. The process moved quickly from there. Eleven days after that preview, the full deacon board, the Future Program Committee, and the finance committee met to discuss the new plan. All eighty-three people in the room voted in favor of the new site. With each meeting along the way, someone in the church reported the developing plans and the unanimous vote to the local media, using the power of the press to help build excitement within the congregation.[8]

The Redevelopment Commission responded publicly to the reports of First Baptist's planned bid on the tract. The week following the vote of the deacons and the committees, the commission formally invited bidders for the 8.5-acre plot FBC wanted. According to the *Observer*, they "virtually laid out a red carpet for bids from FBC." Commission vice chair Wiley Obenshain (member, First Christian Church) said, "Any church of that size locating in our Brooklyn project will do more to elevate it to a higher status than any one thing that can happen."[9] The courting of FBC through the press was helping to solidify the congregation's resolve in its relocation efforts.

Obenshain's comment is loaded with the ways that the politics and theologies of the day were merged into a single project. First, the citation of FBC's "size" was an economic and political marker that served as a smokescreen for a racist policy decision the Redevelopment Commission made to influence the future owner-ship of Renewal land. The commission decided to turn four blocks with diffuse ownership across small parcels into two superblocks. In the process, they took at least forty-seven individual lots, as they existed in 1960, and turned them into a single lot.[10] By repackaging the land into one large parcel, the Redevelopment Commission was effectively limiting bidding to wealthy institutions, which in 1965 meant white ones. Friendship Baptist had, a couple of years prior, struggled to find $18,000 to purchase 2.5 acres on the edge of the city.[11] One-third of that money was a gift from the landowner they purchased from, the Charles Ervin Construction Company. Friendship was one of the more prominent institutions in the Black community. An 8.5-acre lot with a minimum bid of $450,000 had an invisible fence around it marked "Whites Only."[12]

Further, Obenshain's observation that FBC's presence would "elevate" the entire Renewal project to a "higher status" was a way of theologically affirming the political decisions that had come before and the ones that would follow. The Redevelopment Commission had faced intense criticism from many directions—among them, the National Association for the Advancement of Colored People (NAACP), small-government conservatives, and federal administrators—in their eight years of work. In early 1965, they lacked much to show for it, save a half-razed neighborhood. The city planned a new government center at the corner of 3rd and Davidson, but there was no visible progress on it. Now, across 3rd Street from the seat of governmental power, FBC and the Redevelopment Commission were planting a cross atop a high steeple. Whatever the struggles had been, the commission was able to baptize their process with familiar iconography. As American empire had expanded across the world in earlier generations, it went with religious fervor, the fusion of the flag and the cross ready to colonize lands and save souls.[13] The new frontier was an old one, the 238 acres of Brooklyn targeted for theo-political conquest. The political project had a sacred presence that would live beside it indefinitely. FBC would get their site near to the halls of power; the city would help to build a great symbol of the fusion of sacred and secular.

The public solicitation of FBC's bid had at least one other function. While it certainly represented the joint political and theological project of building the Charlotte cityscape, the Redevelopment Commission's welcome of First Baptist was also an act of expedience. What the commission and the city government discovered by 1965 is that they would welcome any bidder with enough funding to purchase a tract. When it came to Brooklyn land, no one with enough money to meet the commission's requirements wanted it. The visions they had collectively dreamed featured large glass and concrete buildings set amid plazas and parks. They foresaw a sibling of busy Tryon Street, with businesses and conventions and streets packed with cars. By February 1965, it was clear that none of those visions was developing, at least not soon.[14] The problem was predictable. For one, white flight not only shifted the population of cities; it also shifted the flow of capital within them. As policy encouraged suburban development, money followed the people and the policy. With all the focus on the suburbs, preferences shifted there. Businesses went to their customer bases.

But even further, by the time the city put the first lots up for auction in Charlotte, the national Urban Renewal program was fifteen years old, and the trends were clear. People and businesses were not moving back downtown. Charlotte leaders could have observed this around the country. In New York, the well-known planner Robert Moses refused to raze an area without pre-negotiated sales. In 1952, Detroit cleared acres of the Gratiot neighborhood, only to be stuck with a vacant site. The same thing happened in Newark, New Jersey. By the time Renewal projects began in Charlotte, the decade-old trend had only accelerated.[15]

The FBC blocks were the third of three lots to go up for public bid around the same time. The other two parcels received four bids total, and the two winners were both the most quintessentially suburban American business possible: car dealerships. One Dodge dealership, one used car lot.[16] The city that leaders had imagined was just going to be oversized stretches of asphalt. They had spent millions of tax dollars, plus untold hours of work and meetings and marketing, either to convince the public or to overwhelm it in regard to the Urban Renewal project. And yet as the trucks hauled away the old neighborhood, no one who could afford the new one wanted anything to do with it.

In that light, news of First Baptist's planned bid must have been a relief for Vernon Sawyer and Mayor Stan Brookshire. It was certainly not a surprise, though, for Sawyer hinted at some coordination between the Redevelopment Commission and the leadership of FBC prior to the auction. The previous two plots opened for public bids had 60-day bidding periods. For the lot FBC was interested in, the auction period would be only 30 days. Sawyer told the *Observer* that the FBC leadership had "assured him that 30 days would be all they needed to prepare their proposal and get it in."[17] It may have been that no one else was interested anyway, but the shortened bid period certainly looked like an official favor offered to the church, directly in public view. Given the fusion of the sacred and the secular happening at the site, who in power was going to argue? And what harm would be done by rigging the auction to achieve a providential end?

First Baptist moved quickly. Only three weeks following the deacons' visit to the First Union boardroom, the congregation hosted an interest meeting to announce the plan formally. There were no surprises and no midweek mailings from opposing parties. All the news had developed in public this time, thanks to the *Observer*. All the committee votes were unanimous. Yet Pastor Bates could not help but display his apprehension in his weekly column published just prior to the congregational announcement. In bold letters, he wrote, "**No vote will be taken at this meeting.**" Other headings on the same page declared "**Discussion Only**" and "**Church to Discuss Moving.**" Prior to the last meeting about moving, Bates had taken a side. This time he kept things spiritual and noncommittal: "If our people will begin now to pray, I believe we shall find the clear and unmistakable leadership of the Lord. . . . If I were afraid of your judgment, I doubt that I would find it in my heart to plan for such a meeting. I have learned some things about you, however, and I know that you will seek God's will above all other considerations. . . . I ask nothing more."[18] The sixteen months since October 1963 had made Bates more cautious in his public communication.

Behind the scenes, Bates and the FBC leadership had pulled together a smart plan that covered all the needed bases. They had the unanimous support of the deacons, the Future Program Committee, and the financial team. They had used the press to help shape the narrative. They had taken their leadership to look over the city blocks where they thought they were headed. They had followed the congregation's directives in site selection. And now they canceled the primary worship service in order to have a public meeting and offer their recommendation. They would leave a full week following the meeting for people to ruminate on what they had heard and not to feel pressured to vote quickly on such a momentous decision.

There was but one step left to finish crafting the narrative, and it was perhaps the most important of all. In October 1963, two friends argued hard against one another, in public, and asked the congregation to take sides. They brought the arguments of their divided committee into the open. They sent opposing letters to more than three thousand members. They risked breaking open the church body in the process. This time, Bill Poe and C. C. Hope would present their committee's findings together. It was an unmistakable sign of unity.

Once more, there were one thousand people crammed into the sanctuary in anticipation. Poe and Hope spoke at length, and by the time they had finished, with many others lending words of support, there were only a handful of questions. C. C. Hope pointed out that FBC's decision was a "beacon" of Baptist work. "A landmark of what Baptists can do and are doing," he said.[19] Surely, Hope and Poe made their case well. But more than their words, their presence together set the direction of the day. Following the few questions, the meeting dismissed to great applause and to the singing of a hymn:

> Lead on, O King eternal,
> the day of march has come;
> henceforth in fields of conquest
> your tents will be our home . . . .
> Your cross is lifted o'er us,
> we journey in its light;
> the crown awaits the conquest;
> lead on, O God of might.[20]

CONQUEST

The following Sunday, February 28, 1965, the congregation once more gathered at a special time. The leadership canceled the early worship service so that the congregation could merge a business session with the main 11:00 a.m. worship service. They wanted everyone present in unity. Pastor Bates let down his guard following the overwhelming spirit of the previous week. "I have been wrong so many times and I shall likely be wrong many times in the future, but the spirit of our church last Sunday will long live in my heart," he wrote.[21] Bates's plan was to speak to the decision in front of the congregation during the sermon and then, as the moderator of the business meetings, to call for the vote. "I would suggest that you bring the children," he wrote to the church earlier in the week. "They will rejoice someday in being able to say, 'I was there.'"[22] Likewise, during the service, C. C. Hope appealed directly to the children in the room: "Remember this: you are sitting at a time of the most historic occasion of the First Baptist Church. Listen to every word that your pastor says this morning. Watch every action that takes place, because somewhere down the road . . . someone may be saying that the people of First Baptist Church on this morning showed great vision and great foresight . . . and you may be one of the ones who can say that you were caught up in that vision."[23] The secretary for the morning took a moment to note the youngest voting members present: John Culbreth, Warren Jarvis, and Jeff Sutton, all age eight. All caught up in a vision.

The first words those boys and the rest of the congregation heard from the pulpit that morning were the Scripture reading from the Old Testament book of Numbers, chapter 13.[24] In that narrative, the wandering Israelites finally reach the border of their "land of promise" and prepare to settle it. One meeting ended with a hymn of conquest; the next began with a story of conquest.

Following the opening Scripture and a song, the people prayed. The speaker of the prayer was not recorded—it was probably Bates—but in his lengthy supplication to God, he said, "We come today to ask thee . . . to open our understanding and give us a view of the land thou hast commissioned us to possess."[25] The issue was already decided. God was at work in history, and everyone in the sanctuary was caught inside it.

At the last big vote concerning a move, all one thousand seats in the sanctuary had been full, and the debate had gone on for three hours. This time, they needed an additional two hundred chairs in overflow spaces. The meeting was short. The vote was decisive. The feeling was overwhelming. As they had done with all their major decisions, the people cast their votes by standing.

As Bates called the question, the people rose to their feet together, in almost perfect unison, to proclaim their intent. They were on the move to a new land.

C. C. Hope and his committee had worked nearly six years to reach this day. They had studied the issue in every way they could, had nearly split the congregation with their first proposal, had lingered for years over this question. And then, in what seemed like warp speed in comparison, they announced a site, publicized it widely, won the courtship of local government, successfully presented the plan to the congregation, and now were moving forward.

In the newsletter that had followed the 1963 meeting, Bates chastised the dissenters for showing up, given their irregular attendance at prayer meetings. In the days following this meeting, he thanked the few dissenters for having the courage of their convictions, despite being outvoted 1,200–11.[26]

One of the lingering questions around Urban Renewal more than half a century later is how a series of events that seems so clearly cruel could have taken place. The question is not "how" in the mechanics of the story, who did what and what policies they used, but about the stories the actors told themselves. How were they reading the Bible? How were they narrating their own lives? How did they imagine the lives of their neighbors, especially those who were Black? Did they think of others at all? The record lacks any evidence that they did. The stories they told themselves, and whom those stories included and rendered invisible, paved the way for the technicalities of policy. They created a narrative that had the power to lift up and to erase before any bulldozer ever rolled.

"WE ARE WELL ABLE"

By 1965, First Baptist had spent years constructing and carefully curating their world around silence. They offered tacit acceptance of the political and economic world around them, including the violent domination system of white supremacy. The specter of silence kept them taciturn for generations. In the Gospel story from Mark 9, Jesus asks the boy's father how long the specter has afflicted the boy. "Since birth," the father replies, but he clarifies the effects of this silencing-as-social-haunting. "Help *us*," the father begs. The story is political. The specter moves across generations, forward and backward, disjoined from a linear progression of time. It casts itself forward to the seventh generation; it flings itself backward for as long or more.

The story operating within First Baptist contained theological and political strategies that reproduced the silencing specter across more generations. One of the strategies to justify the coming trespass was the un-naming of their new place. Naming and renaming are one part of strategies of conquest in settler-colonial regimes. By disregarding or changing a place name, a dominant group exerts power over how the place is remembered. It claims the authority to tell the official story.[27] In the extant public communications from FBC, the word *Brooklyn* was only used a single time.[28] Instead, they called the area the "Urban Redevelopment Area." Only the "re-" in *redevelopment* hinted that the land was full of stories, filled with the memories of Brooklyn neighbors and of the Catawba and Sugaree people who lived there before there was a thing called *Charlotte*. FBC flattened the specificities and intimacies of the space into two letters, an R and an E. Nothing else remained. No story, no other Baptists, no other Christians, no persimmon trees, no school, no funeral home for the weeping, no juke joint for the reveler, no history of struggle, no artists or restauranteurs or preachers or hairstylists or builders or janitors or insurance agents or bank presidents or diplomats, no Abram and Annie North. Brooklyn was only generic government excess land, a place without a name, *tabula rasa* in search of its Manifest Destiny.

When Bates selected Numbers 13 as the Scripture text for the morning of the decisive vote, he made a theological decision that both reflected the congregation's past formation and reproduced that formation into future generations. He had himself been formed by his education at a Southern Baptist seminary, and by the institutions that supported his ministry, to read himself and his congregation into the biblical story in a strange way.

Eighteen months prior, Bates positioned himself as a Moses-like figure, leading his flock toward a "promised land."[29] His people rejected his advice then,[30] but Bates returned to the same source domain of metaphors and characters to instruct and inspire his people. In the story of the morning from the Bible's book of Numbers, Israel's long journey has taken them from the patriarchal promise made to Abram, into four centuries of slavery in Egypt, through liberation from Pharaoh, and into years of circling the wilderness between Egypt and Canaan. In Numbers 13, the Israelites arrive at the borderlands of Canaan. The narrative portion of the Bible's first epic story is nearing its conclusion.

At the border of Canaan, Moses gives instructions to twelve men to go and spy out the land. Forty days later, the spies return. Along with them, they bring a cluster of grapes so large that it requires two men to carry it on poles stretched out between them (v. 23). The land, they say, "flows with milk and honey, and this is its fruit" (v. 27). However, the reconnaissance team reports an issue: "The people who live in the land are strong, and the towns are fortified and very large" (v. 28). The problem is of huge proportion—those they saw were like giants, and to them the Israelites were but grasshoppers. All the people cry out loudly. They will have to turn back.

Caleb, one of the spies, encourages the people to attempt conquest of the land anyway by saying, "Let us go up at once and occupy it, for *we are well able* to overcome it" (v. 30, italics mine).

"We are well able," Caleb tells Moses and the people. Bates echoed Caleb. The advance team had already looked out from the First Union building. They had reported back, Bates was saying, and FBC was more than able to conquer this place. "We are well able to build the church of tomorrow in this city," he said. "We are able financially. . . . We are able spiritually. . . . We are able historically."[31]

Bates read the story upside-down. He told his people that they were like a formerly enslaved, landless people wandering the wilderness and relying on God to work miracles for them to have a home.[32] Nothing about the material conditions at FBC suggested any parallel with the Israelites. Bates could have been primed to see the injustice his church was participating in—he had grown up in a family of sharecroppers. Was he still driven by a childhood narrative of scarcity despite his present reality?[33] For the first time in the record, Bates indicated some missionary purpose for FBC in their movement within the city. They were to be part of God's salvific plan for Charlotte, able to do "what no other church of any single denomination is now planning to do. . . . God alone knows the end of the spiritual impact which shall be ours on the life of this city,"[34] he said. FBC's move stood in the legacy of white Christians who "joined visions of salvation to ideas of the transformation of lands and peoples and together formed visions of Christian missions," as theologian Willie Jennings has identified. "Whiteness formed at this joining."[35]

Bates's sermon wove together the tangled theology of Urban Renewal. On the one hand, the program and those who ran it in Charlotte and around the country operated from the legal and moral precedents established by the Doctrine of Discovery. Those complementary political and theological doctrines asserted the right to land and space by people who fit the category "white." It is easy to see that doctrine operating across the program. Based on Discovery, whites had the right, or even the duty, to use their strength to subdue land and people. Doing so was not only a statement of political power but also an act of Christian charity. Every step that led to FBC's move was consistent with this doctrine.

On the other hand, Bates was encouraging his congregation to see in themselves not strength but weakness. The words of Caleb that formed Bates's refrain—"we are well able"—were spoken as exhortation to a politically weak people. Nothing about Israel's situation indicated that they could conquer a land or a people. They had lived in precarity for many generations. Bates was genuinely caught up in the idea that FBC's move was part of God's work in the world. It was providential, an act of divine favor, not a manner of acting inside the legacy of white Christians taking and remaking places for their own purposes. "This is an open door which our Lord has set before us. We couldn't have done this," he said.[36] In Bates's words, and in the entire scenario at First Baptist, you can see "the way that race has persistently infiltrated and distorted Christian discernment of the work of divine Providence in the modern world."[37] Providence, as it often can be, was not so much God's work in the world as simple self-justification.

Bates, with the work of Vernon Sawyer years before him, showed just how awry the theo-political moment had gone. First Baptist, the Charlotte Redevelopment Commission, and the municipal power of the City of Charlotte reproduced yet again the Doctrine of Discovery, using might to assert dominion over space. As they did, they claimed that God was choosing the politically weak—namely, the people of Friendship and of the whole Brooklyn neighborhood—to undergo redemptive suffering while playing the part of the strong. Friendship, Sawyer had said, was to "lead the city at this crucial hour."[38] And yet still, Bates and FBC and the whole system of power in the City of Charlotte advanced the idea that God was also choosing the politically strong at First Baptist to play the part of the weak, thus justifying the entire program as the miraculous work of God in renewing the world.

"THERE WERE QUESTIONS"

Bates could not stop gushing in the following week's newsletter about how he would "cherish" every moment of the meeting.[39] The Redevelopment

Commission was as happy with FBC's decision as Bates was. Given the rough record the commission had in their efforts to sell Brooklyn land, having a high-profile institution rather than a car lot moving in was a welcome change. But there was still one matter to attend to—First Baptist had not yet purchased anything. They had only agreed to place a bid on land that the commission was selling. The auction was public, with bidding open to any interested party. The commission's change in the length of the auction certainly made putting in a successful bid more difficult by decreasing the available time a potential buyer had to assemble a site plan and find needed financing. So did the nominally Christian environment dissuade other bidders from pursuing the lot against a public narrative that cast FBC's move as having some divine mandate. C. C. Hope later remembered that "one other party was to put a bid on the property, but when the party . . . found out we put in a bid, he told me, 'I'm not going to bid against First Baptist Church' and withdrew his bid."[40] In the end, FBC placed a bid near the minimum, around $450,000 for about 8.5 acres. The auction closed with no other interest in the tract. FBC's offer was accepted.[41] First Baptist Church, together with the City of Charlotte and the Redevelopment Commission, was indeed well able to make and remake the cityscape.

A month after the bid was accepted, the *Observer* interviewed Coleman Kerry about the status of his congregation, having been gone from Brooklyn for eighteen months. Friendship was maintaining an office in a Fourth Ward building that would later be torn down for the Northwest Expressway. They were meeting regularly in homes during the week and held their Sunday worship services at Northwest Junior High School on Beattie's Ford Road. The church was holding on, though things were difficult.[42]

Nevertheless, Kerry played the politics of the day with the reporter. He highlighted his church's excitement to get its new facility off the ground and acknowledged some minor relief from being out of a neighborhood that could be dangerous at times. Most of his parishioners had moved toward the new Friendship plant, he said, and only a few households remained in Brooklyn. He cited the growth in both their membership and their budget since the move. Yet he also acknowledged that money—which is another way of saying *power*—had forced their relocation from Brooklyn. Friendship could have bid on Brooklyn land but simply did not have the resources. "We couldn't compete with larger commercial enterprises or churches with larger memberships," he said, referencing First Baptist. His members wanted to know why the congregations faced differing fates, Kerry said, but Kerry counseled them, publicly anyway, to move on. "There were questions," he said, "as to why First Baptist can move there and we can't. They have to accept the answer. They know we didn't have $400,000."[43] The move was not providential, in other words. It was the exercise of centuries of accumulated power.

CHAPTER NINE

"Churches Can Profit from Urban Renewal"

Southern Baptist Convention (SBC) leadership saw the project at First Baptist Charlotte and recognized in it yet another opportunity for churches looking to expand their footprint. SBC congregations in urban areas had made one of two choices: to move to the suburbs or to stay put. The executives within the SBC noted the strategy at First Baptist Charlotte and its potential as yet another growth opportunity. William Harrell, the secretary of the Church Architecture Department at the Baptist Sunday School Board, wrote a one-page piece for *Baptist Program* magazine in October 1965.[1] The piece was reprinted as a one-page flyer and made available around the country in SBC churches and institutions. The headline: "Churches Can Profit from Urban Renewal."

The article itself sounded like it could have been written in summation of the decision at First Baptist Church (FBC) Charlotte. "Some churches," Harrell wrote of congregations dealing with Redevelopment Commissions, "have moved only a few blocks, secured larger property, and remained in a central location. These churches are now downtown urban churches in the heart of the city." Curiously, he never mentioned FBC or Charlotte directly. Nevertheless, the echoes were unmistakable. "A church that has maintained an outreaching ministry will find the urban renewal program most profitable and helpful," Harrell said. "If churches in the renewal areas approach the planning commission and designers of the rehabilitated areas, these churches can become a part of the renewed downtown and stay in the heart of these cities."

Harrell cited the historic witness of Baptist churches: "Think of some of our downtown Baptist churches which have remained and which could become a part of such a renewal program. For centuries to come they could remain in the heart of the city with a voice, message, and ministry for Christ and Christianity. Cities such as Washington, Nashville, Jacksonville . . . and others can and should always have a Baptist church and a voice and ministry located in the downtown area." Those words could have come, verbatim, from Bill Poe.

Harrell listed several cities where such transactions were taking place. But there's not much evidence that Southern Baptist constituencies were making such moves. It was true that poor congregations often purchased church buildings abandoned through white flight, but that's not what Harrell seems to have in mind. There are a few examples of primarily white Christian institutions using Urban Renewal lands as an opportunity to expand their footprints. In San Francisco, St. Mark's Lutheran Church in the Western Addition purchased Renewal lands adjacent to its building. It used the new territory for several purposes, most notably to build a housing tower for moderate-income people in its notoriously expensive city.[2] In St. Louis, Saint Louis University, a Catholic institution, purchased large portions of the Mill Creek Valley Renewal area adjacent to its campus after other Renewal plans failed to materialize there.[3]

Perhaps the most egregious example of a Christian institution taking advantage of the Urban Renewal program for its own benefit happened in Waco, Texas, at Baylor University, a Baptist school with Southern Baptist Convention ties. There, Waco and Baylor officials worked together beginning in 1957 to declare a neighborhood adjacent to the university campus a slum, with the expressed intent of expanding the campus into that area. The neighboring area was mostly Black; Baylor refused to admit Black students. The city held a referendum on the issue and changed the election rules to allow only landowners to participate, not renters. Despite several years of ongoing protest, Waco and Baylor pushed ahead with plans for a highway, parks, and an expanded campus. In 1966, after the program was completed, the Executive Committee of the Baptist General Convention of Texas, the religious institution most closely affiliated with Baylor, issued a statement clarifying that while it was acceptable from the perspective of church-state separation for a religious body to purchase Urban Renewal lands, any such transaction should clearly be made at a fair price. It was important to Baptist principles that no "Baptist institution initiate action . . . or exercise preferential privilege by virtue of its religious nature."[4] They took their principled position after Waco and Baylor finished the Renewal project.

RELIGIOUS AFFILIATES

By 1965, some of the white churches in Charlotte were beginning to grapple in public with the extent of the social problems around them. They especially were becoming aware of those problems pertaining to race and the ongoing conditions that white supremacy had created in the city. The problems were not new, but white ministers in progressive churches were finally feeling the need to take action.[5] Locally, desegregation of public facilities in Charlotte had already happened in 1963, under a series of public symbolic actions taken by Mayor Brookshire and local Black leadership.[6] Nationally, the political and legislative gains of the civil rights movement won victories with the Civil Right Act of 1964 and the Voting Rights Act of 1965. Even as public institutions finally carved out space for Black participation, most white churches were still holding out. Those that were moving forward were timid and only ready for symbolic action.

At St. John's Baptist Church in the Elizabeth neighborhood, their renowned minister Claude Broach had pushed on his members for some years to consider their relationships to the civil rights movement and to their public commitments for racial justice. Finally, in 1965, the issue became unavoidable in the congregation when word spread of young Black activists attempting to join white churches. Worried church members publicly voiced their doubts about the activists' sincerity. But they also raised questions of church governance: Would a white Baptist church accept a Black member? If so, under what terms?[7]

The limited step of considering Black members was the smallest possible action, yet it remained a difficult sell in some congregations. But as it regarded Urban Renewal and the destruction of the churches where Black Christians already held their membership, the time to take action had passed. A decade earlier, as the planning phases of the project were beginning, white ministers could have offered their voices and their pulpits. None did. As their Black colleagues faced the loss of sanctuaries and Sunday School buildings and the displacement of their membership, no white ministers spoke publicly about the proceedings. By 1965, the bulldozers were rolling on phase 3 of the Brooklyn project. In the press and at city hall, leaders and clergy including Rev. Richard Hildebrandt were praising the work of Vernon Sawyer and his commission for bringing progress and vitality to Charlotte. In their eyes, the projects were going so well that it was time to consider others in the future, including in First Ward, Third Ward, some parts of Dilworth, and the Greenville neighborhood to the north of downtown. The record left behind indicates only ministerial silence.

White churches had made their choices about how—and whether—to engage in the unfolding struggle. Into the Black space of Brooklyn, which was becoming increasingly barren, one white church was moving to establish a new facility. In the white spaces of church sanctuaries and Sunday School rooms, white churches were finally debating whether a Black person would be allowed to join the congregation, and if so, under what conditions. In both moves, white congregations and their ministers assumed that their dominance was a given. It was their inheritance by the work of God.

When white churches began waking to the social problems Urban Renewal either caused or exacerbated, they took a few forms of action in response. Covenant Presbyterian was one of the first to be actively involved, beginning in 1962. Covenant sat on the northern edge of Dilworth, just a couple of blocks from Brooklyn. They joined in a partnership with Brooklyn United Presbyterian in 1962 to begin a daycare. They followed the daycare with a Sunday School. Both met at the Phillis Wheatley YWCA, one block from the site First Baptist would eventually buy (see figure 9.1).[8] How long Covenant's work went on is unclear, but such efforts were necessarily short-lived given the ongoing displacement of the people they served.

It was not until 1966 that Charlotte ministers began an organized effort to assist persons displaced by Urban Renewal. Rev. Page Shelton of the Mecklenburg Baptist Association, a collection of white Baptist churches working together in the county, called together about twenty colleagues from around the city in August of that year to form the Religious Affiliates of the Redevelopment Commission. Black and white ministers from six Christian denominations, plus a rabbi from Charlotte's Jewish community, inaugurated a small association whose goal was to assist families with relocation. They based their work on the example of a similar group in Durham, North Carolina. The group there insisted that ministers offer direct, face-to-face service to poor people rather than organizing their congregations for some larger effort.[9]

In Charlotte, ministers established a revolving fund that would assist those displaced in their relocations. Each minister's congregation was to contribute no more than twenty-five dollars. The Religious Affiliates would loan monies from the accumulated fund to families who needed to pay a deposit with the gas company, for instance. Loans had no interest and were expected to be repaid so that the money could go to another family. A 1967 roster of ministers included twenty-eight pastors or rabbis around the city, including most of

Figure 9.1. A missionary Sunday School group, sponsored in part by Covenant Presbyterian Church, meeting at the YWCA in Brooklyn, near the site of the current FBC. Used by permission of *Charlotte Observer*.

the large Black and white congregations, though First Baptist ministers were not a part. However, when the Redevelopment Commission sent the group a report of their progress in October 1967, it showed only sixteen families had received loans from the Religious Affiliates. The group appears to have folded in only a year or so, even as the work of the Redevelopment Commission was beginning in other neighborhoods. When it came to solving the problems created by Urban Renewal, Charlotte churches lacked the necessary vigor.

PASSING IT ON

First Baptist's movement from North Tryon to Second Ward did not proceed quickly. Even the legal paperwork behind it took more than two years to finally clear. The Redevelopment Commission accepted FBC's bid in June 1965. The title to the land was not deeded over to FBC until November 22, 1967.[10] Less than a week following the transfer of the title, Charlotte City Council appointed W. J. Smith Jr., one of the Four Horsemen at FBC, to fill an open position on the Redevelopment Commission.[11] Smith was highly energetic and involved with numerous public campaigns and work groups, including a chamber of commerce campaign regarding a local sales tax, serving as vice president of Charlotte's United Community Services (forerunner of the United Way) and the Mecklenburg Baptist Association.[12] Shortly after his appointment, he wrote a letter to document his conflicting statuses as a Redevelopment Commissioner and a member of FBC. He declared his intention to recuse himself from any further decision-making regarding FBC, should anything come about.[13]

Smith stayed busy in his capacity on the commission, eventually becoming its chair. But the work proceeded slowly at First Baptist. Various committees worked on design, furnishings, finance, sound—every detail went through groups of members leading the massive project. It took three and a half years of planning and design to reach the next critical step—breaking ground on the new site. [14] As the work developed, Bates used his congregation's success to raise his own profile. In summer 1970, he was elected president of the Southern Baptist Convention.[15]

Following their 11:00 a.m. service on Easter Sunday in 1971, members and ministers of the church made the three-quarters-of-a-mile journey to their lot on South Davidson Street. They had worked six full years since their vote in preparation. Now on a bright April day, the choir gathered in their robes. Children cheesed for the cameras. The congregation filled in the nameless ground that they were ready to build on, where stood only a handful of trees to shade them. Dr. Bates, Dr. Warren, and all Four Horsemen stayed near the center, each awaiting his turn on the program. The service included the hymn "The Church's One Foundation," drawing on a building metaphor appropriate for the morning. They sang the popular camp song "Pass It On." They pledged allegiance to the United States and Christian flags. Three people delivered statements or homilies. Warren spoke to them of "The Heritage of the Past." Bates spoke of "The Challenge of the Century." Between the two preachers and SBC presidents, youth group president David Abernathy spoke to "The Promise of the Future."[16]

Figure 9.2. Groundbreaking program at the new FBC site in Brooklyn, April 11, 1971. See "1st Baptists Break Ground at New Site," *Charlotte Observer*, April 12, 1971. Photo negatives from the *Observer* could not be located for this event. The reproduction of the photo here, however, hints at the spectral nature of the scene. Photo used by permission of *Charlotte Observer*.

It was all promise there, all hope, all future. They prayed and sang and prayed again and then passed the shovels. There was a pair of gold-painted shovels for Bates and Hope and hundreds of plastic toy shovels for the young people. The children opened the ground bit by bit and the older men spade by spade, unaware of what they were opening that would not close and that has not yet closed. They did not know the stories buried in that ground, of tears wept or bloodshed or the seed left from the lime tree in Annie North's yard, stories beyond counting, as "one can neither classify nor count the ghost, it is number itself, it is numerous, innumerable as number, one can neither count on it nor with it. There is but one of them and already there are too many."[17] They did not know, innocent all.

It was a strange resurrection they were proclaiming on that Easter day. They followed one who had been raised from the dead, who had appeared as a ghost, a revenant, a spirit, one who returned from a journey to a place where no one goes and returns, yet by faith they proclaimed the resurrection of his body. And here they were, on this most mystical of days, beginning to dig into the ground of the story that haunts this wide country, and they did not know.[18] They spent their lives chasing the one who is always returning, and now they were excavating something still living, still filled with stories they had wanted so badly not to see, not to know, not to acknowledge, the stories of the ones of whom there *were already too many.* They had avoided naming their place for so long, avoided calling it *Brooklyn*, added to its dismemberment by saying "urban redevelopment area." But now they could not avoid it. They exhumed a story that would be told.

And the children were doing it. At the site of the trespass, the children were performing the ritual transgression on behalf of the elders. "Help my unbelief," said the father of the boy with the silencing spirit, as the spirit moved backward across generations, *the time out of joint.* "Help our unbelief," the children could have said to the parents who wanted them pushing the shovels, over and over scraping the dirt while being asked to dig up the haunting they were helping to create in the world. "Help our unbelief," they might have said to one another. But they lacked the power to heal.

The first service in the new building took place only sixteen months later. The new space was the result of the dedication and labor of dozens and dozens of people within the congregation. It provided most of what they were hoping for. There were three stories of classrooms across two wings, with space for 1,400 in Sunday School. There was a large auditorium, built to begin its life as a sanctuary until a grander sanctuary could be built on the north side of the lot, at which point the auditorium was easily converted into a fellowship hall with even more classroom space. The buildings were constructed in a U shape, leaving a courtyard in the middle for children to play and small groups to gather. Across the front of the courtyard was a long breezeway of columns. All of it was done in a crisp brick made of crushed white marble. Standing out front was a 150-foot-tall bell tower, the gift of Mrs. Guy Carswell.[19] Her $100,000 contribution brought the structure the gravitas the congregation hoped for. It projected a cross high into the sky, astride the new city hall. As Bill Poe had advocated almost a decade prior, FBC was located adjacent to the halls of power.[20]

The structure itself straddled the suburban idyll some had advocated for and the urban setting that others wanted. It was, in evangelical language, *in* the city but not *of* the city. Notably, the building did not adjoin any sidewalks or interact with the urban spaces that were supposed to be growing around it. On two full sides and a portion of a third, the congregation built parking lots.

The other exterior façades featured a driveway from the street to the parking lot and at the front of the building, next to its white-columned entrance, a circular driveway (see figures 9.3 and 9.4). Bright white columns, circle drive: the ghosts of the past haunted even the building itself. The structure, plus courtyard and parking, took up one of two large blocks FBC purchased. Immediately across Davidson Street was the other full block, where in 1961 Mayor Brookshire had swung a sledgehammer in the first act of Urban Renewal's demolition. That block was now fully a surface parking lot.

Where the process of debating and deciding on a move had received extensive coverage a decade prior, the building's opening service garnered far less attention. Local reporting on the congregation's inaugural worship hour there focused on how members were thinking about the new structure's environs rather than the building itself. A member named Mrs. Moss stated that some congregants had heard stories "about assault or purse-snatching in the downtown area and were nervous about attending evening services" at the old Tryon Street location. Mrs. Moss and her husband had been driving a group of elderly members to church of late as the women did not like going downtown alone. A Mrs. Pulliam, the church librarian, pointed out that many women "did not like to leave the church alone, especially in winter months, when darkness came early."[21] Her words echoed closely those of Bates back in 1963, when he advocated relocation so that members could attend "without fear of dangerous streets where traffic threatens by day and uncertainty lurks at night."[22] Mrs. Moss was glad that the new building "was located in [a] more convenient and open area, with convenient and lighted parking nearby."[23]

The worship service was simple, including two hymns, a piece from the choir, Dr. Bates's sermon, and a greeting and prayer from the head of the North Carolina Baptist State Convention. The central hymn of the service was called "Dedicatory Hymn." Together, the congregation sang,

This house we dedicate to Thee,
O Lord, this holy day;
And may its mission ever be
Thy glories to display.
A precious gem of Thy right hand,
A trophy of Thy grace,
Long may its walls in beauty stand,
For Thee a dwelling place.[24]

The centerpiece of the service was a litany of dedication for the building and the bell tower.[25] The dedication framed the significance of the day in FBC's understanding of how God had been working in history, which is to say their words conveyed a doctrine of providence. God had been acting on their behalf, they proclaimed: "With joyful and grateful hearts we dedicate this building and Tower to God, who has loved us, who has blessed us, and who has led us in the task." They quoted from Psalms, saying, "Except the Lord build the house, they labour in vain that build it."[26] And they stated the purpose of the bell tower, the tall symbol staking its claim on the landscape

Carl E. Bates

Figures 9.3 and 9.4. *Previous page:* Pastor Carl Bates stands in front of the new First Baptist as it nears completion. Photo from *Biblical Recorder*, May 20, 1972. *This page:* Worshippers outside the new First Baptist building on its opening day. Photo from *Biblical Recorder*, September 2, 1972. Both photos used by permission.

of Charlotte. "As a comfort to the sorrowing, support to the weak, help to the needy, charity to the wayward, sympathy to the suffering, and as [a] beacon of hope to all people, we dedicate this Carswell Bell Tower," they said.[27]

Bates noted proudly the significance of what FBC had accomplished. He called the church a symbol of hope, an open door for ministry in Charlotte. "If you're interested in finding hope you will find it built on achievement," Bates told the congregation. "Dreamers have never been those to find hope."[28]

C. C. Hope must have had both the greatest sense of accomplishment and the greatest sense of relief in the building that day. Hope had spent fifteen years working on this move, and finally it had reached a conclusion. The church staff reserved a page for him in the program, with a headshot and a chance for him to offer a few words as longtime chair of the Building Committee. His first sentence called back to Dr. Warren, who had taken C. C. into his mentorship years before: "Attempt great things for God and expect great things from God," Hope said, appealing to his Christian mentor. Warren had often written and spoken that sentence during his ministry at FBC, as well as in his 1957 presidential address to the SBC.[29] From time to time, Bates had appealed to the quotation as well.

Here it was, at last: a great thing. A thing that could satisfy Bill Poe and Carl Bates both. There was a nine-acre campus with a new kitchen and more than enough classrooms. There was ample, well-lit parking. Bates got his suburban wish. Poe saw his urban vision fulfilled. The Carswell Bell Tower pierced the sky in sight of the downtown high rises and across the street from city hall.

As the city destroyed Brooklyn, they realigned some streets. First Street in Brooklyn was eliminated. Second Street began a diagonal near the railroad and finished it near Davidson, then ran straight to McDowell. The grid has a disjuncture now, a quirk on the map with a story to tell. If you follow the path of the old 2nd Street, along where the row of businesses stood, you trudge through one FBC parking lot. Across the street you pass into the next parking area, along the windowless exterior of that first sanctuary. When you reach the back of the structure, you stand at the corner of the building where it rests atop the former 625 E. 2nd Street, the home of Abram and Annie North.

CHAPTER TEN

"Our Debts"

Forgive us our trespasses.
—Jesus, traditional rendering of the Lord's Prayer

Forgive us our debts.
—Jesus, Matthew 6:12

Like her great-great-great-great-uncle Abram, and her great-great-great-aunt Hazeline, Tiffany North works as an insurance agent. Perhaps that's a coincidence, just the luck of the job market at the time she was interviewing for work. Maybe not. Legacies pop up unexpectedly—the confluence of aptitude and interest, the dance of nature and nurture. Tiffany did not know of Abram and did not know of Hazeline's résumé before she started the insurance job, but the idea of a legacy makes sense to her.

She's good at the job. No surprise there. But the paychecks don't cover everything. Between raising two adolescents, making the rent in an expensive city, and paying off student loans, one job is not enough.

Tiffany is good at hospitality also, like her great-great-great-great-aunt Annice and other of her North kin. At night and on her days off, she runs a catering business. Lasagna is her specialty. Her version is as good a one as you'll find down South, teeming with vegetable slices and chunked with meat, then baked to oozing. Tiffany's other offerings include soups and baked salmon and party planning. It's all enough to make ends meet but not much more than that. And all the hustling grinds her down sometimes.

Tiffany's mother, Regina, has had a different career path, but her economic conditions are similar. She went to night school at Johnson C. Smith

University, a historically Black school in Charlotte, to finish her degree and has spent thirty years working in law firms. And yet her career keeps hitting invisible barriers: "Every time I try to get a job—because they laid lots of us off due to COVID—it just feels like there's a block. Blocking access. . . . *They* [corporate recruiters] keep saying, 'Oh, we enjoyed you, but the client had someone else that blocked you out of that position.'"[1] Regina keeps moving forward, but the regular theme of the history has not eluded her—the North family striving, the systems around them throwing up roadblocks.

The North family legacy in Charlotte is expansive beyond owning homes and land, though many of the descendants were homeowners.[2] But the properties they owned were the most significant material asset they held. As Tiffany sees it, continuing to hold those properties could have been transformational for her family. "How would that have spearheaded generational wealth?" she asks. "How would that have been able to further along [the next] generations? . . . We are fighting student loans now because everybody got them."[3]

Tiffany notes how the lack of an asset that once belonged to their family had turned into a debt that was difficult to get out from under. What could have been in place to finance education, to move upward, to lift themselves and their community, had been replaced with a usurious debt made necessary by a society that also made paying it off remarkably difficult. North resources were taken in a scheme of redistribution to other public and private institutions, leaving behind accumulating debt where there could have been an appreciating asset. As the material assets disappeared, so did the stories of what had been and how it had come to be. The narratives of triumph and success in the face of unyielding oppression were muted, perhaps in the pain of reliving by memory yet another assault on home and body and spirit.

While Tiffany and Regina struggle, the institutions that profited from the seizure of North properties, and of their entire neighborhood, have helped to keep the stories in the ground. They reap the rising value of the places they inhabit with little sense of the debts that they have inherited by virtue of the places and institutions they occupy. Staying clammed up about the history, keeping the archives inaccessible, and suppressing the public narration of the story make it seem like the story is complete. Silence tries to turn political and economic power inevitable rather than a matter of ongoing choice.

Tiffany's sister Brandi North Williams says that the silences have been costly to her family. "The loss of legacy is a huge cost to us," she says. The damage is connected to attachment to place and the grounding that comes with the knowledge of her family's importance in it—and her own. She describes "a feeling that this is where we've been placed, and so we're gonna live until it's time to die. But I think it gives you so much more to live for to know the connection that you have to the city. I never knew that we were landowners. It just blows my mind, the fact that we did all that."[4]

Brandi is speaking about ownership not only of the land and the place that her people had nurtured. She is also speaking about her connection to the story of Charlotte, about a sense of power and belonging inside that story. Brandi has been fighting for justice for years, but the fight feels different when she is not constantly in the "underdog role, with a feeling of lack and shame."[5] She is part of generations of people who have altered the political economy of the city. That's power. Knowing the legacy charges her work.[6] It deepens her connections to herself, her ancestors, and the place she calls home. It feeds her fire, one planted in her before she was born and that will not be extinguished when she joins the realm of her ancestors.

Along the century-and-a-half of story that has brought us to this point, I have suggested that the history is still alive, that *the time is out of joint*. At this disjuncture, we may note, much is still not well. The cityscape of Charlotte, like the landscape of the country, remains scarred with the evidence of Urban Renewal. Derrida asks, "Is not disjuncture the very possibility of the other?"[7] We live at the edge of a rupture that opens an opportunity for justice. Redress requires multiple accountings, a host of reckonings, visits from innumerable ghosts. They speak of the economic damages visited on the Norths and their Brooklyn neighbors. They press for money and its exchange, the restoration of Black families to some sense of wholeness, and the assumption of risk by white institutions who profited from those families' losses. The specters demand we dig underneath finances into the stories and songs and culture that gave birth to Renewal's injustices. Together, our efforts at economic and theological repair—at changes both political and cultural—may offer us a chance to be whole.

ASSESSING THE DAMAGE

After the Redevelopment Commission forced Hazeline North Anderson to sell her home, she and her husband, Sam, moved to 2028 Oaklawn Avenue. From Hazeline's front porch, she could see her sister Bessie's house. Bessie

Figure 10.1. Regina North (youngest child, center) and siblings, left to right, Agnes, Malia, Patricia (holding Regina), and Reginald. Picture taken ca. 1959 in Hazeline North Anderson's yard at 625 E. 2nd St. Photo courtesy of Regina North.

had bought there nearly fifty years prior, becoming one of the first home-owners in the Washington Heights section (see chapter 3). Across the street and a block over, on Patton Avenue, was her cousin Jacob North Jr. and his family (figure 10.1). Jacob was the son of Abram's brother, Jacob Sr. The new expressway would cut through Jacob Jr.'s neighborhood a few years later, but Jacob was fortunate that his house was spared.

Neither the relative cultural comfort of their new neighborhood nor their good fortune in standing out of the way of the expressway would shield Sam and Hazeline North Anderson and their neighbors from the social forces bearing down on them. The Northwest Freeway blocked their neighborhood off from Johnson C. Smith University, the historically Black college founded shortly after the Civil War that was one center of Black life in

Charlotte. It also created a barrier between them and Clinton Chapel AME
Zion Church, which by then was located across the street from Johnson C.
Smith. The interstate highway cut them off from downtown. White residents
fled nearby neighborhoods like Seversville. When they did, they primarily
sold to investors and speculators angling to make a profit off white fears
of Black neighbors, a strategy called "blockbusting."[8] Among Charlotte's
blockbusters was B. Brevard Brookshire, a founding member of Providence
United Methodist Church, brother of Mayor Stan Brookshire.[9] Landlords
like Brevard Brookshire started crowding people into houses by subdivid-
ing the housing stock into duplexes and triplexes, no matter how small. Or
they might sell at inflated prices to Black families who could get loans, after
using aggressive scare tactics to get white owners to sell cheap.[10] Despite the
end of legalized segregation, Black tenants faced restricted supply in actual
practice. There were few choices besides overpaying. The new chapter that
was opening following Urban Renewal was not going to get easier for those
displaced. They would face similar challenges of ongoing disinvestment by
public and private actors. Communities were dealing with the "root shock"
that resulted from being forcibly transplanted from other neighborhoods.[11]
At the same time, government was building highways, which served as huge
geographic and psychological barriers between Black neighborhoods, Black
cultural institutions, and the economic engine of downtown.

The financial consequences of Urban Renewal and its legacy for Hazeline
North Anderson and her extended family[12] look like this: the city paid the
Andersons $6,300 for their house on 2nd Street. They came up with $200
more and then bought 2028 Oaklawn Avenue for $6,500. The building was
similar, the lot a bit larger. In Brooklyn, their six-room house ("with plumbing," according to the *Observer*) and detached garage sat on about 5,000 square
feet of land. On Oaklawn, their house had five rooms on a 10,000-square-foot
lot (see figure 10.2). Depending on how an individual valued land and the
improvements on the land, you might even argue that the Andersons got a
slight upgrade. On the new larger lot, Sam would have room to grow collards
and tomatoes. "I'm a garden man," he told the *Observer*.[13]

But as municipal and private money went elsewhere, including to the
"renewed" Second Ward, the Andersons saw their investment stagnate in
comparison with the land values in their former home. Sam Anderson died
on September 10, 1967, and Hazeline on February 22, 1976. By the time of
their deaths, their property had not appreciated in value. The trajectory has

Figure 10.2. Sam Anderson stands in front of the home at 2028 Oaklawn Ave. that he and his wife, Hazeline North Anderson (not pictured), purchased following their displacement from Brooklyn. Photo used by permission of *Charlotte Observer*.

not changed. Over the last sixty years, the assessed value of 2028 Oaklawn has remained nearly flat.

The market for land is quite different in the former Brooklyn neighborhood. At First Baptist Church (FBC), the value of their property has increased ninefold, at minimum.

The forced sale of the North property in Brooklyn has, in the intervening years, cost the North family at least $440,000 in equity. That equity has instead been accumulated by FBC. In considering how to make Black families from Brooklyn whole following the destruction of their neighborhood, and then their subjection to multiple decades of ongoing neglect in other neighborhoods, these figures are a good starting point. Further, it is important to note that the tax value of the house on Oaklawn nearly doubled between 2019 and 2023. The 2019 figures show an appreciation of about 3 percent over fifty-eight years. The recent jump in value has many factors, notably the considerable gentrification of the area and its presence in a so-called Opportunity Zone, a Trump-era investment incentive that serves primarily as a tax shelter for real estate investors.

Material difference for Norths and FBC[14]	FBC land	Former North home, East 2nd Street	Former North home, Oaklawn Avenue
Purchase price (inflation-adjusted to 2023 dollars)	$4.27 million (1965)	$64,100 (1961)	$66,200 (1961)
Assessed value, 2019 (in 2023 dollars)	$41 million	$615,500	$68,300
Assessed value, 2023	$40 million	$600,500	$106,000
Appreciation over time	930%	930%	155%
Difference in accumulated appreciation	$35.73 million	$489,600	$49,800

The figures I have presented also suggest, through the case of the Norths, FBC, and the City of Charlotte, the extraordinary cost of white supremacy as it has been built into real estate markets and land use in the United States. These data are but a fraction of the ongoing costs that white supremacy exacts on Black people and neighborhoods and the corresponding accumulated advantage[15] given to white people and our institutions. To get to this point, one might ask the question, "How did removing Black people from a space change its economic (or commodity) value?" The answer can be calculated over the course of the intervening years. The value of former Brooklyn land, in inflation-adjusted dollars, has appreciated nearly tenfold, whereas the value of land where former Brooklyn residents and their descendants moved—often within one or two miles of the former location and sometimes adjacent to other white neighborhoods—stagnated, at least until changing racial geographies of so-called "gentrification" brought white residents into those neighborhoods, a subject we will turn to in chapter 12.

The figures I am presenting show that solving the entrenched problems of systemic racism cannot happen through simply paying economic damages, though paying economic damages is a necessary and unavoidable step.

However, in a culture of white supremacy, space is raced. Placing the North family, or any Brooklyn family, back into a previous location, even to the point of reconstituting the entire neighborhood with its descendants, would devalue the land again. In American society, Black space is worth less than other space because Black people live in it. At the same time, white cultures consider Black people morally deficient, thus creating a feedback loop around the value of Black spaces and their inhabitants. Philosopher Charles Mills calls this "a circular indictment: 'You are what you are in part because you originate from a certain kind of space, and that space has those properties in part because it is inhabited by creatures like yourself.'"[16]

The economic data show not only what one Brooklyn family might stand to gain in the imaginary world where Urban Renewal did not happen. Beyond that, these figures demonstrate the costs imposed by white supremacy that Black people are always paying simply because of the racial identity—and the correspondingly raced spaces—they inhabit. And even further, the figures demonstrate the advantage in wealth and power that white people and institutions gain and hoard simply because of the spaces and racial identity *they* inhabit. First Baptist Church sits on millions of dollars in equity that can be leveraged for a world of opportunities. Half of their land is a parking lot that creates passive income to augment their budget. Likewise, Lee Kinney's real estate firm remains a robust commercial real estate practice that passes wealth across generations of his family. Philosopher George Lipsitz says of these sustained material differences that pervasive racial segregation creates "a geographically organized vulnerability for Black people. Not only are they concentrated demographically, but the processes and power that turn white privilege and power into property, into the accumulations that appreciate in value and can be passed down across generations, also leave Black people with little control over the economic decisions that shape their lives."[17] The values of places greatly exceed their exchange prices as commodities. However, under systems of white supremacy, the presence of Black people creates land that is imprinted with negative value until white people arrive and fulfill the purpose and possibility of the land.[18] The assumption on the part of people who imagine themselves "white" that they—really, we—rightfully dominate the present and future of places in their varied uses and conceptions is a consistent and primarily unspoken characteristic of life in a society organized around white supremacy. The assumption of white spatial dominance played out across the course of this story in Charlotte: the 1912 article suggesting that white people would have to take Brooklyn land eventually; the Presbyterian pastor Richard Hildebrandt advocating for Urban Renewal in part because of "porch-sitting, beer-drinking, undershirt-clad" citizenry; Bill Poe's emphasis on having a Baptist church downtown but never advocating for the Black Baptist churches that were being forced from downtown; Ray King teaching Sunday School and two days later pushing down a house while wearing a suit.

Abram and Annie North did precisely what US culture celebrates as the American Dream. They were born enslaved in an economy that planned for them only to have their work stolen until they died. Over decades, they forged a way into stability, married and raised children, influenced their community, and earned the respect of citizens across Charlotte. They created a space of welcome for neighbors, threw parties and celebrations, founded and nurtured a church, and stayed devoted to their God and their family. When they died, they passed on their estate to their heirs. It became the property of their daughter Hazeline, a solid house in a comfortable neighborhood they had helped to build.

The Norths played exactly by the rule book.

According to the dominant myth of US culture, a house and some land were the surest way to establish generational wealth. And yet, because the Norths were Black and "for no other reason,"[19] their material legacy has been zeroed out by the racist housing policies and practices of the City of Charlotte, the County of Mecklenburg, the State of North Carolina, the United States of America, and by all of its constituent citizens who have believed the lies of whiteness, who have either profited openly and vocally or simply remained silent in the face of obvious injustice.

REPENT AND BELIEVE

The other side of the North story is the story of FBC. It is the story of those made white in the system of racial hegemony. The question of cost has a different calculus on this side of the color line. We own a legacy built on the dispossession of others, an inheritance explained by someone else's disinheritance, a past that is not past, a wavering present.

I asked Regina North to speak to the wavering present. "What would you say to us who live with the advantages taken from your family?"

Regina paused briefly and then with utter conviction said, "Repent."[20]

It's a theological answer. It is also a political and economic one, from a word whose root sense means "to turn around." The conditions that preceded and led to Urban Renewal—which were the conditions of centuries of white supremacy in doctrine and in practice—were built on the meshing of theological beliefs with political and economic practices. Whiteness is precisely the joining of political and economic hegemony to a theological project that would justify the domination of people who declare themselves to be "white" by calling that domination the work of God in the world.

Regina understands that repentance is not disembodied spirituality, nor is it merely individual piety. It is corporate. It is economic. It is political. It is geographic. Repentance is also spiritual and psychological: "If you're talking about giving something monetarily, that can soothe [the guilt] away. But what goes forward is that you need to make sure that it doesn't happen again. I mean, look, we can pay something off and say, 'Oh, I'm done with that!' and then go back and do the same thing over again. You got to know how to put a period behind that sentence. And vow never to have it done again."

There are *somethings-to-be-done*,[21] in other words. More than one thing, more than one type of thing, things that will make demands of us that we will not be able to control. The material experience of haunting continues until the injury is resolved, until the wounding stops. Until we conjure differently.[22] And perhaps beyond that. There is no way to know. But doing the right thing cannot be dependent on getting a painless result.

MAKING REPAIRS

The costs, in the crude measure of land converted to dollars and cents, will never convey the full loss of a space defined by culture and kinship and affection and legacy. But the financial loss can, to some extent, be calculated. Those exiled to other neighborhoods and districts can, to a great extent, be tracked. City archives around the country still contain records of payments and valuations. Directories and phone books still hold the names of residents. Newspapers and church archives and family histories hold obituaries listing descendants. And beyond all those paper records, people from neighborhoods plowed under by Urban Renewal still live and participate in their communities in cities around the country. They hold stores of connections and relationships and stories, all of which can help to restitch the fabric unraveled by various Redevelopment Commissions.

We, as a society, can know some of the damage. We, as white Christians and churches, can understand how we participated and how we have profited. And the institutions responsible can make repairs[23] directed at those whose families were directly harmed, whether they were homeowners or not.

As an act of penitence, FBC Charlotte can offer reparative payments to those on whose land they now sit. The families who lived on those blocks are listed in the city directories easily accessible online and at the public library. Finding those still living and the descendants of those who have died is not a simple task, but it is hardly an impossible one. Part of the process of restoration is lovingly attending to the names and stories of people you do not know. You honor the mystery of what and who has disappeared and await the opportunity to connect gently with those whom you can find.

Myers Park Baptist, the community that nurtured the faith of Medd McNeill, can join the work and offer acts of economic penitence as well.

So can the Presbytery of Charlotte, the institution responsible for Richard Hildebrandt and the now-defunct Wilmore Presbyterian.

So can the other institutions that played roles from small to large, those mentioned in this work, those whose place in the story still remains shrouded in silence, and those in other cities and towns who will learn about their own stories.

The public penitence of making repairs is one way that those who remained silent can try, in a costly fashion, to send the silencing specter on its way. Offering redress is a theo-political act that fits the theo-political sins that white churches set the stage for, encouraged, profited from, and observed in silence. Some will protest that acts of penance are punitive. But restoring communities and their people is not punishment. It is the only way to be free.

Brandi Williams says the love of neighbor compels the work of repair: "I don't understand how you can see the harm that was done to us and not want to make that right."[24] To change course, which is the root sense of the Hebrew term for "repent," requires a commitment to the well-being of the other. It also demands a regard for one's own soul. It is love in action rather than in dreams.[25] When you love your neighbor well enough, the work may be hard, but it is worth it.

If you love your neighbor, the pain of confronting your own people—including your own self—is not too great. Penance is a moral commitment that flows naturally from repentance. It is an act of acknowledging sin beyond the bounds of law. It is an act of belief that calls us to the simple confession of the father of the boy possessed by the silencing spirit: "I believe; help my unbelief!"

Such bold repentance invites another step: returning land. Redistributing real property raises complex questions that have only imperfect answers. To whom would we return the land? What of those who claim title to it now? Is such a move in the realm of political possibility? Surely there are many other questions that a program of redistribution would raise. There are also the righteous claims of those who occupied this land before Europeans settled here. In Charlotte, they include the Catawba and Sugaree people. None of these concerns have easy resolutions, but difficulty does not justify inaction. No solution will be perfect. Of importance in the current context of American Christianity, gifts of land may represent a legacy for shrinking congregations. As Christian churches experience long-term decline across the country, many of them have building and land holdings far beyond what their congregations can sustain. For congregations facing changing identities, and even their deaths, returning land to oppressed communities is an opportunity to confront their histories, to alter their cities, and to restore their souls.

Returning land or making payments based on land values is a question of harm repair or restitution. It is like the framework for reparations to descendants of slavery proposed by William Darity and A. Kirsten Mullen. In their important work *From Here to Equality*, Darity and Mullen say that "restitution is the restoration of survivors to their condition before the injustice occurred or to a condition they might have attained had the injustice not taken place."[26] Within that framework, the City of Charlotte, together with the private institutions and landowners who have profited from Urban Renewal, might track down those who lived in Brooklyn around 1960 and offer their descendants appropriately large checks or pieces of real estate that will satisfy the debt. Such a program would rightly give redress to both renters and homeowners within Brooklyn and other Renewal areas and would do so in a racially conscious fashion for the remnants of that entire community. The harms of Jim Crow, redlining, and Urban Renewal were done along the lines of race, not ownership status. The remedies must be made along those same lines. The cruelties of Urban Renewal came about because the accumulations of the wealthy created difficult conditions that harmed entire neighborhoods. Restitution cannot proceed according to one of the same principles—payments to property owners only and not to renters—that helped the injustice to persist.[27]

Reparations strategies based on restitution are an essential part of what is to be done. But as philosopher Olúfẹ́mi Táíwò points out, such strategies are incomplete and may operate inside some of the same assumptions that gave rise to the injustices they aim to repair. Making economic comparisons for the purpose of noting what has been lost "invites us to view Black suffering in accounting terms."[28] Such comparisons may be necessary as one step toward justice, but they also "tend to 'represent détente with rather than commitment to changing capitalist class relations, including those that contribute to intra- and inter-racial disparity in the first place.'"[29] Programs of economic repair matter because they address the harm done and create some restoration and self-agency inside the communities where that harm has accumulated over generations. But without changing the relations of people and their institutions to one another—relations currently, perhaps indelibly, marked by white supremacy—there simply aren't enough checks in the country to fundamentally alter our future.

A CONFUSING WITNESS

White America's theo-political actions create a confusing witness. So says Rev. Janet Garner-Mullins, who spent her childhood in Brooklyn until her family was forced out in the mid-1960s. She and her mother later moved to Third Ward, and again they were forced out for another Renewal project. So was their church, First Baptist Church-West.[30] She frames the problem as a theological one: "If we say we serve the same God, then how is it your God is telling you to put me out of my house and out of my community so you can buy the land . . . ? And [then] I'm homeless. And I serve God, the same God. I'm a little bit confused how that works."[31]

The theo-political events around Urban Renewal as I have described them cannot be written off as aberrant acts of waywardness, the backsliding of a handful of otherwise decent people who had the misfortune of having their pictures taken at inopportune times and memorialized in the archives. The roots of their actions run deep through the faith their ancestors handed them. They passed that faith on to their descendants. Writing on white evangelicals in the second half of the twentieth century, historian Jesse Curtis observes,

"Americans read Monday morning's paper with the Sunday sermon ringing in their ears. When they picked up their Bibles, they did not put down their political commitments."[32] Faith and political commitments are all knotted up together, sometimes buttressing one another, even becoming indistinguishable, always leaving complex, sometimes troubling, testimonies. Acts of repair must necessarily include changing the theological cultures inside our congregations and institutions. Unless those who are committed to repair address the ideological scaffolding on which we have built, we are bound to repeat the same errors, to be visited by the same ghosts.

"We are well able," Carl Bates preached to his congregation before their fateful vote. He drew the title and the refrain of his sermon directly from the Bible. The message was an exhortation to his flock that they could accomplish, with God's help, a major task. But the culture inside which he wrote that sermon required him to apply his ignorance of the world around him to the biblical story. He read the Bible's foundational Exodus narrative in a way that married the material conditions of the Exodus to Bates's own social location despite a chasm of difference.

Scripture is a story that binds, whether it comes directly as narrative or political drama, as exhortation or poetry or oral tradition.[33] Scripture weaves people together into a common way of life and lineage. Christian gatherings include Bible readings not with the expectation that any one encounter with sacred text will transform a person or group but that many repeated readings over a lifetime will form and discipline a person into the contours of a tradition. The regular reading of Scripture is enculturation, a process of enfolding. Every reading, then, is a potential site of political contestation but also a potential compromise with the current order. Just as the members of FBC carried on a theological debate inside whiteness about their move and its meaning, so were their practices of reading Scripture both constitutive of and at the same time reflective of the dominant political category of whiteness. So it was with all of the other parties included in this story—each brought the text into their political commitments and their political commitments into the text.

Repairing our trespasses, for white churches and Christians, will require us to examine our relationships with our sacred texts. Our readings tend to justify hegemonic power rather than unsettling it. Sometimes our readings of texts overlook their contexts of political and material power altogether, instead spiritualizing or allegorizing ancient drama into immaterial life lessons. Such strategies serve to reinforce power rather than to challenge it. They drive us further from repair, deeper into our debts.

Next to story and Scripture in its importance for teaching culture and ideas is song. When the people of First Baptist needed a piece of music to express their feelings and understandings about their coming move, they turned to "Lead On, O King Eternal," a hymn of conquest. Christian worship services use hymns and songs to teach theology because singing has a long-lasting impact on memory and on collective identity. Patients facing dementia often remember songs and hymns far longer than they remember their own spouses and children. The civil rights movement featured a canon of songs that encouraged, inspired, and united marchers. Many of those songs preceded that movement and are still used in various justice struggles today. Music forms collective identity and instills meaning.[34] The contents of our hymnals and songbooks are not distractions for passing the time. They teach us how to live in the world.

A further element of culture is our relationship to place. First Baptist's history as recounted above fits well inside the relationship of dominant American culture to the places we inhabit. In their story, the congregation moved several times, first in search of stability but then in search of visual and social prominence. Moving and migration are regular occurrences in all of human history, so moving is not surprising in itself. However, the period of white flight came to be characterized not by attachment to place but detachment from it. The importance of particular spaces was not about the place itself—its flora, its built environment, the creeks and the watersheds to which they belong, the neighbors, the animals, the microclimates within it—but rather about its usefulness as an expression of political power. The automobile became the dominant mode of interacting with the landscape. People became detached. First Baptist Charlotte is such an interesting case of this because their move to the former Brooklyn neighborhood highlights the idea of detachment so well. They have a suburban campus in an urban setting, made possible by erasure and forgetting and silence. They got there through a lack of attachment to their former place, both as an entity and as individual households moving from the city in the new chapters of segregation.

The detachment from place remains a salient characteristic of dominant American culture. In the work of repair, one key move is re-placing ourselves. Our sanctuaries are important sites where we can learn to be appropriately attached through our baptism into specific watersheds.[35] Connections to space and place create room for both hospitality and justice, not as masters with dominion but as part of creation.

Inside the culture of white Christians is a long legacy of cultural resources that made it more likely, rather than less likely, that Christians would plan, participate in, execute, and profit from world-changing schemes like Urban Renewal without grappling with the fullness of what they were doing and to whom they were doing it. As they played their various roles, they did so as fully themselves, as whole persons whose lives seemed consistent from Sunday morning in the pews to Wednesday afternoon at the office and Friday evening at home. When Ray King ran the bulldozer while wearing a suit, he was the same Ray King who taught Sunday School. Hell, he may have worn the same suit. When Carl Bates read FBC into the book of Numbers as the grasshoppers rather than the giants, he was not putting on an act inside the pulpit. And when he left First Baptist Charlotte to become a preaching professor at Southern Baptist Theological Seminary in Louisville, Kentucky, he passed to his students the same cultural legacy that he had inherited so that they could pass it on to thousands and thousands in their respective pews.

When the white Christians described in this project acted, they acted *as Christians*, utilizing the resources and content of their faith to make sense of their actions. Among the legacies of the faith of white Christians and churches has been that our conceptions of land and space and place operated silently underneath our more vocal confessions. Christian faith in white-dominant spaces, whether evangelical or progressive, has assumed our sovereignty over places as part of God's work in history. That's a legacy that lives, not only as explored above regarding Urban Renewal but also in the ongoing shifts of urban spaces in the 2020s, including gentrification, where white Christians are often at the visible frontier of the changes to racialized space.[36] Our songs, our tellings of the stories of Scripture, our church structures, our spiritual formation, our displacement—each is an element of a culture that supports our trespasses.

Repair beyond money but including money. And real property. *Reparations and....* The nature of the liability must be reflected in the act of penitence.[37] Among white Christians, what follows our economic offerings is not the washing of our hands nor the soothing of guilty consciences. Rather, we need a series of iterative processes, grounded in a theology of repair, that can help our unbelief. One step reveals, for instance, a story like that of the Norths, grounded in a specific place and time and implying specific economic responsibilities. Another step might look at the cultural resources that help to justify the unjust use of political and economic power in reproducing distorted ideologies of race and class. Each step would reveal yet another to be taken, not in a linear fashion but instead circling around the geography of our churches, the territory of our neighborhoods, the lives of our neighbors, the terrain of our own souls. One action reveals the next, turns up another specter, always involving us in a chase where we seek only to find ourselves pursued.

A CONSTRUCTION PROJECT

What we are seeking, finally, is another way to exist in the world.[38] You might think of that as *redemption*, which is a word with economic and theological meanings. To redeem is to buy back, to release from a debt, to dissolve a lien, to clear from distress, to end a captivity. When a thing is redeemed, a new set of possibilities opens for the future.

Redemption is an economic action of great personal and political import. It is not a transaction, like buying chips from the corner store, but the kind of exchange that clears the ledgers. Redemption opens a possibility that did not exist before, which makes it such a powerful theological concept. While the Israelites suffer under slavery in Egypt, God promises them, "I will redeem you with an outstretched arm and mighty acts of judgment" (Exod 6:6). Jesus, in a decidedly political speech that sets in motion the events leading to his death, declares that a coming apocalypse will shake the foundations of the religious and political world. This, he says, is redemption "drawing near" (Luke 21:28).

Likewise, the father of the boy with the silencing spirit begs for help. Standing in for communities of both the silenced and the silentious,[39] the father wants a different world than the one he and his son currently suffer with. "If you are able to do anything, have pity on us and help us," he pleads (Mark 9:22). Is there a world that is not characterized by the grinding down of people, by the fires of oppression, by the drowning of poor people in floods of debt? Can we create a culture of wise speech and careful listening, of gentle community rather than rigid death?

"All things can be done for the one who believes," Jesus responds (Mark 9:23). Redemption accompanies belief. Release from bondage or debt is incomplete without a person or a political body who will receive it and walk in freedom. The gift comes with strings attached—the work of recovering the lost years, of learning new habits and skills, of imagining some new way of living. "Reparation is a construction project," Táíwò says.[40] The aim of our building will be a set of systems where everyone has a place. And though some will have different roles and goals in that project, each of us will have a part.[41] Belief is active participation in the construction project.

Whiteness names the joining of political, economic, and theological projects of domination for the supposed benefit people who declare themselves to be "white." I have offered a detailed story of how whiteness works in one specific place, at a discrete moment in time. The story, I believe, is generalizable—though the details of varying Urban Renewal projects are different, the trajectory of the story is not. For those of us who are white in a racialized world, and specifically for those who are white Christians, active belief places demands on our lives. Our healing is possible but not outside participatory repair to the world our ancestors damaged in service of empire rather than of life. We engage our belief not only to right past injustices or to make right the present for those who have lived oppressed by our theo-political friendship with the silencing spirit. The work is for ourselves also—the laconic, the reticent, the hesitant, the taciturn, the mum. Our debts are not only to our neighbors whom our thirst for land and space has so often uprooted. They are also across generations of our own people—our ancestors to whom we owe truth, our children to whom we owe wholeness.

Unbelief walks beside faith. "All things can be done for the one who believes," Jesus says. But what of those who do not believe, those who maintain the silence, who perpetuate the injustice, who sit comfortably atop the spoils? What of those who do not welcome justice but block it? We now turn to the strategies and stories that seek to maintain the veneer of innocence and in so doing stifle the construction of a new world.

CHAPTER ELEVEN

"The Innocence That Constitutes the Crime"

It is not permissible that the authors of destruction should also
be innocent. It is the innocence which constitutes the crime.
—James Baldwin[1]

In May 2019, the strategic planning committee at First Baptist Church (FBC) was looking for new projects that would help the congregation grow their profile in the city, especially among the thousands of residents who had moved downtown, or adjacent to downtown, during the decade of the 2010s. FBC had once been full of prominent people, but suburbanization among their main constituency and the long tenure of a hard-line conservative pastor had taken its toll on the congregation. Attendance was down, even as the area around them was showing some signs, sixty years later, of turning into what the Redevelopment Commission had hoped for. Jan Johnson presented the strategic planning team with a simple idea: turn their four acres of parking into a Saturday morning farmers' market. The market would be the only growers' market uptown. It would be within walking distance of thousands of residents. It could attract people from across the community, bridging race and class.[2]

Johnson was thorough in her preparations. She submitted a plan that discussed all of the aspects that would be necessary for the market's success: incorporating a separate entity, personnel, potential vendors, pricing, payments by public assistance (SNAP) benefits, parking. She thought of everything. All those factors made the market an idea that Johnson thought would "touch the community, not by going out to evangelize, but by using the space to serve."[3] Johnson's presentation included a brief history of the land where they would host the market. She didn't know much yet, but she knew the outline of the story and began talking openly about it. Importantly, she never shied away from the difficulty of the area's history. She incorporated her research into the story of Brooklyn as part of the overall project.

Johnson was not only reading in the library and the newspaper archives. She was also asking questions about the story of Brooklyn and First Baptist's presence among her own people at the church. By 2019, she had been a member there for thirty years. Johnson asked a friend who had been a member since childhood about the move to Brooklyn. The friend was present at the groundbreaking in 1971. "What was the day like?" she asked. The older woman recalled it fondly, as any young person might remember the good feelings of a memorable, well-choreographed moment. The excitement had left an impression. There was the choir and the Easter celebration and the shovels and the children digging the dirt.

"Do you remember what they said about Brooklyn?" Johnson asked.

"What's Brooklyn?" the woman responded.[4]

How do 238 acres disappear, and thousands of lives and livelihoods, and all the music that moved through the streets? And how does it stay shrouded in silence? The empty sidewalks would speak, and the oldest trees would testify if someone would listen. Along the way, though, people became sure that there was nothing before. Believing that our lives and our landscapes are but a blank slate requires ways of "convincing ourselves that we aren't *responsible* for (or to) history."[5] Such strategies attempt to preserve political, economic, psychological, and theological distance in individuals and institutions even when they are faced with the knowledge of injustice. Elaine Enns and Ched Myers, drawing on the work of Eve Tuck and K. Wayne Yang, identify a number of these maneuvers. They call them "moves to innocence."[6] In my interviews and interactions with people while researching this project, moves to innocence as Enns and Myers identify them were obvious strategies deployed during conversations. They were not necessarily conscious efforts, but they were nevertheless present and identifiable as culturally constructed norms for dealing with injustices. Among the most salient of those strategies were "personal dissociation," or, as Enns and Myers state it, the condition of "ahistoric individualism [that] understands the self as a free-floating entity neither constrained nor advantaged by the past"; "inheritance without responsibility," the idea that the histories and material benefits of accumulated privilege arrive unencumbered by any liability or accountability; and "willful ignorance," or a chosen and maintained lack of knowledge, often accompanied by a lack of care about one's ignorance. A fourth characteristic that I will call *awareness absolution*[7] became a consistent theme as well. We will return to it at the conclusion of this chapter.

In white Christianity, moves to innocence often find justification through an appeal to providence, the work of God in history. Providence so used becomes an attempt to distance ourselves from knowledge of the social forces that shape the world, from our own personal connections to those powers, and from our responsibility to act in pursuit of justice. Using a thin description of providence for the purpose of self-justification,[8] Christians lean on God to declare their innocence inside fundamentally unjust systems of white supremacy. Appeals to providence inside white churches are often both a justification of power and at the same time a deflection from it for the purpose of maintaining innocence. From a variety of FBC members, I heard a statement that sounded like this: "It may be true that we have accumulated advantage. We did not choose that advantage; we simply have to be good stewards of what God has given us." In a deft move, God has become responsible for injustice, and white Christians for managing the spoils.

In the churches of Charlotte, and in the Christianity of white Americans as a whole, personal dissociation, inheritance without responsibility, and willful ignorance all maintain a veneer of innocence around stories that continue to live and have impact. These moves to innocence, as Enns and Myers have identified them, persist in the ways Christians choose to remember or not to remember, and they impede the ability of people and institutions to move toward justice. Among those I interviewed, a few spoke of small steps away from innocence. They ventured to demand a reckoning with the specters of the past. Small steps alone are wholly insufficient for righting a massive injustice or for altering systems of domination, though they are still necessary acts in the long work of making repairs. However, the idea of moving toward repair eventually conjured another spirit—one who allows speech about the errors of the past but binds the imaginations of those who might step beyond acknowledgment into action.

PERSONAL DISSOCIATION

A confession: I started my research and interviews with the hunch that I would eventually find some dirty business along the way. Surely, I thought, something untoward—even illegal!—must have happened for a prominent church to wind up right in the middle of a storied neighborhood at the same time all the people of the neighborhood were being moved out. During endless hours in the archives, I hoped to find documents that would prove a misdeed, some preserved evidence that could be the basis for corrective action.

The closest thing I could find was a letter from W. J. Smith, one of FBC's Four Horsemen. The letter was dated December 12, 1967, just a week after the official closing of the sale of Urban Renewal land to FBC. In the letter, Smith declared a conflict of interest prior to joining the Redevelopment Commission. After acknowledging his involvement in FBC's purchase of Renewal land, he said, "The contracts between the First Baptist Church and the Redevelopment Commission were entered into prior to my being sworn in as a Commissioner. . . . If any matters should come up in the future between First Baptist Church and the Redevelopment Commission it is my intention to disqualify myself in the consideration of any of the issues."[9]

Hardly a smoking gun. Really, it was the opposite. It was a clear statement of a potential ethical quandary and a documented pledge to act with integrity should such a conflict arise in any further business of the Redevelopment Commission. The letter was evidence of integrity, not the lack of it. Still, it stands to reason that powerful people in a relatively small city all knew one another. Power lunches, conversations after chamber of commerce of meetings, outings on the golf course: there were surely many opportunities to grab some juicy information or to influence an upcoming deal. It was easy to be suspicious that there were backroom agreements and informal phone calls that were never memorialized. I still suspect that there were, but clever people don't make notes of such conversations.

So I called the person most likely to know—Hugh McColl (church membership: Covenant Presbyterian), the retired president and chairman of Bank of America, perhaps the most important single individual in the realm of banking and finance in the United States over the last fifty years. McColl was by far the most powerful figure in Charlotte for several decades and still plays a behind-the-scenes role in civic and political matters, even into his mideighties.[10] He was W. J. Smith's boss and personal friend for many years and knew C. C. Hope, Allen Bailey, and Bill Poe well.

To my surprise, McColl agreed to meet me and suggested a middling coffee shop for a discussion. Per his reputation, he was both affable and overwhelmingly conceited, I suppose the natural consequence of owning the world. But

McColl turned quickly serious when I asked if he found it all strange—the top three executives at one of the largest banks in town at that time, First Union, all went to church together, and then that church wound up as one of the largest landowners of prime real estate in uptown Charlotte following the displacement of more than one thousand families, shortly before one of those men joined the commission charged with taking and selling off the land.

McColl quickly turned stern. "Let me tell you something: W. J. Smith was a straight arrow," he said.

I asked him to clarify that phrase "straight arrow."

"What I mean is that I never met a person of greater integrity than Wilburn Smith. The reason he wound up working for me at NCNB[11] is because someone at First Union asked him to do something improper, so he left.

"If you're trying to concoct some sort of conspiracy theory here, then you're barking up the wrong tree."[12]

I left with half a cup of cold coffee and the nagging sense that McColl was right about W. J. Smith in some way I had not thought about yet. In fact, nothing had gone wrong; nothing untoward had happened because nothing outside the bounds of the policies had to happen. Everything was done properly. It was all documented and notarized and filed in the correct drawers, dealing an administrative death blow to Brooklyn and to the other neighborhoods that would be cleared after it.

David Reule joined First Baptist around 1965 and has been a faithful member since then. For Reule, Renewal's legality cleared both the institutions and the people involved of any ongoing association with the project. "Everything they did was according to the law," he said. "I mean, they followed the law to a T. You can't hardly blame somebody who's been charged with making this Urban Renewal work the way Urban Renewal was supposed to work. You can't now come back fifty years later and condemn them for having done what they were charged to do." Reule was engaging on behalf of the Four Horsemen, and perhaps a bit for himself, in personal dissociation. So was McColl. They had substituted "legal" for *faithful* or *just*. If one played by the rules, no guilt could be imputed. The history was over.[13]

But what is legal is a function of which groups have power and to what ends they want it used. That a thing is legal is not compelling moral or theological reasoning, though it may have in fact been the reasoning deployed. The Christianity practiced in the sanctuaries up and down Tryon Street was silent in tacit support of the result they wanted—expanding empires and growing congregations.[14] Because the powers of the day were aligned in a way to produce that result, they assumed it was just and that the transaction and their involvement with it ended when the papers were signed.

INHERITANCE WITHOUT RESPONSIBILITY

The accumulated advantages that white people and institutions hold have not piled up in a handful of years. They are the inheritance of multiple generations. Part of the work that institutions do is to hold both assets and debts across decades or even centuries. The move to innocence of "inheritance without responsibility" actively accepts all the benefits of our history but has "no sense of accountability to it."[15] Accepting the credits without attending to the debits, though, keeps the accounts out of balance. It creates conditions where emotional responses or acknowledgments become a substitute for repairing the damages done to one group that have become the wealth of another.

As I was learning FBC's history, the church's senior pastor, Robert Welch, still somewhat new to the congregation, encouraged me to share what I was learning with him. On multiple occasions, we carried on long conversations in his office about what happened and what it all meant for his ministry there.[16] During our early discussions, he sometimes deflected from the church's ongoing responsibility. He said, "If [our church] were ever really aware of [the history] and if you ever put two and two together . . . , it certainly is grieving to think, 'This is a person's home. It's their neighborhood.' There were *other churches* that got kicked out or forced out. That is grieving. I mean, it would be grieving for anyone, and I think that's something that our church would grieve over. Whether they grieved over it that day, I don't know."[17]

But his next sentence pivoted away from the grief. Regarding FBC's presence following the forced relocation of twelve Black churches, he said, "I would say that at least a church got the opportunity to be there. That would probably be a positive thing." Neither Welch nor anyone else I encountered at FBC was thinking about responsibility, at least not yet. They were, however, glad to accept the inheritance.

As he continued, he made a clever move to draw God into the action:

> There are a lot of other things that could have been done with this land. . . .
> I mean, somebody could build a high-rise apartment and profit greatly off a
> business like that. At least God chose to put something like [FBC] here that

would hopefully be a beacon and help and a light in a very dark situation where unfortunately, once it had been done, could it be reversed? . . . And so I think that maybe our church would view it somewhat like this: that this was at least a redeeming thing, that God redeemed the razing by bringing a church that would still be here fifty to sixty years later.[18]

Welch invoked the feeling of grief while avoiding any material or cultural changes that would address that hypothetical emotion of his own congregation. He did not even attempt to address the grief of those whose churches, homes, and businesses were forcibly taken, nor the material harms they experienced. The grief stays distant, the damage stays far away, and no one bears the responsibility for redistributing plundered assets nor even of holding any feelings about how past injustices comprise the present.[19] The theological position can be stated plainly: Christians are claiming divine justification for the results of an unjust process. This is not novel. Christians regularly recruit God into situations best described with language other than God-talk. First Baptist's presence in Brooklyn, wrapped in silence, is not evidence of redemption. It indicates an inheritance, the responsibility for which passes from generation to generation. The obligation is not only for the just disposition of a piece of property but also for uprooting systemic injustice muddled with religious virtue.

"Once it had been done, could it be reversed?" asked the born-again preacher.[20] If God, in God's providence, was at work, who would dare try to reverse it? Those questions are expressions of political and theological power. Certainly, some things can be reversed. The Norths' title to 625 E. 2nd Street was revoked through a forced sale, not by providence but by politics. What was done can be undone by power. Perhaps also with the aid of the work of God in history, but that language must be deployed with great care. What white Christians have received as a gift often comes encumbered with liabilities. Christian discipleship includes taking responsibility for the liens that accompany our histories.

WILLFUL IGNORANCE

"What is Brooklyn?"

Jan Johnson remembers the question starkly. It was an honest reply. She was shocked. At the groundbreaking, or the grand opening, or at any other point, Brooklyn was not honored; neither was it disparaged. At First Baptist, it had vanished. It may as well have never existed. Not land, nor people, nor history, nor the presence of their own church had raised the curiosity of the congregation.

Johnson kept asking older members, and the story for those longtime congregants of FBC remained consistent. Most knew nothing. The few with memories of the neighborhood prior to FBC's building there recalled little and had long ago stopped thinking about it. For those who came later, after the opening of the new facilities, there was no knowledge of Brooklyn. The institutional memory of the church held certain stories, but others it had abandoned completely.

"I would guess that one percent of our members knew what I was talking about when I mentioned Brooklyn," she said. "We just don't know."

the American Dream is all innocence and blank slates and the future.[21]

FBC's official account of its own history confirms that the church moved along with full silence around Brooklyn. In 1982, at their 150th anniversary, the church commissioned a history book. In approaching the decade-long process of moving from North Tryon St. to South Davidson St., the book keeps it simple: "During the 1960s the greatest thrust of the church was its relocation to a tract of land on South Davidson and Third Streets, a part of Charlotte's Urban Renewal Development. In a hotly contested decision, the church voted against moving away from the downtown area, then in a strong, cooperative movement, resolved to build again near the heart of the city."

The book goes on to list, at length, the various subcommittees of the Building Committee and all the many members who served on those subcommittees to make the move happen. The section reads like one of the Bible's genealogies, listing name after name, a way of conveying meaning to those on the inside but difficult to understand for those on the outside. The move of a large, volunteer-focused institution took tremendous time and energy. But in FBC's own telling, whatever was "hotly contested," either within the congregation or within the city where it stands, was now well in the distance. All the feelings had cooled, and the important genealogy asserted the unity of the congregation over whatever disagreements may have come in the past. Only one decade following the opening of their new building, and less than two decades after their decision to move into Brooklyn, they had a double forgetting: the story of the place they now occupied was shrouded in silence, and the crisis that brought them there was ancient history.[22]

The congregation's history book, though, was an accurate portrayal of how they had told the story from the very beginning of the Future Program Committee. Brooklyn had never been a part.

"I've never heard of that neighborhood," one former minister's family said to me of Brooklyn. "It has never been discussed in our family."

Likewise, a member who joined in the late 1960s: "I've never heard of that neighborhood. Nope, don't remember it being talked about."

Or another: "I know you've done all the research, but I don't believe what you are telling me. And I have questions about your integrity."

They're not lying. There is no cover-up, no great mystery to be unraveled. There is only the not-knowing, the not thinking to find out, the inability to understand their own documentation. What disappeared remains in plain sight. There is city on every side except for the sparsely built Second Ward. Vacancy among density, un-use amid intensity.

Not-knowing is an ongoing strategy. In January 2021, the Sunday following the January 6 attack on the US Capitol, FBC Pastor Robert Welch demurred from addressing massively important current events in any theological way.[23] He kept his comments in the spiritual and metaphorical realms rather than the material or direct ones until he neared the end of his sermon. Then he said,

> There might be some of you that can remember that right where we . . . sit there were actually fields. It was farmland a long, long time ago. And that farmland, it was transformed into neighborhoods, and houses started popping up, and there were neighborhoods here and neighborhoods there.
>
> But then a few decades ago, those fields of corn, those fields of neighborhoods, turned into fields of concrete. And over those decades, there's been concrete laid upon concrete. And then on that concrete, they put steel covered in concrete, stacked it up on top of each other and threw a bunch of people inside of it. There's concrete everywhere. We are in a field of concrete.[24]

Welch's point had something to do with the difficulty of growing new individual Christians and churches. But in the process, he reinforced, once more, the not-knowing. He erased the Brooklyn neighborhood altogether. He erased the Catawba people who thrived prior to settlers platting out Second Ward. He imagined only a blank space to be placed into production. Any prior details were unknowable mysteries. So mysterious it was that no human ever acted—houses popped up, corn fields alchemically became concrete, some unknown *they* stacked the concrete together. It all just happened. Maintaining the unknowing is part of the scheme for holding on to innocence. It is a strategy for sentimentality when the hard work of making costly moral choices is necessary.

Not-knowing is not neutrality. Racialized ignorance is taking the side of abusive power without having to publicly commit to your choice. Choosing not to know allows the myth of innocence to remain undisturbed within souls and institutions. It creates a standoff with ghosts, the false comfort that if we do not disturb them, they might not redirect the light seeping through the stained glass.

Philosopher Charles Mills calls cultivated not-knowing an "epistemology of ignorance."[25] Such ignorance is inherent in the "racial contract," the established sociality of white supremacy constituted by "a particular power structure of formal and informal rule, socioeconomic privilege, and norms for the differential distribution of material wealth and opportunities, benefits and burdens, rights and duties."[26] For white people inside the racial contract, Mills asserts, "One has an agreement to misinterpret the world. One has to learn to see the world wrongly, but with the assurance that this set of mistaken perceptions will be validated by white epistemic authority, whether religious or secular."[27] Inside the veil of racial ignorance, not-knowing creates a façade of innocence. The participation of religious authority blesses that innocence to white people across religious and partisan divisions. With Urban Renewal, progressive ministers like Richard Hildebrandt and Carlyle Marney failed to challenge the white domination of racialized space, just as evangelicals like C. C. Warren, Carl Bates, and their successors did. For white churches and Christians, their participation as *white* in a public issue over space and place outweighed any other moral or theological considerations, even if they would have made those considerations for other issues, as Marney and Hildebrandt did at the very same time with the civil rights movement.[28] Mills says, "The Racial Contract creates a *racialized* moral psychology. Whites will then act in racist ways *while* thinking of themselves as acting morally. . . . They will be morally handicapped simply from the conceptual point of view in seeing and doing the right thing."[29] Remaining willfully ignorant is "a condition for membership in the polity."[30] With the confidence that it is God's hand that has done the work and not the workings of political economies or systems of racial domination, piercing the innocence becomes even more challenging. The blessing of innocence by religious leaders makes disrupting the narrative of innocence dangerous, for those who would challenge it are accused of working against the very hand of God.

Related to ignorance as a move to innocence is another strategy for justification: the creation of fantastical knowledge. Rather than claiming to know nothing, some white people create myths and fanciful narratives that they hope might justify their own actions or the deeds of their institutions.[31] David Reule and I talked for nearly two hours in his office one day. A copy of Richard Rothstein's *The Color of Law*, a book-length exploration of how public policy has enforced white supremacy in land use and neighborhoods, sat on the shelf next to Reule's desk as we talked. When I asked for his review of it, he said that he had found the book insightful. He also recalled the Brooklyn neighborhood as a hopeless place: "That area down through there, everybody has forgotten that what it looked like was a nightmare. I mean, it was a bad place. . . . If you don't remember what it was like, then you can have all kinds of opinions" about the taking and the razing of the neighborhood. "But *I* remember what it was like. It was a terrible place to live. . . . The arguments [against taking it] come from 'where did those people leave to go to?' Well, *they* helped a lot of them. . . . They didn't run over them with bulldozers. They followed the law."[32]

Reule thought that there was a simple explanation for the discrepancies between what he recalled and what so many Brooklyn residents remembered. Of those Brooklyn residents, he said, "Their memories are faded." Local press, historic association members, and displaced residents and their families were writing hagiographies. "When people die, they might have been scoundrels all their life; then when they die all of a sudden they become saints," he said. Reule had invented a new set of knowledge about Brooklyn containing only minor allowances for the injustices that created legitimately bad conditions, with no room for the goodness that thrived despite injustice, and with no conception of structural problems that originated outside the neighborhood. Whether willful ignorance or fantastical knowledge, the epistemology of ignorance, in Mills's terms, "produced the ironic outcome that whites will in general be unable to understand the world they themselves have made."[33]

EFFORTFUL KNOWLEDGE

As the Uptown Farmers' Market team made their plans, they tried to make the space as economically and racially inclusive as possible. They learned the process for accepting electronic benefits transfer transactions so that neighbors using public benefits would have access. They worked to create an environment that would represent the full diversity of the area within three miles of the market. The team encouraged vendors from many backgrounds to offer their produce and wares. They hired an artist to paint a bright mural of their vision on a nearby wall. They found a corporate sponsor to match SNAP dollars at two to one, effectively tripling the purchasing power of people on public assistance. Even as they made these moves, the team saw that they were stepping into a difficult history that required deep reflection. They were grappling with the idea that their project, for all the good it could do, occupied a contested space in the souls of former residents who still remembered what had been. The team, though they had formed a separate entity not governed by FBC, was also facing the knowledge that their beloved church occupied that space as well. They were committed to honoring what had come before, but they were not sure how to do so. So they set up a meeting with some city officials with some expertise in local history. They wanted to talk about what they'd been learning and how they might commemorate the space they were working in.

"We've thought about calling it the Brooklyn Farmers' Market," they said.

"You need to think about that," one of the officials firmly told them. Which was a Southern, roundabout way of saying "absolutely not." To use the name devoid of any effort at restoration would not have been an honor but an act of aggression. The team knew that there was something to be done.[34] They knew it was time to break silence. But they knew neither what to do nor how to do it. Nor could they fully give words to the disjuncture they were experiencing.

the something to be done is not a return to the past but a reckoning with its repression in the present.[35]

Curious, but also a little wounded from having their idea so firmly rejected, Johnson and her leadership team began digging deeper. They committed themselves, in Johnson's words, "to understanding how they had been so far off" in understanding the history.[36]

"It was stunning," Johnson said, to be sitting on that land week after week and have no conception of what had happened there. "How have I never heard this story?" she asked. What could explain the habitual silence around her? She and the team read history books and old newspaper articles. They spoke with former Brooklyn residents. They showed up for community forums put on by activist groups seeking restitution for Urban Renewal.

They learned, but it was hard to know what to do with the knowledge. One team member, Marvette Monroe (who is Black), said that they had "a goal that we would be able to earn the use of the Brooklyn name." According to Johnson and Monroe, Charlotte mayor Vi Lyles[37] challenged them to honor the legacy by seeking to restore some sense of the community that had been lost. If they could reconstitute some element of how the community functioned, the mayor indicated, they would have done good work. Lyles's encouragement felt to the team like a manageable goal but still only a start.

Among all those I met along the way, the Uptown Farmers' Market team had worked the hardest to undo their ignorance of both the history and the political and theological realities of white supremacy that had shaped and continue to shape the cityscape of Charlotte. They are not reticent to speak about the story that brought them to their current work. They do not fear telling others of their movement from ignorance to knowledge. But the unlearning is a long journey, one that does not generally find support in the spiritual formation of white Christian churches.

INHERITANCE WITH RESPONSIBILITY

As I did research and interviews around Charlotte, I anticipated people cutting me off. I especially thought this would happen at First Baptist, where I assumed our differing ideologies would quickly come into conflict. But every conversation turned into another invitation. The Uptown Farmers' Market team kept asking me to return and teach them what my research was uncovering. Various members kept taking my interview requests by phone and in person. Staff members relished conversations along the way, often taking meetings with me. Pastor Welch turned me loose in the archives and kept engaging with the findings. And one day, Welch and I finally encountered the ghost.

That afternoon, we had talked for nearly an hour. Over the course of several months, we moved slowly, me revealing some information as I found it, holding some back for later as we waded deeper into troubling waters. This day, he had read a draft of the early history presented in this book, and we reached a moment in our meeting where I wanted to help him put the pieces together. "You recall Abram North, from the writing I sent you?" He did.

"And Hazeline, his daughter, was the first homeowner forced to sell to the city," I started. He finished my thought.

"And that's the home that was located at the back corner of our education building," he said.

"That's right."

"Wow," he said, and he slumped into the couch. He'd seen the specter. In the room. With us.

Pastor Welch stammered trying to get the words out. "I mean, Greg, I think this is—this is—uncharted territory. Also, like, still—I'm still like—I don't know. And I'm just—it's one of those things. I've just been here for two and a half years, and I didn't know all this kind of stuff.

"I think, I think, I think what you're saying is, the very first home that sold, in Brooklyn—the forced sale—it was on our property. That's something we need to say. I want . . . I want . . . I want that to be said, so that we . . . we . . . we're aware of it at the very least."[38] People in the presence of a specter aren't known for their elocution. The haunted room lacked the oxygen the both of us needed to make sense of the moment.[39]

Two months later, Welch convened a small group of his congregants, primarily older ones who had been part of the church for multiple decades. I spoke to the group for an hour, telling them the whole story, none of which they knew in any detail. They showed some interest but otherwise didn't seem to acknowledge or understand their association to my presentation. To my surprise, when I finished, Welch started to speak with great conviction. He was pushing them about the *something to be done*: "I want you to hear clearly what we are learning here. None of us in the congregation made the decisions of Urban Renewal that led to the destruction of all those homes and churches. But the result has been that our church paid four million dollars for this land that is now worth eighty million, and other people got hurt in the process. And we've got to figure out what to do about that."[40] Welch was making the connections. It appeared that his encounter with the story of Urban Renewal, in his space, was doing what Gordon describes: "It is leading you elsewhere, it is making you see things you did not see before, it is making an impact on you; your relation to things that seemed separate or invisible is changing."[41] Welch saw the material consequences and started naming them. He saw the spiritual legacy of silence in the congregation. As their leader, he took his role seriously and used it. He placed on a group of congregants, for the first time, their responsibility as actors in a story that they still have the power to change. But the acknowledgment of responsibility is not the practice of it. Sometimes acknowledgment takes the place of acting responsibly.

PERSONAL ASSOCIATION

The alternative to personal dissociation is the refusal to plead innocence in terms of individualized responsibility. A lack of legal culpability is a distraction, ethical uprightness inside a system of destruction a sleight of hand. The protest that we ourselves were not there only convinces the descendants who still hold the plunder, never the plundered. With systems of domination, the constructions of the past continue to offer benefit to some for generations to come. Dissociation relies on a contradiction in thinking about history. White people and institutions accept accrued benefits as the gift of generations yet publicly deny that they have any material effect. When it comes to the present and the future, the innocent always worked hard for what they have, with little recognition of how we "continue to benefit from historic arrangements in the present."[42]

Association requires public moves away from innocence and toward responsibility in community. The transgressions of Urban Renewal happened in public. The theological speech that supported the programs happened in public. And while there were certainly individualized, internalized consequences with the people on every side who encountered the program, the damage was done in public, through systemic measures. The devastation was open and visible. It was as loud as a wrecking ball through a brick sanctuary. So must the association be. "Personal association" is not privatized but rather the recognition that people operate inside systems and that change inside systems is the responsibility of individuals using their positions in them.

As I was interviewing people for this project, I kept looking for someone with historic ties to First Baptist whose narrative arc pointed toward personal association. Perhaps there was someone for whom the scales had fallen from their eyes, someone who had devoted considerable energy to educating themselves and others into active antiracism. I wanted someone who would not equivocate, who would willingly associate themselves with haunted territory. All the better if it was someone who was there, who had cast important votes only to realize later that they had been taught wrongly, that they lived inside a legacy they still had to unlearn, and that the legacy required public work, not just private reflection.

I thought I found that person, a good antiracist who could exemplify motion toward repair and healing. I invested numerous hours in conversations and email correspondence and sending writing samples. In the end, the white liberal could not manage the discomfort, could not face their fragility, could not become morally or theologically serious about addressing our trespasses. The initial promise of our conversations turned into dragging feet, excuse after excuse for why this might not be the right time, concerns over how family members might react, righteous indignation over imagined grievances, grave concern for the legacies of people long dead without corresponding concern for those still being robbed, the desire to move quietly and privately around what was done loudly and publicly.[43]

Whispered confessions on a full-throttle bulldozer.

Preserving blamelessness in desecrated spaces.

Fear over courage, sentimentality over truth, chaos over community.

That's the liberal. That's the white antiracist.

It was the white liberals who showed up earlier in this story and resuscitated Urban Renewal in Charlotte. Their emissaries were McNeill, the member of the great white liberal church, with the aid of his luminary pastor Marney; and Hildebrandt, the liberal preacher who sometimes said the right things and still got caught up in the destruction. The people you thought might be innocent turn out not to be, and you're in their ranks. You know yourself in this story, know that it is calling you to a kind of work you cannot fully imagine, work that will bring you close to legacies and people and places that were familiar but now made strange. You were scared but trying to steel yourself to confront your own ancestors. Says Avery Gordon, "Therein lies the frightening aspect of haunting: you can be grasped and hurtled into the maelstrom of the powerful and material forces that lay claim to you whether you claim them as yours or not."[44]

The work is risky. Especially because you can't control it. It hurts to hear the things no one trained you to understand, things implicit or hidden for generations. You find out that you are living off a contested inheritance, as were your beloved parents or grandparents, as were so many of the heroes who dominated your childhood. Whiteness, says Willie Jennings, is "a forming toward a maturity that destroys."[45] A maturity that razes, paves over, and displaces and still gets to associate itself with purity rather than depravity. A maturity that gets to privately and easily correct harms that were done publicly and painfully. It is, Jennings goes on, "a diseased understanding of maturity,"[46] a maturity that never ripens, the time never being quite right, justice never being convenient, though it will be soon, once we white folks do a little more preparation, build a little more awareness, have a little more time to reflect.

Behind the silences and the strategies for appearing innocent, as they show up in white Christians, is finally unbelief, lack of faith, the fear that the world as it currently exists may die away, and as it does the debts placed on us may come due. Our faith is in a world we control. But we know our impotence. Gordon says that "haunting can galvanize the middle class, can wrench it from its particular kind of stupor, can shift its investments away from the private world of family and work. An encounter of tremulous significance, or pro-fane illumination, is what is required to tear such a veil."[47] Jesus castigates his disciples as they struggle to cast out the silencing spirit: "You faithless genera-tion, . . . *how much longer* must I put up with you?" (Mark 9:19, emphasis mine). You can hear in his words the echo of "the ancient lament of the Exodus God against a people who refuse to abide in the divine liberation."[48] Jesus's words surely sound like those of the descendants of Brooklyn, like the query posed by Brandi Williams in chapter 10: "I don't understand how you can see the harm that was done to us and not want to make that right." *How much longer will you look without seeing? How long will you speak without having anything to say?*

AWARENESS ABSOLUTION

For all my discussion of silence, there has been no shortage of words about race over the last decade. Not every word has been wise, but the discourse of race and racism is not absent. Even as it regards Brooklyn, and Urban Renewal nationally, there have been hundreds of articles exploring the con-nections of urban highways and housing issues to the history and present of Urban Renewal. Many of those note the connection of Black Lives Matter demonstrators sometimes blocking highways precisely in the places where neighborhoods were plowed down for the ease of commuters. There are plenty of words but no fewer highways.

Beyond personal dissociation, inheritance without responsibility, and will-ful ignorance, there is another move to innocence that is inaction in disguise. Enns and Myers call it "exoneration by conscientization," the idea that knowing and analyzing the problem is doing something about it. While "analysis and critical literacy are indeed necessary," they say, "they are not sufficient for our work: knowledge alone doesn't empower change, healing, or response-ability."[49] They note the tendency for this move to innocence to be more common on the American "left" than among conservatives. Yet as my interviews progressed, I noted that people across the ideological spectrum were always ready to appeal to conscientiousness but rarely ready to make repairs.

Pastor Welch thought his people would grieve the knowledge of Urban Renewal if they only knew.

The Uptown Farmers' Market team rightly recognized that "anyone serving on their committee needed to understand the history well and couldn't [turn away] from the responsibility that comes with that."[50]

White antiracism groups like those organized at Myers Park Baptist since 2018, and facilitated by well-meaning white people—including me—encourage people to raise their consciousness about race and pervasive systems of white supremacy.

All those efforts are essential. There is no corrective action without clear understanding. And yet acknowledgment is not accountability. The zeal of conversion wanes. Fires in the belly languish. Pastor Welch told his people that they had inheritance with responsibility—"We have to figure out what to do"—but the months that followed his impassioned speech saw no growing awareness, no moves toward repair, none of the challenging public work that might help to settle the debts of history.

Is hearing the story yet another move to innocence? Even worse, has bearing witness become a way of reinscribing power as it is, an act of entrenching rather than uprooting white supremacy? "The endeavor to bring pain close exploits the spectacle of the body in pain and oddly confirms the spectral character of suffering," says Saidiya Hartman.[51] Our obsession with acknowledging stories of suffering or naming the land of the dispossessed taps into "the pleasure of indignation yielded before the spectacle of extreme violence."[52] Asks Hartman, "Is the act of 'witnessing' a kind of looking no less entangled with the wielding of power and the extraction of enjoyment?"[53]

Learning history, raising consciousness, and waking up, for white Christians, cannot be only about empathy for those harmed. Inside our constant focus on the *other* is the hidden satisfaction of our own power. The drive for awareness is merely amusement unless we know ourselves on the bulldozer, in the council chambers, casting the vote we wish we hadn't cast, exploiting tenants, drawing redlining maps, singing our conquest songs and reading our conquest stories, knowing ourselves as part of *them*, refusing to plead innocence as the descendants of the authors of destruction. And, knowing ourselves and our institutions, to act. To write new songs, to read the Scriptures anew, to sell our property to our tenants, to give back the ill-gotten gain, to destroy the bulldozers and the wrecking balls, to confront the legacies within us that made those things part of our faith, part of our witness in the world.

"How long has he been this way?" Jesus asks the father of the boy silenced. This *how long* question is an inquiry of solidarity and compassion, connected to the tradition prominent in the psalms of lament that protest personal and political troubles. The answer to this *how long* is "from many generations" and in more ways than we count yet count. The confrontation with the silencing spirit is both individual and corporate. In Myers's helpful terms, it is about political bodies and the body politic.[54] As surely as the ills of white supremacy have been coded into the skin of individual bodies, they have also been inscribed into cityscapes.

CHAPTER TWELVE

The Ghosts of Christians Present

His disciples asked him privately, "Why could we not cast it out?"
—Mark 9:28

Whiteness is ownership of the earth, forever and ever amen!
—W. E. B. DuBois[1]

I was sitting in a pew at First Baptist Church (FBC) on a Sunday morning, and I heard the silence. Outside it was bright and warm, the kind of May day that holds the promise of North Carolina's goodness. But oddly, the sanctuary was dim. There are four narrow stained-glass verticals on each side of the hall and one narrow horizontal connecting them across the top. They light as a rainbow, one green, the next blue, then purple, then red as they progress toward the back of the hall. For a sanctuary that holds more than 1,500, there's not much natural light. What enters comes mostly from the stained glass at the front of the sanctuary—where Jesus approaches a woman sitting next to an empty tomb, his arms open—and by three crosses in stained glass at the rear. Everything is filtered when it comes in, the outside obscured and transformed to rose and verdant green.

The guitars and drums clamored over the silence but could not conceal it. It was the day following yet another white supremacist terror attack, this one a shooting at a grocery store in Buffalo, New York, by an eighteen-year-old white man filled with racist rage. The event was yet another of the unceasing shocks that rock this country regularly and as a matter of political choice.

I don't expect preachers, including myself, to turn preaching into current events mad libs. A worship service does not have to read from each week's headlines to fulfill its purpose. A church does have to live in its political context, though, and to speak faithfully to it, whether in prayer or in preaching or in music. I had been watching the sermons weekly for months on end, and I heard in the music what I had observed in my interviews and in the preaching and in the archives. At FBC, they were not capable of talking about the immense injustices around them, much less the one inside which they lived. The congregation was too distracted by heaven to be rooted on earth.

The irony nearly swept me down the sanctuary's sloped floor. The actual earth below us had been re-formed by a series of events that forever altered the landscape and the people who had called it home. Yet the ones who opportunistically planted themselves in it had not dug down into any particularity about the place—what it is, who was there, what came before, how the scars on the land might be acknowledged and addressed. We were surrounded by all the standardized fare of white, middle-class American life. Golf shirts and khaki pants. A cop outside as a symbol of protection. Slick video presentations. This sanctuary could be plopped down on any lot in Charlotte's vast suburban landscape, and little would change. The nature of the place was inconsequential to their existence in it.[2]

Behind the irony came sadness. Some of it was for the people of Brooklyn, but I was also, a bit self-indulgently, sad for myself. I had spent half a decade aiming to help the congregation to see themselves, to know, to discern what they might speak and do. I was sad about my own failure. I hit roadblocks at many turns, was boxed out and held at a distance. I encountered unanswered emails, text messages never read, and calls not returned. Some people would talk but could not see the problem. Others could see the problem but didn't find it problematic. Still others knew the issues but refused to talk. I had managed a few achievements along the way, but the theological work had not gone deep. The reckoning I hoped to provoke was not on the horizon at all. In fact, it seemed to be the opposite. As I neared the final days of completing the writing, the archives suddenly became unavailable. The open doors were closed. The silencing spirit held.

"This kind can only come out through prayer," Jesus said.

This is not a silence to pass on.[3]

WHY COULD WE NOT CAST IT OUT?

I planned to write about the contours of my city, its street grid and its steeples, about neighborhoods present and neighborhoods absent. But I know that this work, like most work that requires long silences and persistent reflection, is also about the terrain of my own soul.

I wanted to hover around the edges, an apparition slipping by unnoticed. And yet the further I wrote, the deeper I went in the archives, I found the words of Saidiya Hartman rolling in my head. "The conviction that I was living in the world created by slavery propelled the writing of this book," she wrote in a new preface to her classic *Scenes of Subjection*.[4] Those words were echoing in me while I watched the razing of a century-old church in my west Charlotte neighborhood. It had started as the all-white Enderly Park Baptist Church but, following white flight, became home to Mount Carmel Baptist Church, an important Black congregation with a long west side history. It then housed an upstart congregation, the complex sort of place where poor people found spiritual freedom and yet were subject to financial exploit by preachers with great sneakers and luxury cars.[5] Leadership ran the place into desolation. It could not be saved. That's the sort of thing that sometimes happens in poor neighborhoods, where there's little safety net, if any. On our side of town—what a former mayor called "the catchment area of Urban Renewal"—there's no recovering from serious financial errors.

While the bulldozers turned that eight-hundred-seat sanctuary to a pile of rubble in a couple of hours, nearby houses were selling for well north of a half-million dollars. Prices had tripled in just over five years. The new construction had signs up to indicate who was supposed to buy them, including renderings with little people on the porches, and the little people were always white, every one of them. The best architects around could draw up a kitchen fit for the year 2250 but could not possibly imagine Black people continuing to live in Enderly Park. I knew it, but Hartman made it clear: I was living in the world created by Urban Renewal, which is also the world created by slavery. I live in that world. The story of that world is not yet finished.

I saw it also in Marshall Park, back in the old Brooklyn neighborhood, just behind First Baptist Church. It was a Monday night in 2020, and a small group of Charlotte activists was leaving the park. We gathered there to remember Jonathan Ferrell, shot and killed by Charlotte-Mecklenburg Police in 2013.[6] Many Charlotte protests and community gatherings begin in Marshall Park. I don't know if participants can narrate the history of the space, but something about it—its poor planning, its lack of visibility, its twenty-four-hour emptiness, the noise of the nearby expressway, the lack of amenities or programs—lets people know that something used to be there. That it is haunted. That where the pond and fountain are now used to be an alley called Watkins Lane, where Reynard Wright lived for many a year, where his mother raised her kids in one of dozens of duplexes squeezed in together, built with profit in mind rather than mothers or sons. On one edge of the park, next to McDowell Street, was the original building of the United House of Prayer for All People, with its brightly colored tile steps and unusual architecture. Across the way, where 1st Street was when there was a 1st Street, is the remnant of Second Ward High School, the pride of Brooklyn. The gym remains, restored after five decades of subsidized neglect. Next to it sits the Mecklenburg County Aquatic Center, a facility with a pair of indoor pools. Pools, pond, fountain: the city is trying to drown something that refuses to die.

Gatherings like the one for Jonathan Ferrell are among the few uses the park gets. Which is to say that people go to Marshall Park for remembering. They intuit that its covering of concrete is a weak suggestion of a blank canvas. Even the natural world itself has joined in maintaining a real presence. A flock of chimney swifts roosts in a magnolia there each fall. Migrating swifts return to the same place on the way south generation after generation. They typically spend the night in a chimney, but when the one their ancestors roosted in gets knocked down, they settle for what shelter they can find nearby. Specter-like, they always return.

I left the park that night walking toward its western edge, at First Baptist Church. A friend and I walked together, and when he peeled off, I stood alone at this space that had occupied my thinking for years. It was early evening. I looked past the building, toward 2nd Street. The light was wavering.

i see you are not there.[7]

The streetlight across the way was next to a magnolia tree. The tree stood in the place where a man drove a bulldozer into a dream; where a few years before that, Vernon Sawyer's people knocked on the door, and Hazeline North Anderson answered; where a few years before that, Hazeline wept over her mother, Annie; where a few years before that, the pear tree out back had produced its best crop ever; where before that, Abram had breathed a last, exhausted breath; where George and Abram had played catch; where Henry had died; where the telegram about Lavinia had arrived; and where the kids had filled a bucket with blackberries from the vines behind Jacob's Ladder School; and Abram and the people of Clinton Chapel had built a house for the North babies; in the place where Abram North, free, and Annie Carson North, freefreefree, had purchased every single one of

52,800 square inches of soil and planted themselves there. Through the asphalt, the land hummed.

The wavering and the humming and the refracted light reflect a *something to be done*. Many somethings. What is to be done is not primarily about me, nor about First Baptist, nor about Myers Park Baptist, and yet the things to be done cannot be done without us, and we cannot be whole without doing them. I know, though I do not want to know and though I cannot *not* know and still be myself, that even as a visitor, I feel at home at First Baptist Charlotte, that the space connects to my own Southern Baptist upbringing, my own nurture in faith amid white evangelicalism and "evangelical whiteness."[8]

And I know, as I near the cornerstone of the education wing, where that morning parents dropped their children off for preschool, where on Sundays young kids like me bounced in for Bible lessons with characters moved across felt boards, that at this particular corner of this particular building, a great rejection happened.[9] This soil under my feet Abram North claimed title to, after being born into a world that tried to claim title to him. The world aimed only to exhaust him, tried to deny all the joys he persisted in, the thousand slaps of ball into leather, the fathomless laughs at silly children, the habit of etching his own words into the archives by writing letters to editors. At this site, worlds collide again and again, and I know that I have been to this Sunday School and that I must reckon with how I am in this story, and how it is changing me, and what hauntings I carry.[10]

I did not want to write myself into this story, but I know that I am a part of it. In 2005, I moved to Enderly Park, a neighborhood three miles west of the old Brooklyn area. Many folks with roots in Brooklyn wound up in Enderly Park. When my spouse and I arrived, the neighborhood had dealt with forty years of disinvestment, the beginnings of which coincided with the arrival of Black neighbors here in the aftermath of Urban Renewal. Blockbusting, corporate redlining, exploitative landlords. All the strategies used across the country to maintain white spatial domination happened here. I moved here with some liberal Christians, all of us white, who were ready to agitate for justice. We were also naïve about our own whiteness. No one had told me. We didn't talk about race in the conservative Southern Baptist church of my youth and barely did in the liberal seminary I graduated from.

The next decade and a half were a consistent cycle of action and reflection. I was always unlearning something from years of miseducation and always trying to put liberative practice in its place. You might think that fifteen years would be enough time to make a significant difference in the regular cycles of displacement that sweep across cities and uproot the poorest residents.

But in spring of 2021, while a global pandemic raged, I watched out my window as vehicle after vehicle lined up for the showing of a house a couple doors over. The parade went on for four hours, with tight twenty-minute appointments. One white couple pulled up and went inside. Another arrived just as the previous one exited. After just half a day on the market, the house was sold for nearly half a million dollars, more than twice the top purchase price ever for any other home on our block.[11]

Seeing the price tag on that small but sturdy house was shocking, though it was not surprising. The strategy of long-term disinvestment in cities eventually gives way to rapid reinvestment. That's how you maximize profit. The result is another manner of Urban Renewal. Over just a handful of years, there has been an exodus of poor people, almost all of them Black, forced from the neighborhood as it suddenly becomes desirable to people with money, almost all of them white. Our neighborhood had prepared for this for several years. We argued for better policy, created and preserved affordable spaces, and even started a community land trust.[12] Still, for all the advocacy, organizing, and preparation, the result was a tidal wave of money crushing the neighborhood quickly and efficiently. The family who formerly lived in that little house on our block that sold for a record price then spent eighteen months hopping between hotel rooms. They were a mom, an adult son, and a preteen in search of stability in a city that would not offer it. They drowned in a rapid and widespread wave of displacement.

Even when you can see it coming, there's no way to be fully prepared for the day the bulldozer pulls up on your block. Nor is it surprising to see churches, especially white-dominant ones, at the forefront of the visible efforts to remake the neighborhood. As the first signs of reinvestment in our district started to appear, white Christians poured in. A financial company run by a well-meaning Christian bought up acres and acres of property. A charter school followed, pouring resources into a semiprivate facility in an area where public schools have lacked adequate buildings and support for years. Nonprofits, often explicitly Christian, either moved here or started here, often displacing small neighborhood groups that had long struggled to find adequate funding. One franchise of Elevation Church, a massive multisite operation where a single pastor preaches at one location and the message is transported by hologram to two dozen other locations, moved in. Alongside them were new businesses that served a mostly white clientele, often expressing social missions. Breweries, daycare for dogs with a bar attached, coworking, yoga, CrossFit, restaurants, multiple coffee shops.

Everyone was so nice. They all did their work with cloying earnestness accompanied by fervent prayer. And soon, they held the land. White Jesus is funny, always calling people to new territory when the real estate deals are at their best.

The process is often called *gentrification*.[13] It is a strategy made possible by Urban Renewal and redlining and zoning inequalities and blockbusting, the inevitable consequence of a society built on the commodification of land for the purpose of profit. Gentrification is one more recent form of W. E. B. DuBois's observation that "whiteness is ownership of the earth forever and ever, amen!"

I am not innocent. I am a white man, a Baptist minister, a homeowner in a Black neighborhood. I moved in long before it was fashionable, but that's no guarantee of good results or even of good intentions. I've tried to be in solidarity with those who are poor, but some folks think I'm just an early adopter of this form of exploitation. They might be right. I came here influenced by past and present radicals like the Catholic Workers, but given the merger of white Christianity and white supremacy, that influence does not absolve me. My family and my organization have done a decent, though imperfect, job of solidarity rather than charity. We helped start the land trust mentioned above, which has attracted tens of millions of dollars of investment in affordable, inclusive neighborhoods. We've written article after article, spoken at forum after forum, preached sermon after sermon, and bent the ear of anyone who would listen. We exhausted ourselves along the way. We made extraordinary friends and left behind a trail of alienated people, some of whom are our new neighbors. Nearly two decades later, the results of our work have mattered deeply to a lot of people, including ourselves. But the scale of the repairs necessary to make our neighborhood right still overwhelms. And we are still white.

Why could we not cast this one out?

"We cannot exorcize that by which we ourselves are still possessed," Ched Myers says.[14] Over the course of this work, I've shown how white Christians participated in Urban Renewal in Charlotte, namely, by actively engaging every phase of the project, from the planning to the profits. I take those characters to be consistent with the Christianity practiced by white Americans as a whole, both then and now.[15] White-dominant Christianity works from the assumption that white Christians rightly possess every space and place where they are. Those are the terms by which our society operates. Though it has not always been obvious to me, I am one of *them*, those white Christians who accumulate land and advantage and opportunity, sometimes without even trying. I cannot separate myself from the issue. I cannot live in a different body or claim a different status in society or have different ancestors.

In American society, you can try to breach what Charles Mills calls the Racial Contract, only to find yourself stuck inside it without your consent. Mills says that "all whites are *beneficiaries* of the Contract, though not all whites are *signatories* to it."[16] Even dissent from the terms of the Contract takes place inside it and thus from a position of dominance over nonwhite people, who are "the objects rather than the subjects" of the contract.[17] The agreement is a trap. Morally, cognitively, and politically, it binds and limits the creation of an alternative. And yet to acquiesce to it is to willingly be the "faithless generation" of Mark 9, or in Mills's words, to continue "rewriting" the Racial Contract rather than "tearing it up altogether."[18]

I lament the loss of beloved neighbors, and at the same time the renewed interest in this space by people who look like me has profound material benefit to me. I do not want the housing equity that has magically appeared next to my name in the past several years. I have seen the costs imposed on others to create that equity and would gladly give it up. But whether I want it or not is irrelevant. I have it. It comes attached to me.

The material benefits of whiteness, even as they are unevenly distributed, cloud the thinking and the moral judgment of white people. Those benefits impair us, both personally and politically, from knowing—the "epistemology of ignorance" at work—and from acting morally. The moves to innocence (see chapter 11) that try to preserve distance from the issues are themselves evidence that this thing called *whiteness* is hurting our souls. Moral philosophers call this *moral injury,* "the failure to live in accordance with our deepest moral aspirations, and . . . the diminishment that comes from our own actions as well as the actions of those against us."[19] Womanist theologian Chanequa Walker-Barnes further says that "moral injury consists of how we are impacted when our actions violate our beliefs about what it means to be a good person."[20] Our trespasses do not only affect those we harm. They also hurt the souls of those doing the harm, both individually and collectively.[21]

To sustain the moral injury of whiteness is to live with the distorted imagination that those things that you should know are not acceptable—the destruction of people's homes, the razing of a neighborhood, separate and unequal schools, and so on—are neutral or given or inevitable or not worth resisting. Or, worse, that they happen for the overall good of society.[22] Our people hurt people, we hurt people, and as we did, we dulled our moral imaginations about whether it was even possible to act in a different way. For white people who begin to struggle against the structures and habits of whiteness, the contradictions can be maddening. The condition against which we strive has stolen our ability to envision something beyond whiteness or even to think and speak our way out of a world distorted by the ideology of race. We lack the structures to become different people. The condition is totalizing, leaving no part of us unblemished. The challenge we face is like that of the father in the story of the silencing spirit: whether to desperately seek the help that can restore our communities or whether to leave our children possessed.

Whiteness as moral injury should not be conflated with victimhood. The central harms of the story I have presented happened to the people of Brooklyn and to those other neighborhoods around the country subject to Urban Renewal projects. Casting the perpetrators of those events as victims in some way distorts and misrepresents what actually happened. We know that we cannot be innocent, but we lack the structures to collectively change ourselves and our history. The contradiction creates a peculiar wound. It will not heal easily, perhaps not at all. The wound has been built into our cityscapes and into our souls through inalienable national myths about property rights and the Dream. Walker-Barnes says, "It's a wound, but it's a very convenient one. . . . [It is] a wound to one's humanity that you're not able to experience full compassion, you're not able to envision full justice. But that actually works in your interest materially."[23] The wound hurts so good. The clearest conviction many white folks have is not that *we* need to be healed but that more people should be wounded like us. Whiteness has a missionary character that exports our destruction as though it were maturity and tries to make it the standard for the world.

Whiteness is an injury, but it is a tricky kind that, as Walker-Barnes told me, "precludes repentance."[24] It renders sin silent by focusing on individuals when no one did anything wrong. The systems do our sinning for us.[25] The nature of the injury is that it keeps itself from being seen. It makes you unable to speak about it. In Mark 9, the disciples ask Jesus why they could not cast the silencing spirit out. In his first words within the story, Jesus calls his companions a "faithless generation." Their impotence has to do with faith. The faith he is speaking of is not something internal, felt as a strength of emotion or an otherworldly confidence, or at least it is not only internal. The faith Jesus is talking about makes a material difference in human suffering. In the case of the boy silenced, marginalized in his community, subjected to violence, living on the edge of danger at every moment, what faith does for him—even when exercised by another person—is to restore him to that community, to raise him from the edge of death back into life.

The Gospel story and the history that we live inside invite us to see whiteness as a structure for unbelief. The society and the people formed inside this structure consistently produce two hauntings—one of the silenced, the other of the silentious. Those who have been silenced work and wait for their restoration. Those of us trained into habitual silence, which is to say into whiteness, are unable to understand our impotence precisely because our faith has been built with an architecture of unbelief. We live inside the very thing we want to cast out. In contrast to the faithless disciples in the story is the father of the boy. "I believe; help my unbelief!" he cries. Hearing his supplication, Jesus demonstrates what belief does—it restores, it repairs, it heals, it raises up, it attends to bodies and spaces and not just souls. Belief chases the specter that holds the future[26] and makes possible a new story, a new imagination, the arrival of a new world.

THIS KIND CAN COME OUT ONLY THROUGH PRAYER

The quietude typically associated with prayer hardly seems an adequate response to a society in need of exorcisms. Silencing spirits helped entrench segregation, perpetuated serial displacement, and malformed the souls of the habitually silent. White Christians loosed a deluge of global capital and roaring bulldozers into the world. Quiet, private speech with God is not sufficient for the task of stopping them. Prayer in that way might be part of the problem, not the solution. But this is not a unique problem, nor a novel one, and yet Jesus, with his face set toward Jerusalem and a political confrontation with the Roman Empire, counsels prayer rather than provocation.

Prayer seems an especially feckless response until you realize that the thing is in you as well. The silencing spirit is a political condition that removes people from their communities, that creates bifurcated economies of desperation and hoarding across generations, that makes truthful speech about the material conditions of the world costly to the point of death. The subjects of a vast and violent empire are all touched by this spirit, none more so than those of us descended from the authors of destruction. Prayer, at the very least, is intensive internal examination. You might call it reflection or introspection or meditation or contemplation. In prayer, we aim to discover what it is that lives in us.

In an individualistic culture, the emphasis of prayerful examination is to root out personal sin from the human heart. This is a worthy goal. Buried in every imperial subject are lies we have believed, prejudices we have upheld, and temptations to domination. Prayer may help us to uncover those short-comings. But the fervent examination of our interior lives is not the only mode of prayer. So is the careful inspection of the institutions in our body politic in all their theological and economic failings. Such work is done in part through public history, by consistent and ever-deepening engagement with the past that describes our present. It is done by cultural criticism that looks at the current arrangements of our economy and politics without flinching and describes them in ways that can exorcise the spirits that destroy.

The public work of rigorous self-examination must be done at the level of society at large. But not only there. Large-scale practice takes root in local institutions. Local groups produced redlining maps. They planned and executed Urban Renewal projects. All politics, as the saying goes, is local. Repair requires the full commitment of smaller institutions, from city and county governments and businesses to churches and religious bodies. Inside those institutions are archives and records that are filled with stories and testimonies. They are also filled with gaps. One way to cast out the silencing spirit is to find out what your people said and what they did not say, whether by ignorance or intention. Those are the things you probably still are not saying, the things you still have not discerned. They are the things that will come back, for "what is unconscious is bound to be repeated."[27] The silences cross generations. The gaps are a legacy themselves, and they cannot be undone without "a painstaking excavation of our political unconscious."[28] The work of public history and public confession creates a space to address the past and the present.

I'm still talking about knowing and critiquing and examining things past and present, though. What I want to know runs into the future: whether an alternative politics is possible. A different set of theo-political commitments might end the displacement, or return the systemically silenced to speech, or help the habitually silent find new words. At stake in an alternative politics could be an end to gentrification, for instance, or the elimination of the land- and place-based exploitation that is part of the very foundations of racism.

These are issues of belief and unbelief.[29] Though my focus across this work has been on Christians and their participation in Urban Renewal, questions of belief are not only the domain of Christians. They are collective questions germane to a society where neighbors live together across theological and religious boundaries, where ostensibly secular government institutions still privilege certain Christian discourses and institutions, where the common wealth of the country requires coalitions that can cast visions of creative futures and map out steps to achieve them. An alternative politics begins with the belief that a different future is possible, one where all our neighbors have secure places in thriving neighborhoods.

In the story of the silencing spirit that has framed this work, belief and prayer are companions. For Mark's story of Jesus, though, prayer is not secret speech meant to increase personal piety. Rather, prayer is a manner of "engaging the Powers in the apocalyptic struggle over history."[30] Myers helpfully points out that the two other places in Mark where Jesus calls his disciples to prayer both occur in the context of political struggle. In the first (11:24–25), he wants them to "envision a different world in which the exploitative Temple State is overthrown." In the second (14:32–42), he wants them to stay awake as the violence of the Roman police state bears down on him.[31] The exhortation to prayer sets the stage for a confrontation with the politics—and the religion—of domination.

Confrontation comes in multiple forms. Sometimes it is fierce resistance and open defiance. At other times, it is slowly building alternative structures that make thriving possible. For most social movements, both streams happen alongside one another. Some activists throw their bodies in the way, while others work on new methods for structuring our cities and neighborhoods, ones that will not produce so many specters. In Enderly Park, I think of my neighbor Frank. As I am completing this book, he is in the process of purchasing a house for the first time through the work of Charlotte's West Side Community Land Trust (CLT). Frank has lived in Enderly Park for twenty-five years. He has served as neighborhood association president, eyes on the street, caring neighbor, father, and occasional crank during that time. His smile disarms, and his quick wit tolerates no phoniness.

Frank's leadership here has not shielded him from displacement by the rising land costs sweeping through the neighborhood. He had to move in 2018 when his landlord nearly doubled his rent, exceeding what his Housing Choice Voucher would cover monthly or what his fixed income could sustain.[32] Even while he was facing displacement, Frank was meeting with a group of neighbors in Enderly Park and across several west Charlotte neighborhoods to establish West Side CLT. The CLT concept, used in more than two hundred localities across the nation, establishes local control and modified homeownership to benefit poor people who are easily displaced.[33] Homeowners purchase homes at reduced prices and fixed rates of equity. The CLT organization controls the land the homes are built on through a board whose by-laws stipulate that majority control of the organization is held by those experiencing the problem that CLT is trying to solve. The organizational structure stops the speculative patterns that have made Black communities in particular easily displaced by the whims of real estate investors.

West Side CLT is creating a microsystem to mitigate against the conditions of white supremacy. Where the aftermath of Urban Renewal, and its ongoing reinvention in new forms like gentrification, had left devastation, activists and neighbors are building on different terms than those imposed by a domination system. Those oppressed are taking control of their places. Wealthy allies have divested themselves of land and houses and money to build the resources of the organization. The neighborhoods where the land trust is at work develop an infrastructure for economic justice. The families who are a part of it are better able to resist displacement thanks to their collective power. The public sees the trust's witness through its subversion of an economy built around land as commodity.

West Side CLT is not a perfect solution, nor are community land trusts in general. Even with modifications, they still rely on the logic of capitalist homeownership. In 2023, West Side CLT is nearing a decade of existence, and developing a large enough number of units to impact Charlotte's enormous housing problem is still a long way off. Nevertheless, it is an important material and cultural intervention that addresses the present in full view of the past. It is a manner of conjuring differently, one of many strategies needed that might help us to believe that we can become different people.

The story of the silencing spirit, like the story of FBC Charlotte and of Christian participation in Urban Renewal more broadly, wavers between belief and unbelief. It is a story of time out of joint, where generation upon generation is revisited by the hauntings that follow us. We live with the specters of the silenced and the silentious until we conjure a "reconstructed future."[34] Is there an alternative possible to the economics of gentrification, the politics of conquest, the theology of domination?

help my unbelief.

In the trembling space between faith and doubt, belief and unbelief, humans finally require aid. To whom do we ask whether there is an alternative? It is not to ourselves. We know our own impotence too well. We require now a revenant, some spirit who might come back and raise us up.

CODA

On the western edge of Uptown Charlotte stands Pinewood Cemetery. From its founding, Pinewood Cemetery has been adjacent to a space supposedly called Elmwood Cemetery. For most of its existence, Pinewood had a separate entrance at a hard-to-reach corner of Uptown near an industrial site and some train tracks. Elmwood was more accessible by way of 6th Street and several stately, if modest, stone entrance markers. The two areas were separated by their naming and by a wire fence until 1969.[35] The separation was merely a way for white people to keep fooling themselves.[36] I guess they thought they could maintain their conceit for all eternity by putting a porous gate between them and Black Charlotte.

No one is fooled. All those white folks are buried in Pinewood Cemetery.

On a Saturday in January 2022, my two adolescent boys and I were walking around the cemetery. We were seeking the last trace of Abram and Annie North. It was North Carolina's version of winter—gray, cold but not bitter. A bit of breeze had moved down from up north. We plotted out imaginary grid lines across the various areas of the cemetery's expanse so that we could move methodically, trying to touch every square and read every marker. The city maintains few records of who is buried where in the Pinewood section. If you want to find a specific grave, you just walk, acre after acre, in hopes that there is a tombstone, and that if there is one, its markings are still clear. Many of the older stones have been washed smooth by years of wind and rain. Others are yellow-green from mosses living in the indentions made by letters and numbers.

The boys and I walked section by section, hoping with each step that the next stone planted into the ground would hold the name North. We read hundreds of names and dates, each one its own saga left mostly to the imagination. We stepped gently around broken pieces on the ground. We did not find what we sought.

Later that day, my wife and I returned for one more try. A date, of sorts. We zigzagged around on foot, moving apart and back together, apart and together, with no luck. We finally gave up and got back in the car.

I was winding pensively around the driving path when I spotted the marker. The root ball of a stump, its brittle tentacles reaching into the ground, was grasping a flat white stone carved deep with the letters AB NORTH. The marker sat at the top of a plot, outlined in stones, with room for a half-dozen caskets. One small stone in the middle lay flat in the earth, a brown nameplate again marked AB NORTH. And that's it. Abram's head, his feet, and the tacit assumption that Annie and young Henry and baby Alma are resting here as well, in their final patch of dirt. They are surrounded by towering willow oak trees draped with wisteria. On the retaining wall nearby sat three unhoused Black men. They talked among themselves and ate sandwiches provided by a service agency.

A half-mile east of the cemetery is the Byzantine dome of the old First Baptist Church, now a theater. In winter mornings, the sun rises behind the cathedrals of commerce towering to the southeast. Just behind the towers stands the newer FBC in Second Ward. As the day dawns, their shadows trespass across Pinewood Cemetery and the grave of Abram North.

Appendix

Key Scripture Passages

Mark 9:14–29

[14]When they came to the disciples, they saw a great crowd around them, and some scribes arguing with them. [15]When the whole crowd saw him, they were immediately overcome with awe, and they ran forward to greet him. [16]He asked them, "What are you arguing about with them?" [17]Someone from the crowd answered him, "Teacher, I brought you my son; he has a spirit that makes him unable to speak; [18]and whenever it seizes him, it dashes him down; and he foams and grinds his teeth and becomes rigid; and I asked your disciples to cast it out, but they could not do so." [19]He answered them, "You faithless generation, how much longer must I be among you? How much longer must I put up with you? Bring him to me." [20]And they brought the boy to him. When the spirit saw him, immediately it convulsed the boy, and he fell on the ground and rolled about, foaming at the mouth. [21]Jesus asked the father, "How long has this been happening to him?" And he said, "From childhood. [22]It has often cast him into the fire and into the water, to destroy him; but if you are able to do anything, have pity on us and help us." [23]Jesus said to him, "If you are able!—All things can be done for the one who believes." [24]Immediately the father of the child cried out, "I believe; help my unbelief!" [25]When Jesus saw that a crowd came running together, he rebuked the unclean spirit, saying to it, "You spirit that keep this boy from speaking and hearing, I command you, come out of him, and never enter him again!" [26]After crying out and convulsing him terribly, it came out, and the boy was like a corpse, so that most of them said, 'He is dead." [27]But Jesus took him by the hand and lifted him up, and he was able to stand. [28]When he had entered the house, his disciples asked him privately, "Why could we not cast it out?" [29]He said to them, "This kind can come out only through prayer."

Numbers 13:21–33

[21]So they went up and spied out the land from the wilderness of Zin to Rehob, near Lebo-hamath. [22]They went up into the Negeb, and came to Hebron; and Ahiman, Sheshai, and Talmai, the Anakites, were there. (Hebron was built seven years before Zoan in Egypt.) [23]And they came to the Wadi Eshcol, and cut down from there a branch with a single cluster of grapes, and they carried it on a pole between two of them. They also brought some pomegranates and figs. [24]That place was called the Wadi Eshcol, because of the cluster that the Israelites cut down from there. [25]At the end of forty days they returned from spying out the land. [26]And they came to Moses and Aaron and to all the congregation of the Israelites in the wilderness of Paran, at Kadesh; they brought back word to them and to all the congregation, and showed them the fruit of the land. [27]And they told him, "We came to the land to which you sent us; it flows with milk and honey, and this is its fruit. [28]Yet the people who live in the land are strong, and the towns are fortified and very large; and besides, we saw the descendants of Anak there. [29]The Amalekites live in the land of the Negeb; the Hittites, the Jebusites, and the Amorites live in the hill country; and the Canaanites live by the sea, and along the Jordan."

[30]But Caleb quieted the people before Moses, and said, "Let us go up at once and occupy it, for we are well able to overcome it." [31]Then the men who had gone up with him said, "We are not able to go up against this people, for they are stronger than we are." [32]So they brought to the Israelites an unfavourable report of the land that they had spied out, saying, "The land that we have gone through as spies is a land that devours its inhabitants; and all the people that we saw in it are of great size. [33]There we saw the Nephilim (the Anakites come from the Nephilim); and to ourselves we seemed like grasshoppers, and so we seemed to them."

Notes

FOREWORD

1 Scott Beyer, "How the US Government Destroyed Black Neighborhoods," *Catalyst*, April 2, 2020, https://catalyst.independent.org/2020/04/02/how-the -u-s-government-destroyed-black-neighborhoods/; Liz Ogbu, "Reckoning and Repair in America's Cities," US News & World Report, February 15, 2022, https://www.usnews .com/news/healthiest-communities/articles/2022-02-15/reckoning-and -repair-in-cities-divided-by-racism-and-exclusion; Brent Cebul, "Tearing Down Black America," *Boston Review*, July 22, 2020, https://www.bostonreview.net/articles /brent-cebul-tearing-down-black-america/.

2 Digital Scholarship Lab, "Renewing Inequality," *American Panorama: An Atlas of United States History*, ed. Robert K. Nelson and Edward L. Ayers. https://dsl.richmond.edu/panorama/renewal/#view=0/0/1&viz=cartogram &text=about.

3 Eduardo Bonilla-Silva deftly explains this in his book, *Racism without Racists: Color-Blind Racism and the Persistence of Racial Inequality in America* (Lanham, MD: Rowman & Littlefield, 2021).

CHAPTER ONE

1 The Charlotte Sanborn maps label the street as "Watkins Alley." Wright called it "Watkins Lane" instead. I am adopting Wright's name for his street. The Sanborn company began making detailed maps of thousands of American cities and towns shortly after the Civil War. The maps were used by fire insurance companies but now are of enormous historical value for tracking changes to the built environment over time. Local libraries or university archives often house those map collections.

2 Reynard Wright died on September 11, 2020, while this work was in production. His shaping of my imagination is reflected across the work.

3 Thomas W. Hanchett, *Sorting Out the New South City: Race, Class, and Urban Development in Charlotte, 1875–1975*, 2nd ed. (Chapel Hill: University of North Carolina Press, 2020), 130. Hanchett cites the earliest reference to the area as "Brooklyn" coming from 1897. He also notes several other connections that might help explain the name on pp. 303–4, note 50. Brooklyn became a borough of New York City in 1898. Prior to that, it was a separate municipality.

4 The Charlotte City Directories of that era provide an estimate of owner-occupied residences. They show that about 10 percent of residences were occupied by owners in 1960. A *Charlotte Observer* story of the same period estimates owner occupancy at 7 percent, a similar figure. See "Brooklyn Homes Give Owners High Returns," *Charlotte Observer*, January 11, 1960.

5 See Rose Leary Love, *Plum Thickets and Field Daisies* (Charlotte, NC: Charlotte Mecklenburg Library) for firsthand descriptions of Brooklyn. Text available at https://tinyurl.com/2p9a3enc.

6 Avery Gordon, *Ghostly Matters: Haunting and the Sociological Imagination* (Minneapolis: University of Minnesota Press, 2008), 16.

7 This paragraph is built from my interview with Richard Campbell, Ivy's son. Richard was a brilliant storyteller and gifted musician. He died on November 10, 2022. His memory remains a blessing.

8 The story I am referencing here is Mark 9:14–29. Over the course of this work, I will return to this story repeatedly. I will sometimes use the phrase *Mark 9* as a shorthand reference for it. For those without a Bible handy, the text is printed on the back of this book.

9 In Mark's Gospel, exorcism and healing stories like this are always political. See Ched Myers, *Binding the Strong Man: A Political Reading of Mark's Story of Jesus* (Maryknoll, NY: Orbis Books, 1988), 26–31, 140–49, 190–94.

10 Eve Tuck and C. Ree, "A Glossary of Haunting," in *Handbook of Autoethnography*, eds. Stacy Holman Jones, Tony E. Adams, and Carolyn Ellis (Philadelphia: Routledge, 2018), 639–58, 642; Elaine Enns and Ched Myers, *Healing Haunted Histories: A Settler Discipleship of Decolonization* (Eugene, OR: Cascade Books, 2021), 36–41; online lecture from Myers, "Always More Ghosts to Return? Healing the Haunting of Racism in America," https://tinyurl.com/3xvw3yrs. I am deeply indebted to Ched Myers and Elaine Enns for their remarkable work and its intellectual and spiritual impact on me. Their influence runs deep through this book. Through their work, I learned of Avery Gordon, Eve Tuck, and other social critics and theorists using the concept of haunting. My research and understanding have been heavily developed from their intellectual and spiritual guidance and from my constant reference to their bibliographies. See the Acknowledgments section for more on their influence.

11 "We search for what has disappeared that has seized hold of us," says sociologist Avery Gordon. Her work *Ghostly Matters* has been a constant companion as I have worked through the stories presented in this book. The quote in this footnote is from Gordon, *Ghostly Matters*, 6, 81.

12 Gordon, *Ghostly Matters*, 17.

13 This is a common Old Testament statement, especially in the books of Joshua and Judges, though usually found in the positive. After a period of conflict, where an enemy arises, eventually peace is restored. The narrator tells the story of the lack of peace and its restoration and then closes a story with the formula "and the land had rest forty years." See, for example, Judg 3:11, 3:30, 5:31b, and so on.

14 Gordon, *Ghostly Matters*, 17.

15 Gordon, *Ghostly Matters*, 28.

16 Shakespeare, *Hamlet*, act I, scene 5, line 190. This line is the quotation that serves as the epigraph for Jacques Derrida, *Specters of Marx* (New York: Routledge Classics, 1994). This volume will be cited throughout my work.

17 See Derrida, *Specters of Marx*, 46–48.

18 I will provide extensive detail about the federal Urban Renewal program, its local implementation in Charlotte, and its long-term results in the rest of the work below. For overviews of the program, see chapters 4 and 5.

19 The photo comes from the Urban Renewal project in Charlotte's Greenville neighborhood, some ten years following the beginnings of the razing of Brooklyn. Nevertheless, the power of the photo has made it a regular representation of the Renewal projects across Charlotte.

20 Despite the commonplace display of the photo above in public discourse about Urban Renewal within Charlotte, few people know the accompanying photos that put together a fuller picture of this demolition. Among the crowd were Black neighbors standing on the porch of the house next door and white officials and onlookers watching the ceremony from the yard of the house being destroyed. For some of those photographs, see "Renewal Bash Begins," *Charlotte Observer*, July 22, 1970. Readers should note that although the local association usually connects the photo to the Brooklyn Urban Renewal project, this photo comes from the later Greenville neighborhood Urban Renewal projects.

21 Gordon, *Ghostly Matters*, 102–3.

22 The picture and accompanying photos are in both *Charlotte Observer* and *Charlotte News*, July 22, 1970.

22 See "Party Chief King Sees JFK Easing Up on Civil Rights," *Charlotte Observer*, July 9, 1963.

24 Gordon, *Ghostly Matters*, 8.

25 Michael Graff and Nick Ochsner, *The Vote Collectors: The True Story of the Scamsters, Politicians, and Preachers behind the Nation's Greatest Electoral Fraud* (Chapel Hill: University of North Carolina Press, 2021) tells the story that involves this pastor, Rev. Dr. Mark Harris. Harris won the North Carolina 9th Congressional District election in 2018. The election was never certified, however, due to a "ballot harvesting" campaign in two rural eastern North Carolina counties that raised significant questions about fraudulent practices. The election was eventually held again, but Harris dropped out of politics rather than run another campaign. Even prior to that case of election fraud, though, Harris was well known in Charlotte for his far-right politics.

26 For an important study of how the loss of neighborhoods to Urban Renewal has had a long-lasting impact in Black communities, see Mindy Fullilove, *Root Shock: How Tearing Up City Neighborhoods Hurts America, and What We Can Do about It* (New York: New Village, 2004).

CHAPTER TWO

1 "South Carolina Conference Appointments," *Charleston Daily Courier*, November 22, 1854.

2 "M.E. Church South," *Greenville Enterprise*, December 8, 1859.

3 There is no record of how Kennedy and Ledbetter met, but her uncle was a well-known Methodist preacher in South Carolina, Henry Willis Ledbetter, a possible source of connection. Thanks to J. Michael Moore for the research assistance.

4 "South Carolina Conference," *Keowee Courier*, January 5, 1861.

5 US Civil War soldier records and profiles, 1861–1865.

6 "A Dear Mother Gone," *Star of Zion*, January 28, 1904. How Kennedy came to own title to the Norths, and why, is unknown. There was a plantation owned by one Richard Laurens North, a physician, in St. Bartholomew's Parish, South Carolina, near Walterboro, which is very likely the place where Sarah, Allmond, and their children were enslaved. The 1850 census shows R. L. North holding fifty-four enslaved people captive. Slave schedules did not generally include the names of enslaved people, but there are teens roughly the age of Sarah and her husband, Allmond, the father of the North children, listed in that schedule. See *Seventh Census of the United States*, St. Bartholomew's Parish, Colleton County, SC Schedule 2. Allmond North remained in Walterboro, having had his family forcibly taken away, and continued to live there after the Civil War. Richard Laurens North was a leader in organizations in defense of slavery in the Walterboro area. See "Meeting at Walterborough," *Charleston Daily Courier*, September 11, 1835; "Meeting at Walterborough," *Charleston Mercury*, September 12, 1850; "St. Bartholomews," *Charleston Mercury*, July 24, 1851.

7 There is a photo of Rev. F. M. Kennedy from his time in Charlotte in the William Wynn Mood Photo Album, South Carolina Methodist Collection at Wofford College. Interested readers can find it easily online. I decided not to reproduce it because I was never able to locate photos that clearly identified Abram North or other members of his family. I am nearly certain that Abram is in one photo of a large group, located in the archives of Clinton Chapel AME Zion, but it is impossible to know which of the more than one hundred people in the panoramic photo is him.

8 See Hanchett, *Sorting Out*, 17.

9 For more on Charlotte in the early period of Reconstruction, see Janette Thomas Greenwood, *Bittersweet Legacy: The Black and White "Better Classes" in Charlotte, 1850–1910* (Chapel Hill: University of North Carolina Press, 1994), 38–56.

10 Eric Foner, *Reconstruction: America's Unfinished Revolution, 1863–1877*, updated edition (New York: Harper Perennial, 2014), 119–23.

11 Foner, *Reconstruction*, 165.

12 Foner, *Reconstruction*, 153–75. There is much important historical work documenting how dependent the United States was on the cotton trade as the source of the country's wealth, both in the South, where enslaved people produced the crops, and in the North, where bankers and traders generated profits off the Southern economy. Two essential works are Edward E. Baptist, *The Half Has Never Been Told: Slavery and the Making of American Capitalism* (New York: Basic Books, 2014); and Sven Beckert, *Empire of Cotton: A Global History* (New York: Vintage, 2014).

13 Foner, *Reconstruction*, 153–54.

14 US Bureau of the Census, *Ninth Census*, "Population by Race and Nativity." Cited in Hanchett, *Sorting Out*, 41.

15 James E. Brunson III, *Black Baseball: A Comprehensive Record of the Teams, Players, Managers, Owners, and Umpires* (Jefferson, NC: McFarland, 2019), 297, 299. Brunson lists North as a member of the Charlotte Recruits, one of the first teams in Charlotte. Also listed on the roster is North's brother Jacob.

16 US Bureau of the Census, *Seventh Census*, "Steele Creek, Mecklenburg County"; and US Bureau of the Census, *Eighth Census*, "Steele Creek, Mecklenburg County." The Slave Schedule attached to the 1850 census shows nine enslaved persons held by the Smiths. The 1860 census shows twenty-two.

17 "Death of Mr. S. P. Smith," *Charlotte Observer*, October 18, 1896.

18 US Bureau of the Census, *Ninth Census*, "Charlotte City Ward 1."

19 "Death of Mr. S. P. Smith."

20 I will refer to the congregation by the name it was using inside the timeline of the text as it progresses. The congregation originated in 1832 as Beulah Baptist. It changed its name in the 1880s, following a move to Tryon Street, to Tryon Street Baptist Church and eventually settled on First Baptist Church in recognition of its chronological position as a "mother church" among the other churches it was birthing. However, this name is not without contest. In 1867 or 1868—documentation varies—a group of Black members separated from the congregation and became independent. They took the name First Baptist Church and were often identified as First Baptist Church, Colored. I will identify that body throughout by their current name, First Baptist Church-West.

21 See "Former Mayor of Charlotte Dead," Charlotte's *Evening Chronicle*, January 28, 1911; "Commander Smith of Meck Camp Dead," *Charlotte News*, April 28, 1912. Also of note, the elder Benjamin Rush Smith, father of Samuel and his brother, Benjamin, placed an ad in the *Charlotte Democrat*, on September 15, 1857, under the heading "Valuable Plantation for Sale." The ad indicates that Smith was selling the land and building but perhaps intended to maintain title to the enslaved persons when he moved to the West. Such conditions make it likely, though not certain, that he intended to become active in the trade of enslaved persons as a primary business rather than as a planter.

22 See John Marvin Crowe, *Biography of a Thriving Church: A History of First Baptist Church, Charlotte, NC, 1832-1952* (Charlotte, NC: First Baptist Church), 13-19, 25-37.

23 Smith and fellow member William Boyd were primarily responsible for the pastoral search, according to Crow. They issued several job offers (*calls* in the Baptist lingo) that were turned down. The pastor who accepted, a Rev. J. B. Boone, stayed only two years. For more on the congregation's pastoral history, see Crowe, *Biography of a Thriving Church*, 25-59.

24 For one incisive and cutting essay on Presbyterianism in Charlotte, see W. J. Cash, "Close View of a Calvinist Lhasa," *American Mercury*, April 1933.

25 Crowe, *Biography of a Thriving Church*, 61.

26 See Thomas W. Hanchett, "Building History," *Charlotte Magazine*, December 28, 2020.

27 US Bureau of the Census, *Ninth Census*, "Charlotte City Ward 1." Anasha Smith is listed in this census as "mulatto." Anasha and Kate Smith, Samuel's wife, are the only two persons in the household listed as born in Virginia. It seems likely that she was enslaved to Kate's family in Virginia prior to Kate's marriage to Samuel and trafficked to North Carolina with Kate at the time of her marriage, which predated the Civil War.

28 This map, called the "Beers Map" for its cartographer, is in the North Carolina Collection at the Louis Round Wilson Special Collections Library, University of North Carolina at Chapel Hill, and available online at https://tinyurl.com/y6xk3fnu.

29 Greenwood, *Bittersweet Legacy*, 32-39, 72-75, 157-76.

30 Formerly called East Avenue.

31 Hanchett, *Sorting Out*, 32.

32 Hanchett, *Sorting Out*, 32.

33 See *First Baptist Church: A Century of Christian Witnessing: 1867-1967* (Charlotte, NC: First Baptist Church-West, 1967), 2-3; Crowe, *Biography of a Thriving Church*,

20–21. Concern about power and leadership is one of the ways that First Baptist Church-West frames this decision. Their church historian and archivist, Dr. Herman Thomas, spoke directly about this to me multiple times in different conversations. The three history texts at FBC do not address the separation in the same way, glossing over numerical and power differences, nor did the two FBC staff members I heard recounting the separation. They chose to narrate the story in terms of kindness and generosity rather than power.

34 On the creation of Black churches as one embodiment of Black political, religious, and economic freedom, see Foner, *Reconstruction*, 88–119. The First Baptist Church-West congregation was displaced by an Urban Renewal project, namely the Third Ward Renewal project, which eventually resulted in construction of the freeway loop known as I-277. Curiously, the freeway went near their property but not through, though they were forced to sell anyway. Today the congregation is called First Baptist Church-West. They are located on Oaklawn Avenue in west Charlotte, between the McCrorey Heights and Oaklawn Avenue neighborhoods, both historically Black. For the story of the congregation, see *A Century of Christian Witnessing*.

35 *White supremacy* is the term that describes the global system of racism that privileges white people and institutions over everyone else. I'll use the term regularly across this work. With it, I am not referring to individual people, as in Ku Klux Klan members, though they are part of white supremacy also. Rather, I am describing a set of interlocking political, economic, psychological, and religious systems that confer benefits to people who are made "white" inside those systems. All of us who are white inside white supremacy benefit from those interlocking systems, even if we are not mean people and even if we don't want the benefits the system affords us.

36 North, in the limited written record, never cites this kind of interaction. My imagination here is informed by personal stories that Charlotte civil rights leader Charles Jones often told me. During the sit-ins of the early 1960s, of which Jones was one of the lead organizers, he would get calls from Black women who were working in the homes of Charlotte's elite. They would report to Jones on the conversations of politicos and business leaders during dinners and meetings. Those persons would speak freely around the household servants, who would then inform Black leadership to help mold strategy for the movement. These kinds of stories are common and demonstrate one way in which white supremacy has seeded its own demise at times, by white people refusing to acknowledge the intelligence of the Black, Indigenous, and other people of color around them.

37 Across the archives, Annice Carson is varyingly called Annice and Annie. *Annie* seems to have been the more common later in her life, and I will generally defer to it when referring to her.

38 Interview with Helen Kirk, May 26, 2021.

39 Brunson, *Black Baseball*, 297, 299. On the importance of baseball in Black culture at the time, see Brunson, *Black Baseball*, 15–34.

40 "22 Years Ago," *Charlotte News*, March 27, 1900.

41 US Bureau of the Census, *Tenth Census* (1880), Charlotte, North Carolina, 30. The North address was 275 2nd St. Clinton Chapel AMEZ Church was near the corner of 3rd and Mint, just a block away.

42 Only a month following Lee's surrender, AME Zion missionary E. H. Hill came to Charlotte and helped organize the congregation, making it the first Black institution in Charlotte founded fully outside of white influence. Various church documents show

Annie North as one of its founders. This is memorialized publicly in a granite memorial in front of the church's present location at 1801 Rozzelle's Ferry Road in Charlotte. Clinton Chapel and other churches became important hubs within Charlotte's Black community, and in Black communities around the country, for more than just worship. Churches were key meeting places and played a central role as locations for working out Black political strategy and building Black political and economic strength. For more on this dynamic in Charlotte, see Greenwood, *Bittersweet Legacy*, 43–44.

43 Greenwood, *Bittersweet Legacy*, 43–47.

44 Greenwood, *Bittersweet Legacy*, 52–55.

45 Foner, *Reconstruction*, 564–601, is a terrific overview of this era. Zeb Vance, mentioned above, appears in Foner's text several times. The North Carolina legislature attempted to appoint Vance to the US Senate in 1870, during Reconstruction, but the Senate refused to seat him. Nevertheless, Foner reports, one Black Republican wrote, "It seems that we are drifting, drifting back under the leadership of the slaveholders. Our former masters are fast taking the reins of government" (444). For more on Vance and similar Southern politicians at the end of Reconstruction, see 569–75; for a biography of Vance, see Gordon D. McKinney, *Zeb Vance: North Carolina's Civil War Governor and Gilded Age Political Leader* (Chapel Hill: University of North Carolina Press, 2013); on Vance and the so-called Redemption campaigns, see Greenwood, *Bittersweet Legacy*, 63–75.

46 George Lipsitz, *How Racism Takes Place* (Philadelphia: Temple University Press, 2011), 15.

47 Crowe, *Biography of a Thriving Church*, 61.

48 Crowe, *Biography of a Thriving Church*, 35–38.

CHAPTER THREE

1 Clinton Chapel was located at the corner of Mint and 3rd Streets until about 1950. Their property there was purchased by Duke Power Company. According to the newspaper article about the sale, Duke planned for a parking lot on the site following the razing of the building. The theme of displacement for the purpose of parking lots will again arise in chapter 5. Additionally, the article notes that Realtor Lee Kinney assisted the transaction. Kinney will also return below, first as one of the real estate men charged with drawing the Charlotte redlining maps (chapter 3) and then as the first white landowner to sell his Brooklyn area property (chapter 3). The former Clinton Chapel site is now Romare Bearden Park. See "Church Tract Sold to Duke," *Charlotte Observer*, July 4, 1950.

2 Alana Semuels, "Segregation Had to Be 'Invented,'" *Atlantic*, February 17, 2017; Hanchett, *Sorting Out*, 116–27.

3 US Bureau of the Census, *Tenth Census* (1880), Charlotte, North Carolina, 30.

4 Hanchett, *Sorting Out*, 116–22.

5 *United States Register of Civil, Military, and Naval Service, 1863–1959*, 1885, vol. 2, 758.

6 Quoted in Foner, *Reconstruction*, 93. The existence of an openly partisan Sunday School in churches would be unusual in any congregation today and likely was in 1893 also. However, ideological and partisan alignments are often clear in practice while remaining unstated.

7   For Cunningham's letter, see "The Post Office Janitorship," *Charlotte Observer*, June 17, 1893. See also Greenwood, *Bittersweet Legacy*, 147–84. Cunningham was one especially public crusader in the cause of joining upper-class Black interests with white Democratic interests. In May 1893, he wrote to the Charlotte-published AME Zion newspaper *Star of Zion*, saying, "If the Negroes of the South will ever get better treatment in the future than we have in the past, we shall have to expect it through the majority of the best white people, who are Democrats, of course." His use of the term "best" was not a naïve flattery of white elites. Rather, it was encoded language commonly locally in that time, used as part of the appeal to middle- and upper-class whites to identify with wealthier Black families by identity with class rather than discard them through racial categories. The "better" classes, meaning the wealthier or more "respectable" ones, had developed a short record of working together on local issues following Reconstruction, with prohibition movements being the most common collective issue. The success of these appeals for the Black community had been limited, but the strategy persisted. The quotation inside this footnote is from Greenwood, *Bittersweet Legacy*, 173.

8   Greenwood, *Bittersweet Legacy*, is one of only a few lengthy studies of Charlotte history of this era. In it, she tracks the language of the "better classes" to show the origins, the halting effectiveness, and the eventual defeat of class-based appeals in the period from Reconstruction to the establishment of Jim Crow. She also examines the Fusion movement, chronicles its successes, and discusses the long-term results of its defeat.

9   "The Post Office Janitorship." Cunningham's purpose in writing to the *Observer* was to warn local Democrats of North, who Cunningham said was searching for another postal job under a Democratic postmaster, despite his strong affiliation with the Republican-Populist cause. Writing to the largest paper in town raised an internal conflict to a new height by taking the argument out of its context inside the Black community and its institutions and putting it into view of the general public.

10 On the roots of Republican-Populist Fusion in North Carolina, see Greenwood, *Bittersweet Legacy*, 77–113, 147–84; Hanchett, *Sorting Out*, 70–88, 152–59. Greenwood's discussion of the Fusion movement and its precursors is especially informative.

11 Records at the time of the sale number this property as 611 E 2nd Street. Charlotte's street grid was renumbered in the early 1900s, when the lot numbered 611 became 625.

12 James L. Hunt, "Fusion of Republicans and Populists," in *The Encyclopedia of North Carolina*, ed. William S. Powell (Chapel Hill: University of North Carolina Press, 2006), 487–88; Greenwood, *Bittersweet Legacy*, 177; Hanchett, *Sorting Out*, 81–83. For a poignant look at the Fusion movement and its current manifestations in North Carolina politics, see Rev. Dr. William J. Barber II with Jonathan Wilson-Hartgrove, *The Third Reconstruction: How a Moral Movement Is Overcoming the Politics of Division and Fear* (Boston: Beacon, 2016).

13 Jeffrey Crow and Robert Durden, *Maverick Republican in the Old North State: A Political Biography of Daniel L. Russell* (Baton Rouge: Louisiana State University Press, 1977), 50.

14 *Charlotte Observer*, February 28, 1897, cited in Hanchett, *Sorting Out*, 83.

15 Greenwood, *Bittersweet Legacy*, 184.

16 Quoted in Greenwood, *Bittersweet Legacy*, 184.

17 "Democracy Is Immortal," *Charlotte Observer*, November 5, 1898.
18 The *Charlotte Observer* issued an apology in 2006 for its participation in these events. See David Zucchino, *Wilmington's Lie: The Murderous Coup of 1898 and the Rise of White Supremacy* (New York: Atlantic Monthly Press, 2020), 81, 343.
19 Zucchino, *Wilmington's Lie*. This story is a crucial one in the state's history but one that until recently has been glossed over or altered by nearly every official accounting. As a child growing up in North Carolina, I learned nothing about this event, though it affected state politics for a full century afterward. When accounts of it were public, it was called a "race riot," as though there was culpability across both Black and white people in Wilmington. There was no such culpability, no blame to spread. The rebellion was organized and executed entirely by white people and entirely for the purpose of white supremacy.
20 Hanchett, *Sorting Out*, 116–22.
21 Crowe, *Biography of a Thriving Church*, 63–64.
22 See "New Church Is Dedicated," *Charlotte Daily Observer*, May 3, 1909.
23 Myers Street School, known locally as the "Jacob's Ladder School" because of the large staircases across its outside, attracted Black families from across Mecklenburg County to move into Charlotte so they could send their children to climb higher at the only school for Black children in the county.
24 *Twelfth Census of the United States*, Charlotte, North Carolina, Ward 2, 33; for information on Myers Street School, see Hanchett, *Sorting Out*, 128–29.
25 "Suburb for Negroes," *Charlotte Observer*, September 22, 1912.
26 James Cone, *The Spiritual and the Blues: An Interpretation* (Maryknoll, NY: Orbis Books, 1992) is a profound meditation on, and exegesis of, the connections and continuities of Black American music.
27 Glenda Elizabeth Gilmore, *Gender and Jim Crow: Women and the Politics of White Supremacy in North Carolina 1896–1920* (Chapel Hill: University of North Carolina Press, 1996), 166. North Carolina Mutual is one of the most important businesses in the history of North Carolina. It was a Black-owned insurance company, based in Durham, that became immensely successful. Archives from NC Mutual are located in special collections at Duke University and University of North Carolina-Chapel Hill. For more on NC Mutual and its social role within Black communities, see Walter B. Weare, *Black Business in the New South: A Social History of the North Carolina Mutual Life Insurance Company* (Urbana: University of Illinois Press, 1973).
28 "Abraham North Injured," *Charlotte News*, August 18, 1905; "Abram North, Sexton of Trinity Church over 15 Years," *Charlotte News*, May 4, 1913; "Honor Aged Negroes," *Charlotte News*, April 1, 1928.
29 *Twelfth Census of the United States*, Charlotte, North Carolina, Ward 2, 6.
30 Charlotte City Directory, 1912. John Riddick worked as a porter and janitor for Southern Railroad. He died of heat stroke in 1924, at which point Hazeline moved back into the family home.
31 "Married but a Week," *Charlotte Observer*, June 30, 1909, reports "the marriage was an event in colored circles," and one imagines that the celebration was indeed quite festive. In an interview with the archivist at Clinton Chapel AME Zion, Helen Kirk, Ms. Kirk recounted her memory of going to tea parties and events given by Annie North at the North household. She could recall Annie North as a vivacious woman who enjoyed entertaining. It is important to point out that as of my writing in 2023,

there are still people alive with active memories of formerly enslaved persons. Interview with Helen Kirk, May 26, 2021.

32 "Married but a Week"; "Wedded a Week—Then Suicide," *Charlotte News*, June 30, 1909; "Took Carbolic Acid," *Charlotte News*, July 3, 1909. Thomas-Hazell was a graduate of Biddle University, now Johnson C. Smith University, a historically Black university near downtown Charlotte. He was a Presbyterian minister and pastor of the People's Presbyterian Church in Denver, Colorado, at the time of his marriage to Lavinia North.

33 In "Locals," June 8, 1916. I learned of this through Hanchett, *Sorting Out*, 141, and through the careful reading and incredible memory of J. Michael Moore; Mecklenburg County Register of Deeds, Book 358, p. 305. The address was 1017 Beattie's Ford. Today the house still stands. As of 2023, it is used as a community economic hub for small businesses run by Historic West End Partners, an important local organization run by J'Tanya Adams. See https://westendclt.com for more info.

34 On the history and importance of Washington Heights, and the development of other Black suburbs, see Hanchett, *Sorting Out*, 134–44.

35 Hanchett, *Sorting Out*, 133–34; Greenwood, *Bittersweet Legacy*, 240.

36 Both the MIC building and Grace AMEZ are still standing, two of only four buildings remaining from the Brooklyn area pre-Urban Renewal. They are now part of the Brooklyn Collective, which seeks to use them in a way consistent with the vision of MIC, which invested especially in the creation and thriving of Black businesses in Brooklyn and in other Black neighborhoods in Charlotte. See https://www.brooklyncollectiveclt.org/.

37 Moreland appears to have owned several homes, including a residence at 700 E. 2nd Street and at least one other property at 310 S. Davidson. That home, on the current site of First Baptist Church, would later become the first house razed in Charlotte's Urban Renewal projects. See "1st Slum Dwelling Given the Ax," *Charlotte Observer*, December 21, 1961.

38 The iterations of Charlotte *Sanborn* maps show these types of buildings springing up relatively quickly, likely as investment properties. Watkins Alley, Reynard Wright's street (from chapter 1), has no residents listed in the 1914 city directory. In the 1915 city directory, there are fourteen residences and by 1920, at least twenty-two. These were all duplexes, poorly built, likely by the same landlord.

39 Thomas W. Hanchett, "Bathrooms, Building Codes, and Slum Clearance," a chapter from an unpublished book provided to the author and used by permission.

40 "Tribute to Good Negro," *Charlotte News*, May 14, 1929; "Honor Aged Negroes."

41 Katherine McKittrick, "Mathematics Black Life," *Black Scholar* 44, no. 2 (Summer 2014): 16–28.

42 Interview with Brandi North Williams.

43 Richard Rothstein, *The Color of Law: The Forgotten History of How Our Government Segregated America* (New York: Liveright Publishing, 2017), 63; Kenneth T. Jackson, *Crabgrass Frontier: The Suburbanization of the United States* (New York: Oxford University Press, 1985), 196–97.

44 Quoted in Kenneth T. Jackson, "Race, Ethnicity, and Real Estate Appraisal: The Home Owners Loan Corporation and the Federal Housing Administration," *Journal of Urban History* 6, no. 4 (August 1980): 419.

45 Most New Deal policy interventions were shot through with white supremacy. The Social Security Act, for example, passed through Congress only with a caveat that certainly types of employment would not qualify for Social Security benefits. The largest portion of workers within the types of worked excluded were Black, notably domestic servants and agricultural workers. Likewise, the GI Bill, while not directly racist in its language, proved to be a program that overwhelmingly benefited white veterans and excluded Black ones.

46 Jackson, *Crabgrass Frontier*, 193.

47 Rothstein, *Color of Law*, 63.

48 Jackson, *Crabgrass Frontier*, 196.

49 The HOLC was an urban intervention. Rural interests were served by the Emergency Farm Mortgage Act, passed one month prior to the creation of the HOLC.

50 See Jackson, *Crabgrass Frontier*, 197; for specific examples of anti-urban bias in Charlotte's redlining maps, see Hanchett, *Sorting Out*, 230–31.

51 Hanchett, *Sorting Out*, 229. Among the eleven men they met with was developer Lex Marsh Jr. Within just a couple of years from that meeting, Marsh would go on to be one of a group of twelve founding members of Myers Park Baptist Church, an institution that will make several appearances later in this study.

52 Hanchett, *Sorting Out*, 230–31; Jackson, *Crabgrass Frontier*, 201–3.

53 Hanchett, *Sorting Out*, 229–32; Rothstein, *Color of Law*, 63–64; Kevin M. Kruse, *White Flight: Atlanta and the Making of Modern Conservatism* (Princeton, NJ: Princeton University Press, 2005), 60. University of Richmond has compiled a remarkable set of resources called "Mapping Inequality" about redlining, including maps, local information, and national overviews, available at https://dsl.richmond.edu/panorama/redlining.

54 Hanchett, *Sorting Out*, 230.

55 Kenneth Jackson points out that most of the direct damage done by redlining was not done directly by the HOLC but instead by private banks and lenders who adopted the HOLC's system of appraisal and risk assessment. Private lenders would refuse to lend in entire cities like Newark, New Jersey, based on redlining maps. Over the course of thirty years of redlining, which formally ended in 1968, the accumulated effect of a private credit freeze far exceeded the amount of loans the HOLC refinanced. See Jackson, "Race, Ethnicity, and Real Estate Appraisal," 430. For an important assessment of how private business practices of banks and real estate undermined Black wealth, see Keeanga-Yamahtta Taylor, *Race for Profit: How Banks and the Real Estate Industry Undermined Black Homeownership* (Chapel Hill: University of North Carolina Press, 2019).

56 For an overview of the FHA's creation and its long-term effects in US housing, see Jackson, *Crabgrass Frontier*, 203–18.

57 Hanchett, *Sorting Out*, 232–36; Rothstein, *Color of Law*, 64–67.

58 Rothstein, *Color of Law*, 64–67.

59 Quoted in Kruse, *White Flight*, 61.

60 Kruse shows how Black real estate agents couldn't join the same associations or even use the same language because of the control of real estate boards and listing systems by white people. Black agents in Atlanta called themselves "realtists" rather than the copyrighted term "Realtor." See, e.g., Kruse, *White Flight*, 63–64.

61 Among the most important books that show, in detail, how the economy of the entire country—not only the South—was built around the cotton trade are Beckert, *Empire of Cotton*, and Baptist, *The Half Has Never Been Told*.

62 "What comes into stark focus as we study [Black banks] over time is the tangible barrier to prosperity presented by segregation, racism, and government credit policy. The effects of these forces on [B]lack banks demonstrate that successful banking and wealth accumulation would remain perpetually elusive in a segregated economy. Housing segregation, racism, and Jim Crow credit policies create an inescapable economic trap for Black communities and their banks. Black banking has been an anemic response to racial inequality that has yielded virtually nothing in closing the wealth gap." Mehrsa Baradaran, *The Color of Money: Black Banking and the Racial Wealth Gap* (Cambridge, MA: Belknap, 2017), 1–2. Baradaran is not levying a criticism at Black banks nor those who started them but rather at the society that made Black banks, and other institutions in Black society with parallels in the dominant white society, necessary and yet made it impossible for them to have the kind of success in building and distributing wealth that such institutions had in dominant culture.

63 "Rites to Be Thursday," *Charlotte Observer*, August 14, 1940.

64 Lev 19:9–10.

65 Alexandra R. Murphy et al., *Jean-Francois Millet: Drawn Into the Light. An Exhibition Catalogue* (Williamstown, MA: Clark Art Institute, 1999), 77.

66 Ione Crummy, "The Subversion of Gleaning in Balzac's *Les Paysans* and in Millet's *Les Glaneuses*," *Neohelicon* XXVI (1999), 15.

67 Bradley Fratello, "France Embraces Millet: The Intertwined Fates of *The Gleaners* and *The Angelus*," *Art Bulletin* 85, no. 4 (December 2003): 685.

68 I am grateful to Dr. Tara Dudley for helping me make these connections. Dr. Dudley is a leading historian of African American interiors. In personal correspondence, Dudley noted that the presence of these reprints in varying places across the country raises a number of questions needing further research, including who printed them, how African Americans saw them, and whether they were specifically marketed to African American families. See HHM and Associates, Historic Furnishings Report, Martin Luther King Jr. Birth Home, Martin Luther King Jr. National Historical Park, Atlanta, Georgia, Volume I: Historical Data, January 2021; "A Saving Cache," *Washington Post*, August 20, 2000; "Vivian Hewitt, Who Amassed a Major Collection of Black Art, Dies at 102," *New York Times*, June 22, 2022.

69 Derrida, *Specters of Marx*, 10.

CHAPTER FOUR

1 The common language for churches hiring a pastor is *calling*.

2 *One Hundred Years of Working for Christ: The Centennial History of Friendship Missionary Baptist Church, 1890-1990* (Charlotte, NC: Friendship Missionary Baptist Church, 1990), 11–22; Charlotte City Directory, 1954.

3 "Kerry to Speak," *Charlotte Observer*, December 7, 1947.

4 *One Hundred Years of Working for Christ*, 16.

5 *One Hundred Years of Working for Christ*, 16–17.

6 Union National Bank was founded in 1908 in Charlotte. The organization became First Union National Bank after merging with First National Bank of Asheville in 1958.

7 Information on C. C. Hope's life from interview with Joan Hope, April 6, 2023. See also "FDIC, First Union Exec C. C. Hope, Jr.," *Charlotte Observer*, March 3, 1997; "C. C. Hope, Jr. Dies at 73; An FDIC Director," *New York Times*, March 3, 1997.

8 Interview with Nancy Kistler, September 24, 2020.

9 Crowe, *Biography of a Thriving Church*, 53–59; see also "Arkansas Man, Native of NC, Offered Post," *Charlotte Observer*, November 8, 1943; "News from the Charlotte Area," *Biblical Recorder*, November 17, 1943.

10 "Doctor Casper C. Warren," *Biblical Recorder*, December 22, 1943.

11 Figures from US census data, cited in Hanchett, *Sorting Out*, 2. On the geography and built environment of Charlotte's postwar growth and development, see chapter 5 and Hanchett, *Sorting Out*, 224–56.

12 "Dr. Warren Opens Service as Pastor," *Charlotte Observer*, December 6, 1943.

13 Crowe, *Biography of a Thriving Church*, 54; "News: Personalities and Events," *Biblical Recorder*, July 18, 1945.

14 "Editorial Brevities," *Biblical Recorder*, September 19, 1945.

15 In every interview I conducted with current and former First Baptist members, the salient characteristic of the church was its sense of community or camaraderie among members. Even those who left under some sense of duress or disagreement spoke repeatedly of the warm fellowship nurtured there among the membership. On Warren's creation of church programs, see Crowe, *Biography of a Thriving Church*. He has an extensive list of Warren's accomplishments during the first decade of his tenure there. The book was published in 1953; Warren remained until 1957. Those accomplishments are heavily administrative and programmatic, including, in Crowe's words, the building of a church staff, the enlargement and improvement of the property, an effort to enlist a large number of people in active service through the church, a perennial program of evangelism, a major emphasis on missions, an appreciation of the church's educational program, and so on. Crowe lists thirteen significant accomplishments in building the programs of the church. See pp. 54–58.

16 From "Rejoice," an unpublished paper written by FBC member Nancy Kistler, on her recollections of FBC and its pastors. Quotation from p. 6. Paper provided to the author by Ms. Kistler.

17 All of my interviews with current and former FBC members and staff mentioned "the Four Horsemen." These men were significant local leaders in Charlotte politics. They also held significant power within the congregation, as detailed below. Their power was not always well used, as those interviews demonstrated. In an interview with Robert Welch, June 10, 2021, Welch indicated that the power of the so-called "Four Horsemen" became significant enough that it resulted in a large conflict and the early termination of Rev. Dr. Charles Page's first pastorate at FBC. Page returned only a few years later, after that conflict had been adequately addressed. Former pastor Joe McKeever also claimed the same about his pastorate, immediately following Page's first pastorate there. When McKeever did not respond as those men, and a small group of others, wanted regarding certain theological questions, McKeever sensed that his tenure was doomed. Interview with McKeever, January 25, 2022.

18 Following World War II, the Veterans' Administration (VA) began "guaranteeing mortgages for returning servicemen. It adopted FHA housing policies, and VA

appraisers relied on the FHA's *Underwriting Manual*. By 1950, the FHA and VA together were insuring half of all new mortgages nationwide." From Rothstein, *Color of Law*, 70; see also 70–72, 85–91, 177–83. The VA did underwrite loans for Black veterans, but the terms were different and were not advantageous to borrowers in the way loans written to white veterans were.

19 Theological engagements with the suburban shift will be part of the reflections in chapter 7. On the history of suburbanization in the country, see Jackson, *Crabgrass Frontier*; on the policy movements that created segregated suburbanization, see Rothstein, *Color of Law*; on race and geography, see Lipsitz, *How Racism Takes Place*; and Katherine McKittrick, *Demonic Grounds: Black Women and the Cartographies of Struggle* (Minneapolis: University of Minnesota Press, 2006); on suburbanization and the creation of the so-called "inner-city," see Arnold Hirsch, *Making the Second Ghetto: Race and Housing in Chicago, 1940–1960* (Chicago: University of Chicago Press, 1998).

20 The basic thesis of Kevin Kruse's important book *White Flight* is that the white flight phenomenon not only was a spatial rearrangement of American cities but also remade the political landscape of the country, in particular the party affiliations and the strength of white conservatives. Kruse's book details Atlanta while mapping its story onto the country at large.

21 One important study of race and housing in the 1940s and '50s is Hirsch, *Making the Second Ghetto*. Hirsch argues that the politics of neighborhood change in Chicago during that period "pioneered" the policy concepts that would come to define the country's Urban Renewal program. Hirsch says, "The legal framework for the national urban renewal effort was forged in the heat generated by the racial struggles waged on Chicago's South Side" (xviii). On the specifics of suburbanization and the entrenchment of segregation in Charlotte, see Hanchett, *Sorting Out*, 223–56.

22 Taylor, *Race for Profit*, 10.

23 Taylor, *Race for Profit*, 10–11.

24 Truman's statement available at https://tinyurl.com/5cekenxx. Text of the act available at https://tinyurl.com/4559cd56.

25 With the passage of the Housing Act of 1954, the name Urban Redevelopment Administration was changed to Urban Renewal Agency (URA). The policies that became the outline of the federal Urban Renewal program were built on ideas largely developed and attempted in Chicago, the city that by many measures was the most segregated in the United States. The Housing Act of 1954, in particular, was directly related to Chicago's attempts to clear Black neighborhoods, usually with only minimal effort to house those displaced by Renewal projects. Important literature around Chicago and the development of Urban Renewal policy includes Hirsch, *Making the Second Ghetto*; Beryl Satter, *Family Properties: Race, Real Estate, and the Exploitation of Black Urban America* (New York: Metropolitan Books, 2009), 36–63; and Andrew J. Diamond, *Chicago on the Make: Power and Inequality in a Modern City* (Oakland: University of California Press, 2017).

26 On this policy and its potential effects, see interview with Vernon Sawyer in Special Collections, UNC-Charlotte. My thanks to Tom Hanchett for helping me to see this aspect of the program, one that has generally gone unnoticed. Interview available at https://tinyurl.com/yp2jzuh2.

27 In its actual lending practices, there is some data that shows that the HOLC did lend in redlined neighborhoods at similar rates as it did in neighborhoods graded as more risk-worthy. Jackson, *Crabgrass Frontier*, contends that the most significant damage was done to redlined neighborhoods not by the HOLC itself but instead by the private banks and lenders who used redlining maps in making lending decisions. See pp. 202–3. The distinction may be slight, given the long-term effects of the redlining maps.

28 Jane Jacobs, *The Death and Life of Great American Cities* (New York: Vintage, 1992), 301.

29 Jackson, *Crabgrass Frontier*, 227.

30 State-level "enabling legislation" was required in North Carolina, as it was in certain other states, in order for local municipalities to enter into federal contracts with the URA. In North Carolina, the enabling legislation passed following the 1949 Housing Act severely curtailed the ability of cities to conduct projects with the URA. See below for details of Charlotte's initial attempts, which failed due to the state legislation.

31 The University of Richmond has a set of resources at the *American Panorama* site. One study, called "Renewing Inequality," has aggregated data from Urban Renewal projects across the country. It features data, maps, sources, and links from all cities and towns that had Renewal projects from 1956 to 1966. Likewise, their "Mapping Inequality" resources tracks redlining around the country. The site is a terrific beginning point for anyone wishing to examine their own locality. See https://dsl.richmond.edu/panorama/.

There is a fascinating subplot from Charlotte on conservative resistance to accepting federal monies, and the eventual acceptance, led by Mayor Herbert Baxter (member, Myers Park Methodist), of subsidized funding for large-scale development projects. For a detailed look at the story, see Hanchett, *Sorting Out*, 224–56; and Hanchett, "Bathrooms, Building Codes, and 'Slum Clearance,'" part of his unpublished work on affordable housing in Charlotte, provided by email correspondence. One notable anecdote there includes Baxter convincing city powers to accept 1944 Federal Highway Act dollars for the construction of Independence Boulevard, a high-speed road through portions of Brooklyn and white working-class Chantilly. The project's results, after years of construction, were dubious at best. "Saves three minutes," proclaimed the *Observer* on the day of its opening. See "Saves Three Minutes: Independence Link Opened to Traffic," *Charlotte Observer*, November 24, 1955.

32 The NACCP's ten-point plan also called for at least one Black member of the school board. That would not happen for another twenty-two years, when Rev. Coleman Kerry Jr. would be appointed to the school board under the chairmanship of Bill Poe, one of the Four Horsemen at First Baptist Church. The Charlotte-Mecklenburg Board of Education occupies a central place in the struggles for racial justice in the 1960s and '70s. While it falls outside the scope of this study, Matthew Lassiter's fine study of suburban politics in the South during the period, *The Silent Majority*, is an important work. See "NAACP to Push Improvement Program," *Charlotte News*, January 23, 1950.

33 "NAACP to Push Improvement Program." The italics are mine.

34 "Council Slates Study of Slum Clearance," *Charlotte Observer*, August 2, 1951. Contemporaneously with Charlotte, other North Carolina cities were engaged in a similar process, including Greensboro, Raleigh, and Fayetteville.

35 The 1951 Redevelopment Commission and its local church membership included Irwin Belk (Myers Park Presbyterian), Paul Younts (elder, Westminster Presbyterian), G. Douglas Aitken (founding member, Avondale Presbyterian), Pete McKnight, and George Sibley (Myers Park Methodist).

36 "Plan Eradication of Squalid Areas," *Charlotte Observer*, November 16, 1952.

37 "Fund to Start Slum Clearance Approved," *Charlotte Observer*, February 29, 1952.

38 North Carolina is a "Dillon's Rule" state, an arrangement whereby the state charter indicates that all municipalities and their elected officials serve at the pleasure of the state legislature. Under this arrangement, state law always trumps local law, and municipal rights to pass ordinances and enforce local statutes are subject to the determinations of the state legislature.

39 "Slum Test Has Anchor in Council," *Charlotte Observer*, July 30, 1953.

40 "Death Knell Sounded for Redevelopment Plan in Charlotte," *Charlotte Observer*, August 6, 1953; "Slum Clearance Plans of Three NC Cities Die," *Charlotte Observer*, August 6, 1953.

41 "Prayer Meeting Discontinued," *Biblical Recorder*, March 8, 1944.

42 "Church to Dedicate Education Building," *Charlotte Observer*, April 4, 1953; "Dedication of Building Held," *Charlotte Observer*, April 6, 1953.

43 "Charlotte Area," *Biblical Recorder*, June 7, 1944. *Biblical Recorder* is the newspaper of the Baptist State Convention of North Carolina.

44 Warren had steadily worked his way toward this position through leadership on numerous boards and committees of Baptist institutions, including the North Carolina Baptist State Convention, Wake Forest University, the Southern Baptist Theological Seminary, and the SBC's powerful Executive Committee. Crowe cites him as especially impactful as a fundraiser for these institutions. See Crowe, *Biography of a Thriving Church*, 58–59.

45 Interview with Bill Leonard, June 24, 2021.

46 A seminary professor of mine, Rev. Dr. Cecil Sherman, now of blessed memory, often said that the most important word in "Southern Baptist Convention" was *Southern*.

47 Notable among segregationist pastors were men like Douglas Hudgins of First Baptist Church Jackson, Mississippi, and W. A. Criswell of First Baptist Church Dallas, Texas. On Hudgins, see Carolyn Renee Dupont, *Mississippi Praying: Southern White Evangelicals and the Civil Rights Movement, 1945–1975* (New York: New York University Press, 2013), 113–20; and Charles Marsh, *God's Long Summer: Stories of Faith and Civil Rights* (Princeton, NJ: Princeton University Press, 1997), 82–115. Dupont shows how pastors like Hudgins used nonracial rhetoric in ways that allowed their members to uphold racial terror and segregation without the pastors themselves having to use directly racist language. Criswell served as president of the SBC in 1969–1970, immediately preceding FBC Charlotte pastor Carl Bates in the role.

48 Notable among those were Will Campbell, who stayed in consistent trouble with segregationists for his agitation in his home state of Mississippi, and eventually across the South, and Clarence and Florence Jordan, who started Koinonia Farms, an interracial farming commune in the south Georgia town of Americus. Both Campbell and Clarence Jordan were Southern Baptist ministers, as well as relatively prominent authors.

49 For text of the resolution, see *1954 Annual of the Southern Baptist Convention*, p. 55, available at SBHLA and at https://tinyurl.com/3z24s8f6.

50 On response to the SBC's statement and *Brown*, see Dupont, *Mississippi Praying*, 63–79; Marsh, *God's Long Summer*, 98–100. Both selections highlight Rev. Douglas Hudgins of FBC Jackson, Mississippi, whose theological training, like C. C. Warren's, was at Southern Baptist Theological Seminary in Louisville, Kentucky.

51 Interview with Bill Leonard, June 24, 2021.

52 Warren, "This Challenging Hour: 1956 Presidential Address to the Southern Baptist Convention," available in *1956 Proceedings of the Southern Baptist Convention* in SBHLA and at https://tinyurl.com/hyvbv3s2. Bates will be a subject of this work below. His correspondence during his presidency is consistent with the above paragraph. It is filled with equivocation. For every letter chiding him for acceptance of liberals is another chastising him for coddling racists. Nearly every response is a lukewarm encouragement for the writer to maintain their zeal.

53 Warren, "This Challenging Hour," 71. The $334 million figure is not inflation-adjusted. In 2021 dollars, that figure is near $3.6 billion, a staggering amount.

54 Warren, "This Challenging Hour," 72.

55 Warren, "This Challenging Hour," 72.

56 Warren, "This Challenging Hour," 73.

57 Warren, "This Challenging Hour," 74.

58 Interview with Bill Leonard, June 24, 2021. Leonard is regarded as one of the foremost Baptist historians in the country. His work has documented Southern Baptist life extensively, especially during the time period in question through the time of the split of the Southern Baptist Convention in the 1980s, when the conflict between the liberal and conservative wings finally reached its conclusion. Bill J. Leonard, *God's Last and Only Hope: The Fragmentation of the Southern Baptist Convention* (Grand Rapids, MI: Eerdmans, 1990) is one important work for understanding the origins, the drama, and the lasting impact of that conflict.

59 Interview with Bill Leonard, June 24, 2021.

CHAPTER FIVE

1 Warren, "Now Therefore Perform," President's Address to the 1957 Southern Baptist Convention. Published in *Proceedings of the 1957 Southern Baptist Convention*, available at SBLHA and at https://tinyurl.com/mryh7u8n. Quote cited twice on p. 73.

2 Warren, "Now Therefore Perform," 72.

3 Warren, "Now Therefore Perform," 72. Warren seems to have reversed the two phrases from Carey. Carey was active in the late eighteenth through the mid-nineteenth centuries.

4 "Church's Pastor Search Near End," *Charlotte Observer*, May 4, 1959; "Accepts Pastorate at First Church of Charlotte," *Biblical Recorder*, June 13, 1959.

5 "Bates Given Mementos of Decision." *Biblical Recorder*, January 16, 1971; Mike Scott, "Inside History: From Swampy to Swanky, the History of a New Orleans Hotel at Poydras and Baronne," nola.com, November 12, 2019, https://tinyurl.com/ywfym3xm.

6 "The Rev. Carl Elkanah Bates, 85, Former Southern Baptist Leader," *New York Times*, January 10, 2000.

7 Interview with Nancy Kistler, other background interviews.

8 "New First Baptist Pastor, Dr. Bates, Takes Over Post," *Charlotte Observer*, July 18, 1959.

9 "Sawyer Pioneer in Urban Redevelopment Field," *Charlotte Observer*, December 15, 1958. Norfolk was among the first cities in the country to undertake a federally funded Urban Renewal project and had at least six different projects in various stages by 1961, the date at which Charlotte finally commenced demolitions on its first project. According to the University of Richmond's database "Renewing Inequality," by 1966, clearance projects in Norfolk had displaced an estimated 5,194 families, 85 percent of whom were people of color.

10 "Slum Rehabilitation Outlined for City," *Charlotte News*, November 21, 1957.

11 The literature on the Doctrine of Discovery and missionary conquest is voluminous. Some important works include Willie James Jennings, *The Christian Imagination: Theology and the Origins of Race* (New Haven, CT: Yale University Press, 2010); George Tinker, *Missionary Conquest: The Gospel and Native American Cultural Genocide* (Minneapolis: Fortress, 1993); and at a more popular level, Mark Charles and Soong-Chan Rah, *Unsettling Truths: The Ongoing, Dehumanizing Legacy of the Doctrine of Discovery* (Downers Grove, IL: InterVarsity, 2019).

12 Charlotte City Council Minutes Book 37, 334, November 27, 1957; "Council Names Slum Group," *Charlotte Observer*, November 28, 1957.

13 "Chamber Seeks Commission on Urban Renewal," *Charlotte News*, November 26, 1957. Membership included James H. Glenn (chair), Elmer Rouzer (vestryman, Christ Episcopal), Irwin Belk (Myers Park Presbyterian), James A. Malcolm (member, St. Patrick's Catholic), and Claude Q. Freeman (member, Christ Episcopal). As a side note, city council member Martha Evans (member, Myers Park Presbyterian) nominated both a Black member and a white woman for the commission. Other council members did not take her seriously and elected the white men listed above instead.

14 "Brooklyn Area Blight Study," 4. Published by Charlotte-Mecklenburg Planning Commission. A copy is preserved in Fred. D. Alexander Papers, box 40, folder 12. File accessible electronically at https://tinyurl.com/yhrku5rz.

15 Various planning documents and reports are available in the Redevelopment Commission collection and in the Stanford R. Brookshire papers at J. Murrey Atkins Library, University of North Carolina at Charlotte. A variety of them is available in an online collection at https://tinyurl.com/2dhtd5y5.

16 "Brooklyn Area Blight Study," 4.

17 Charlotte City Council, Resolutions Book 3, 445, January 18, 1960.

18 Charlotte City Council Minutes Book 39, 222.

19 Charlotte City Council Minutes Book 39, 216.

20 See, e.g., "Sifford Stands Against Urban Redevelopment," *Charlotte News*, December 13, 1957. Sifford, chair of the local parks commission and member of First Presbyterian Church, was an outspoken critic of Urban Renewal, according to the paper, because his apartment building on East 3rd Street brought him $8,500 a year in profits.

21 See Rothstein, *Color of Law*, 93–99, 115–37.

22 These patterns, as they have become entrenched, are often referred to as a "crescent and wedge" shape, where the southeastern "slice" of the city map, if divided as a pizza, contains extreme concentrations of wealth and the largest concentrations of white residents. Around that wedge sits most of the rest of the city, with far less wealth and containing almost all of the city's nonwhite residents. As of my writing in 2023,

there is some indication those patterns are shifting, but they remain present. Visual representation of data available through maps at https://mcmap.org/qol/.

23 NAACP Branch Department, Geographical File, Charlotte, NC 1960–1965, in Manuscript Division, Library of Congress. Report filed to Charlotte Redevelopment Commission, January 7, 1960. A letter with similar concerns was sent from Alexander to the Housing and Home Finance Administration on April 23, 1956. Letter archived in Kelly Alexander Sr. papers, box 29, folder 25.

24 One particularly tense meeting occurred at Charlotte City Council on December 4, 1961. Several NAACP speakers spoke to the council regarding the lack of housing options available to Black families, even as they were being displaced from Brooklyn. For an accounting of that meeting, see "Public Housing Sought for Negroes," *Charlotte Observer*, December 5, 1961; and Charlotte City Council Minutes Book 41, 183–84, December 4, 1961.

25 The 1960 NAACP report clearly described the problem of constrained supply and high demand, resulting in inflated prices. For national context, see Rothstein, *Color of Law*, 93–99. For a deeper look at the interdependence of public policy and private institutional practices in creating and maintaining housing inequality, see Taylor, *Race for Profit*, 1–54. Importantly, Taylor notes that the differences in housing available to white and Black families were not, as commonly claimed, evidence of two separate housing markets, but "instead, there was a single United States housing market that was defined by its racially discriminatory, tiered access—each tier reinforcing and legitimizing the other." See p. 37.

26 "Public Housing Sought for Negroes."

27 Federal oversight quickly saw Charlotte's inability to provide adequate housing and responded by suspending the city's ability to get the second phase of its project approved without better planning. See "Slum Aid Snagged on Alternate Housing," *Charlotte Observer*, October 9, 1962.

28 FBC Business Meeting records, January 1958–November 1962. The report is dated November 5, 1958; a subsequent report was filed on December 7, 1958. Also see *Church Voice*, April 28, 1960. *Church Voice* was the title of the First Baptist Church of Charlotte's newsletter.

29 "Brooklyn Plan Approved," *Charlotte Observer*, April 26, 1960.

30 *Church Voice*, May 5, 1960.

31 *Church Voice*, May 12, 1960.

32 One interesting coincidence for this work is that Abram North had spent some time working for Cameron Morrison prior to Morrison's governorship from 1921 to 1925. See "Honor Aged Negroes." Morrison's legacy is complex. He was a member of the Red Shirts, a group that worked against the Fusion movement, sometimes violently. He later instituted racially progressive policies on some issues during his time as governor.

33 Second Presbyterian merged with another congregation to form Covenant Presbyterian in the Dilworth neighborhood. Some churches decided to stay, including First Presbyterian Church. In 1951, already sensing the draw of the suburbs to white congregations and their members, Rev. Dr. Charles Kraemer preached a sermon titled "We Do Not Plan to Move." Lois Stickell, *200 Years in the Heart of Charlotte: A History of First Presbyterian Church* (Charlotte, NC: First Presbyterian Church of Charlotte, 2021), 199.

34 Bates letter to Carlyle Marney, August 31, 1960, Carlyle Marney papers, box 8; Bates letter to FBC members, October 24, 1963, in FBC Business Meeting Minutes, December 1962–December 1965.

35 In *The Racial Contract*, Charles Mills speaks of how Black spaces, in white settler conceptions, are sometimes judged to be empty or if not empty, not properly *peopled*: "There is just no one there. Or even if it is conceded that humanoid entities are present, it is denied that any real appropriation, any human shaping of the world, is taking place." Charles Mills, *The Racial Contract* (Ithaca, NY: Cornell University Press, 1997), 49.

36 "Site Problem Facing Church Congregation," *Charlotte Observer*, November 7, 1960. The italics are mine.

37 Saidiya Hartman, *Scenes of Subjection: Terror, Slavery, and Self-Making in Nineteenth-Century America*, revised ed. (New York: W. W. Norton, 2022), 37.

38 Hartman, *Scenes of Subjection*, 38.

39 *One Hundred Years of Working for Christ*, 17.

40 "Site Problem Facing Church Congregation."

41 Charlotte City Council Minutes Book 39, 223, January 25, 1960. See also "Opponents of Urban Redevelopment Give Views," *Charlotte News*, January 19, 1960.

42 *Charlotte Observer*, November 7, 1960.

43 Mecklenburg County Register of Deeds, Book 1547, p. 121; Mecklenburg County Register of Deeds, Book 571, p. 129.

44 "Brooklyn Homes Give Owners High Returns," *Charlotte Observer*, January 11, 1960. As of 2023, the inflation adjustment from 1960 to 2023 is about 10 times, so annual revenue of $210,000 with less than $10,000 in taxes due annually.

45 "City Buys Little Piece of Brooklyn," *Charlotte Observer*, August 11, 1960.

46 Hanchett points out the discrepancy in appraisal in "Bathrooms, Building Codes, and 'Slum Clearance,'" an unpublished work provided to the author. Whether the pattern established in the two above transactions continued is extremely likely, but that data is a bit unclear. Deeds for a short period in the late 1950s through the early 1970s obscured transaction values, making data hard to track without other sources. It is right to assume that such inequality was persistent without evidence to the contrary. According to Vernon Sawyer, in a 2004 interview, Lee Kinney was one of the negotiators who bargained with homeowners on behalf of the Redevelopment Commission! Interview at https://tinyurl.com/8zk55cvf. It is important to note that valuing Black property less than white property is a common feature of real estate practice in the United States. That Hazeline North Anderson received far less money for her property is unjust, but it is not unusual. For explorations of this history and practice, see Lipsitz, *How Racism Takes Place*; Mills, *The Racial Contract*, 41–62; Sheryll Cashin, *White Space, Black Hood: Opportunity Hoarding and Segregation in the Age of Inequality* (Boston: Beacon, 2021), 38–73. Cashin reminds readers of one way the phenomenon persists as common sense in real estate markets. In 2019, then-president Donald Trump announced a HUD policy change by tweeting, "I am happy to inform all of the people living their Suburban Lifestyle Dream that you will no longer be bothered or financially hurt by having low income housing built in your neighborhood." Cited in Cashin, 69. Trump's appeal, stated as the "common sense" of the real estate market, is that the presence of poor people devalues real estate. Given both US history and Trump's personal history of both housing discrimination and

making racist statements, it is easy to conclude that the term "low income" is working as a marker for both race and economic status.

47 The Andersons' relocation will be covered in chapter 8.

48 There is a secondary story of those who did fight the appraisals of their property, most of them white, and the one particular lawyer whose young career developed around fighting eminent domain cases, Henry Harkey. Harkey had a personal stake as he was a significant landowner in Brooklyn. He worked on behalf of clients against seizure by eminent domain or for higher payouts to those whose property was seized. In the case of Urban Renewal projects, most of those were white landowners, not only because most landowners were white but also because Black landowners were far less likely to have the resources and time to hire a lawyer, given the necessities of moving and reestablishing themselves in new communities. Of interest to this study, Harkey was a member of Myers Park Presbyterian Church. See "Brooklyn Homes Give Owners High Returns"; "Henry Lee Harkey, Lawyer, Dies," *Charlotte Observer,* January 7, 1989; "Resolution and Memorial in Honor of Henry Lee Harkey," in archives of Mecklenburg Bar Association and available at https://tinyurl.com/yz9hcbp2.

CHAPTER SIX

1 The quote is from George D. Younger, *The Church and Urban Renewal* (New York: J. B. Lippincott, 1965), 27. The other criteria included, in Packer's words, "adequate local codes and ordinances for buildings, plumbing, electrical installations, and housing; a comprehensive community plan; effective administrative organization; and sufficient financing." Among these, notably, Charlotte had been at the forefront of adopting a municipal housing code, though its enforcement, or lack thereof, led to deplorable conditions in numerous places. See also Scott Greer, *Urban Renewal and American Cities: The Dilemma of Democratic Intervention* (Indianapolis: Bobbs-Merrill, 1965), 35–64; Mark I. Gelfand, *A Nation of Cities: The Federal Government and Urban America, 1933–1965* (New York: Oxford University Press, 1975), 173–94; and Hanchett, "Bathrooms, Building Codes, and 'Slum Clearance.'"

2 Federal funds were temporarily suspended in 1962 over the issue of providing adequate housing. The Redevelopment Commission was forced to rework their planning in order to access any further funds or to have the next phases of the Brooklyn project approved.

3 Roster dated July 18, 1961, in Stanford R. Brookshire Papers, MS 40, box 2, folder 5. For Grier identified as a major landowner in Brooklyn, see "Brooklyn Homes Give Owners High Returns."

4 Letter from Walter Keyes of Housing and Home Finance Agency, dated July 26, 1961, in Brookshire Papers, MS 40, box 2, folder 5.

5 Letter from HHFA dated August 15, 1961; letter from Brookshire to HHFA dated August 17, 1961, both in Brookshire Papers, MS 40, box 2, folder 5. I was unable to locate congregational affiliation for Brown and Bivins.

6 Strawn eventually served for nearly two dozen years on the board of Charlotte Housing Authority (CHA). CHA named a public housing complex in the cleared area of the Dilworth Urban Renewal project for Strawn. See "Mr. Zeb C. Strawn" obituary in *Charlotte Observer,* May 1, 1987.

7 "More Skills Urged for Negroes," *Charlotte Observer*, February 8, 1963.

8 See Crisler's report to Strawn, dated December 10, 1962, in Brookshire Papers, MS 40, box 2, folder 5; Charlotte City Council Minutes Book 42, 259–66, October 15, 1962; on the Charlotte program's suspension and subsequent adoption of new public housing programs, see "Slum Aid Snagged on Alternate Housing," *Charlotte Observer*, October 9, 1962; "Urban Renewal Plan Is in Real Trouble," *Charlotte Observer*, October 11, 1962; and "Mayor to Propose New Public Housing," *Charlotte Observer*, October 13, 1962.

9 An agenda and several attachments from the meeting are in Brookshire Papers, MS 40, box 2, folder 5. Former iterations of the committee appear not to have met or been active.

10 From an undated paper called "Redevelopment in Charlotte," published by the Redevelopment Commission. Avery Hood Papers, MS 399, box 2. Note that the goal quoted above is not a bad one, but it is also a far distance from what Renewal projects actually did.

11 Both quotes from attachments to August 7, 1962, meeting agenda in Brookshire Papers, MS 40, box 2, folder 5.

12 McNeill provided semi-annual reports of his subcommittee's work to Brookshire and CCUR chair Zeb Strawn. The extant reports are located in Stanford R. Brookshire Papers, MS 41, box 2 of 6, folder 2:5. I will cite them in the following as "McNeill Report," followed by date and page number. This citation from McNeill Report, December 26, 1962, 1.

13 McNeill Report, December 26, 1962, 2. Today the Cordelia neighborhood uses the name Villa Heights.

14 McNeill Report, December 26, 1962, 5.

15 "Youth Corps Gives Boy Job, Money, New Outlook," *Charlotte Observer*, August 11, 1966.

16 See Hanchett, *Sorting Out*, 54–67, for more on the development of Dilworth.

17 The 1964 yearbook of the Dilworth Rotary Club is in the archives at Dilworth United Methodist Church. Each member, including McNeill, has a full page of biographical information. Of note for this study, the most common church membership in the club by far is Myers Park Baptist, also McNeill's congregation.

18 McNeill Report, December 26, 1962, 5–6.

19 McNeill Report, December 26, 1962, 6.

20 McNeill Report, December 26, 1962, 6.

21 McNeill Report, December 26, 1962, 6.

22 McNeill Report, December 26, 1962, 6.

23 McNeill letter dated April 15, 1963, in Brookshire Papers, MS 41, box 2 of 6, folder 2:5. The capital letters are McNeill's.

24 McNeill letter, April 15, 1963; Martin Luther King Jr., *A Testament of Hope: The Essential Writings and Speeches of Martin Luther King, Jr.*, ed. James M. Washington (New York: HarperCollins, 1986), 299, 295.

25 McClernon letter to Rouzer, November 19, 1962, in archive of Myers Park Baptist Church, folder 1962.

26 In fact, McClernon's sentence quoted above is copied directly from the piece by Lyle Schaller, "Urban Renewal: A Moral Challenge," *Christian Century*, June 27, 1962. All

quotes through the end of current paragraph are from that article. Schaller was trained in urban planning but went on to become an ordained minister and a wildly successful church consultant. A 1989 poll cited Schaller as the most influential Christian in the country, ahead of Billy Graham and popular priest and writer Henri Nouwen. See "Church-Growth Analyst Leads in Survey of Influential Figures," *Los Angeles Times*, November 25, 1989; "Rev. Lyle E. Schaller Dies at 91," *New York Times*, March 26, 2015.

27 Mark Wild, "Liberal Protestants and Urban Renewal," *Religion and American Culture: A Journal of Interpretation* 25, no. 1 (Winter 2015): 110. Wild is perhaps the only historian who has written at length about the Renewalists. For a book-length treatment, see Mark Wild, *Renewal: Liberal Protestants and the American City after World War II* (Chicago: University of Chicago Press, 2019).

28 From a report in the National Council of Churches archive, quoted in Mark Wild, "Liberal Protestants and Urban Renewal," 110–46.

29 McNeill Report, June 19, 1963, 1.

30 McNeill Report, December 26, 1962, 4, 6–7. The television appearances were primarily on Charlotte station WSOC. Their archives only date back to the mid-'70s, so those recordings appear to be lost, and no transcript is known.

31 McNeill Report, June 19, 1963; McNeill Report, December 19, 1963.

32 Among those are "Elderly Can Help Fight Slums, Minister Says," *Charlotte Observer*, July 17, 1964; "City 'Litter Squad' Holds Pep Rally," *Charlotte Observer*, November 11, 1964; and "Grier Heights Bugged on Litter," *Charlotte Observer*, December 25, 1967.

33 *Charlotte News*, August 10, 1963.

34 "Youth Corps Gives Boy Job, Money, New Outlook."

35 "Youth Corps Gives Boy Job, Money, New Outlook." The archives contain several undated flyers that were distributed around neighborhoods, including Brooklyn, advertising these projects. See Brookshire Papers, MS 40, box 2, folder 6.

36 "Mayor Urges Home Fix-Up," *Charlotte Observer*, March 27, 1964.

37 "Hildebrandt Legacy of Giving and an Honest Word," *News of Orange County*, February 28, 2015, https://tinyurl.com/49tyartk.

38 "Community Improvement Is Sought," *Charlotte Observer*, July 19, 1963; "Cleaning Up the Queen's Domain," *Charlotte News*, August 10, 1963.

39 For further reflection on how American housing markets, under the rules of capitalism, create artificial scarcity that inevitably results in substandard housing for those who are poor, see David Madden and Peter Marcuse, *In Defense of Housing* (New York: Verso, 2016).

40 McNeill Report, December 19, 1963, 6.

41 "'War on Slums'—Minister; 'Profit Vital'—Landlord," *Charlotte Observer*, January 20, 1964.

42 "Mayor Urges Home Fix-Up."

43 "Mayor Urges Home Fix-Up."

44 Hildebrandt appears in several other reports in the *Charlotte Observer*, including "Improvers Compare Notes," November 27, 1963; "Community Anti-Blight Meeting Set," April 28, 1964; and "Elderly Can Help Fight Slums, Minister Says," July 17, 1964.

45 The text of Hildebrandt's speech is in the Stanford R. Brookshire Papers, MS 41, box 2 of 6, folder 2:5.

46 Stanford R. Brookshire Papers, MS 41, box 2 of 6, folder 2:5.

47 Letter from Strawn to Brookshire, dated January 30, 1964, in Brookshire Papers, MS 41, box 2 of 6, folder 2:5.

48 "People Want a New Look," *Charlotte Observer*, April 12, 1964.

49 "People Want a New Look."

50 McNeill Report, December 19, 1963, 6.

51 In a recorded interview, architect Tebee Hawkins, a member of Myers Park Baptist and a part of the architectural firm that designed the sanctuary, recounts the acquisition of the walnut trees by the head architect, who was based in Philadelphia. The interview is available at https://tinyurl.com/2j3azxdw. The sanctuary was completed in 1952. For more detail on the sanctuary and its construction, see Marion Ellis, *By a Dream Possessed: Myers Park Baptist Church* (Charlotte, NC: Myers Park Baptist Church, 1997), 40–45.

52 Luke 4:20–21.

53 Citizens' Committee resolution dated December 17, 1965, in Brookshire Papers, MS 41, box 2, folder 2:6.

CHAPTER SEVEN

1 My interview with Ken Poe, February 4, 2021, provided the basis for this scene.

2 See, e.g., Rothstein, *Color of Law*, 177–94; Jackson, *Crabgrass Frontier*, 190–218, 231–45.

3 Hanchett, *Sorting Out*, 241–45; Hanchett, "US Tax Policy and the Shopping Center Boom of the 1950s and 1960s," *American Historical Review* 101 (October 1996): 1082–110; Norman B. Ture, *Accelerated Depreciation in the United States, 1954–1960* (New York: National Bureau of Economic Research, 1967); Jackson, *Crabgrass Frontier*, 231–71. Hanchett, in the pages cited, succinctly shows the underappreciated role that federal tax policy known as *accelerated depreciation* played in giving rise to the suburban strip mall. This policy changed the development industry by making new construction much more profitable than renovating older buildings. It did this by allowing building owners to write off depreciation of a long-term asset in as little as seven years. This essentially turned new commercial development into tax shelters, allowing investors to build new, avoid taxes through accelerated depreciation, and then sell once they had fully depreciated a property. They would then move on to the next project. Hidden policies like this have had a profound effect on the American landscape, but their role remains mostly unknown. In this case, they encouraged further sprawl by making urban areas less and less attractive to builders, not because of location or condition but because of tax policy.

4 Steering, whereby agents showed homes to Black clients only in Black neighborhoods and white clients only in white ones, was a common practice in real estate, and in some accounts still is, though now with more subtlety ("The schools here are / are not very desirable"). Prior to 1950, the National Association of Real Estate Boards included in their ethical code the duty of real estate agents never to introduce into a neighborhood "members of any race or nationality, or any individual whose presence will clearly be detrimental to property values in the neighborhood." Though the ethical code changed in 1950 to remove such racist language, the practice remained. See Kruse, *White Flight*, 60–61; Rothstein, *Color of Law*, vii–viii.

5 This theme in Poe's life is part of the enormously impactful school desegregation debates, which Poe presided over as chair of the school board during the late 1960s and early 1970s. For an in-depth history of the story and Poe's impact in both resistance to busing and then full-throated acceptance of it following the board's defeat in the US Supreme Court, see Frye Gaillard, *The Dream Long Deferred: The Landmark Struggle for Desegregation in Charlotte, NC*, 3rd ed. (Columbia, SC: University of South Carolina Press, 2006), where Poe is a primary character. For a look at how Poe and the desegregation of Charlotte schools shaped suburban politics nationally, see Matthew Lassiter, *The Silent Majority: Suburban Politics in the Sunbelt South* (Princeton, NJ: Princeton University Press, 2006), 119–221.

6 These three letters have been preserved in the business meeting records at First Baptist Church. They are in a bound collection of minutes labeled "December 1962–December 1965." I will refer to the three letters in the material to follow as "Bates Letter," "Hope Letter," and "Poe Letter," plus date and page number. Regarding the Poe letter, it alone of the three is signed by multiple people, and there is every reason to think that it came from multiple people. However, the full record indicates that Poe was first among equals here and likely the loudest of the voices present. In recognition of his significant role within the congregation's leadership, I will refer to that letter as his, with knowledge that there were also other voices behind it.

7 Hope letter, October 24, 1963, 4; Bates letter, October 24, 1963, 2.

8 Hope letter, 1.

9 Hope letter, 4.

10 Bates letter, 1.

11 The obvious reason for this is that a pastor of any church, at such an early point in their tenure, would not have the political capital to support such a drastic move. This was especially true for Bates, who had already made a number of members angry by firing a beloved and long-tenured church musician just as Bates was beginning his ministry at FBC. The members who disagreed took quite a while to warm up to Bates in the aftermath of that staffing change. This incident reported in group interview with FBC members, August 25, 2021.

12 What Bates means by "the many facets of our situation" is unclear. The appeal to providence is a consistent theme that runs throughout this study and raises complex theological issues. Appeals to providence can be used to justify obvious power moves, distracting from hegemony by making God the primary subject of an action rather than the political actors and systems governing a place. At other times, though, appeals to providence help Christians make sense of good results that come from difficult circumstances. One can hear such appeals, for instance, at Friendship Baptist (now Friendship Missionary Baptist), where God is cited as having worked unexplainable good out of a situation of oppression. That both Friendship and FBC appeal to providence to help make sense of a period where they stand on opposite sides of both the process and the result highlights the complexity, and the precarity, of the idea. For a lengthy study of the doctrine of providence and the structures of race in the United States, see Matt R. Jantzen, *God, Race, and History: Liberating Providence* (Lanham, MD: Lexington Books, 2021).

13 Readers familiar with the Charlotte area will note that several features of the built environment have the name "Providence," especially Providence Road, which runs through Charlotte's most well-heeled neighborhoods. For clarity, readers should

note that my discussions of providence are always theological and not in relation to specific roads or neighborhoods in Charlotte. Any exceptions will be noted clearly in the text.

14 Bates letter, 2.

15 Num 13:27. The story cited from Numbers will become quite important later in the narrative, when Bates not only implies the story but preaches directly from it regarding FBC's movement of location.

16 Jennings, *The Christian Imagination*, 93; Jantzen, *God, Race, and History*, 17. In plain terms, a doctrine of providence seeks to resolve the question "Who's in charge here?" For Christians, the simple answer is that God is ultimately in charge. The doctrine helps to negotiate the difficulty of understanding the sufferings and injustices of the world while still affirming the goodness and control of God in the universe. In the hands of hegemonic power, providence becomes a horror, an uncritical justification for political and economic domination. For more on this, see Jantzen, *God, Race, and History*; Jennings, *The Christian Imagination*.

17 Brueggemann offers a helpful synthesis of the rhetorical issues in the "land of promise," a dominant theme of the Pentateuch and really of the entirety of the Bible: "The traditions of *land promise* and *land violence* (twin claims that are decisive for the tradition and cannot be separated out) are not given us in the final form of the text as reportage. Rather, the final form of the text is completely removed from what may have been the 'happening' of land, and now function as a belated ideological rationale for the subsequent community of Israel. Thus, even though the land promises in the tradition are in purportedly old traditions, they are now to be completely understood in terms of subsequent ideological claims of important use to a later interpretive community." Walter Brueggemann, *The Land: Place as Gift, Promise, and Challenge in Biblical Faith*, 2nd ed. (Minneapolis: Fortress, 2002), xiv. A survey of postcolonial readings of the Pentateuch will be helpful in clarifying ongoing issues with the ideology of land promise, particular in the context of white congregations. There is a wide body of such literature. One such study referenced below is Pekka Pitkanen, *A Commentary on Numbers: Narrative, Ritual, and Colonialism* (London: Routledge, 2018); Brueggemann also helpfully points out that Deuteronomy is "insistent and repetitious in its connection between *land possession* and *Torah obedience*." Torah issues important constraints that have failed to chasten settler-colonialism by white Christians in the current age. See Brueggemann, *The Land*, xvi.

18 Jantzen, *God, Race, and History*, 17.

19 Bates letter, 2.

20 Kenneth Jackson observes that US culture and its visions of the good life were in fact deeply influenced by television, which during the period discussed here had started showing suburban life with a nuclear family as the dominant norm. Even the popular program *I Love Lucy*, which started its run based in Lucy and Desi's urban apartment, switched settings to a single-family detached suburban home, reflective of this cultural emphasis. See Jackson, *Crabgrass Frontier*, 278–82.

21 See chapter 3 on Rev. C. C. Warren and the Southern Baptist strategy for handling the civil rights era with a focus on growth and construction.

22 Carolyn Renee Dupont shows clearly how Southern ministers negotiated racial politics by coded language and strategic silence on racial issues. She uses the example of Douglas Hudgins, pastor of First Baptist Church in Jackson, Mississippi. A similar

dynamic is at play here with Bates and FBC Charlotte. See *Mississippi Praying*, 113–20. See also Marsh, *God's Long Summer*, 82–115.

23 Bates's words here prefigured what Enns and Myers call "personal dissociation" as a strategy for maintaining an individual or a group's innocence in histories of oppression. Personal dissociation is one "move to innocence" that creates an individual or individuals who are "unaccountable to a history which is not 'my fault'; disinterested in how I continue to benefit from historic arrangements in the present; and concerned chiefly with my personal future." See Enns and Myers, *Healing Haunted Histories*, 214–15. Enns and Myers are drawing on Eve Tuck and K. Wayne Yang, "Decolonization Is Not a Metaphor," *Decolonization* 1, no. 1 (2012): 9–28. Such moves are the subject of chapter 11.

24 Winter was among the Renewalists mentioned above in chapter 4. His *The Suburban Captivity of the Churches: An Analysis of Protestant Responsibility in the Expanding Metropolis* (Garden City, NY: Doubleday, 1961) is a book-length study on churches dealing with changing urban geography in their ministries.

25 Bates letter, 2.

26 The other signers of the letter were R. M. Alexander (Rod), W. B. Cummings, Mrs. F. W. Newman, and Carl C. Wagner. Locating the first names of the women in this study has sometimes been challenging due to the conventions of the day. Occasionally I have failed to find those names, as in the case of Mrs. Newman. My apologies to her and to the reader.

27 Poe letter, October 23, 1963, 1.

28 Poe letter, 2.

29 Interviews with Ken Poe, Kistler, and FBC history group.

30 Those interviewees actually claimed that FBC had members from *every* high school, a claim that is obviously untrue given the segregated school system and the segregated nature of FBC. But within the racialized world where FBC members circulated, the claim of their geographical dispersion being joined together at the church probably is true. Interviews with Ken Poe, Ebbie Bailey, and the FBC history group.

31 Poe letter, 2.

32 My interview with Ebbie Bailey had an unusual moment when I raised the term *class* in a question for her about the divisions in the church. She gently chastised me—"Don't use that word!"—in a moment that seemed quite uncomfortable for her. She was willing to acknowledge economic differences but thought they should not be discussed openly. This moment struck me as further evidence of how a silencing specter still worked in the congregation and its members. Silence about economic differences, or at least a refusal to attach language to economic differences, would not resolve the material gaps among households. But it would preserve a sense of innocence for those of means, especially those who had achieved great economic success and might be seen as traitors to their working-class roots. Additionally, the Bates letter cited in the section above contains this interesting section: "My heart cries out when I hear reference made to 'classes' of people." Clearly, rhetoric about class was operating within the congregation, and not everyone was comfortable with it.

33 "This Is Joe . . . One of Thousands Indebted to City Rescue Mission," *Charlotte Observer*, April 23, 1960.

34 Poe letter, 2.

35 *Church Voice*, May 24, 1962. The context of this statement was referring to segregation. Bates saw the issue not as a matter of policy or governance but as hatred or contempt within an individual's heart. In that same letter, he went on to further cite alcohol consumption as a major issue, again framed in terms of individual consumption.

36 Poe letter, 3.

37 Greater Mt. Sinai Baptist was later displaced by the Urban Renewal-funded Northwest Expressway project. First Baptist Church-West (the current name) was displaced by the Belk Freeway project in 1977, despite the fact that the freeway was not built directly onto their site.

38 Ibram X. Kendi's work builds out the notion of racist ideas or policies or actions, using the word *racist* as a descriptor for those things that produce racially differentiated outcomes. Kendi's history of racist ideas is a deeply important work in understanding the origins of various forms of racism that persist in American society today. See Ibram X. Kendi, *Stamped from the Beginning: The Definitive History of Racist Ideas in America* (New York: Nation Books, 2016); and Ibram X. Kendi, *How to Be an Antiracist* (New York: One World, 2019).

39 "Church Buys Building Lot," *Charlotte Observer*, May 15, 1961.

40 "Brooklyn Church Gets New-Home Cash," *Charlotte Observer*, September 3, 1961.

41 I was told that the check was indeed quite small, but I was unable to confirm its amount. Letter from Brookshire to Friendship reprinted in Friendship's 1963 program commemorating the history of the church and the closing of the Brooklyn location. Accessed through archives at Friendship Missionary Baptist Church and by FMBC member/historian Brenda Porter-Dewitt.

42 *Church Voice*, October 17, 1963.

43 FBC business meeting minutes, October 27, 1963. C. C. Hope obviously was not a Charlotte city bus rider.

44 FBC business meeting minutes, October 27, 1963.

45 "First Baptist Church Will Stay Downtown," *Charlotte Observer*, October 28, 1963. That quote reads more clearly as "The downtown church is a mix of all classes and types."

46 FBC business meeting minutes, October 27, 1963.

47 FBC business meeting minutes, October 27, 1963.

48 FBC business meeting minutes, October 27, 1963.

49 FBC business meeting minutes, October 27, 1963.

50 FBC's documentation indicates that during Bates's and Warren's tenures, the pastor served as the moderator of business meetings. That practice is a little unusual but not unheard of.

51 FBC business meeting minutes, October 27, 1963.

52 FBC business meeting minutes, October 27, 1963.

53 Bates letter.

54 "Charlotte First Votes to Stay Downtown," *Biblical Recorder*, November 9, 1963.

55 Interview with Ebbie Bailey.

56 "Future Program Report Rejected," *Church Voice*, October 31, 1963.

57 Crowe, *Biography of a Thriving Church*, 60–67.

58 "Future Program Report Rejected."

59 Jackson, *Crabgrass Frontier*. Jackson's work is referenced throughout this study. It remains one of the more important accounts of the suburbanization of the country, even forty years after its publication.

60 Among the ideas that I persistently heard while interviewing subjects for this work was the relation of parking to the planning and razing of Brooklyn. Representatives of several Black churches told me something like this: "We were told that churches would not be able to remain because we didn't have sufficient parking to match the new plans for the area." I could not confirm that exact messaging, but it comports with what happened in the area in the aftermath of Urban Renewal. Most, if not all, construction there until about 2000 was surrounded by several acres of surface parking.

61 Kruse, *White Flight*, 234–58; Rothstein, *Color of Law*, 93–99; Lipsitz, *How Racism Takes Place*, 26–28; Taylor, *Race for Profit*, 25–54; Hanchett, *Sorting Out*, 206–56.

62 See, e.g., Jesse Curtis, *The Myth of Colorblind Christians: Evangelicals and White Supremacy in the Civil Rights Era* (New York: New York University Press, 2021); Marsh, *God's Long Summer*; Dupont, *Mississippi Praying*.

63 Kenneth Jackson says of the ongoing architectural changes in cities and suburbs, "With increased use of automobiles, the life of the sidewalk has largely disappeared, and the social intercourse that used to be the main characteristic of urban life has vanished. Residential neighborhoods have become a mass of small, private islands; with the backyard functioning as a wholesome, family-oriented, and reclusive place." See *Crabgrass Frontier*, 279–80.

64 Jackson, *Crabgrass Frontier*, 281; Rachel Krantz-Kent, "Television, Capturing America's Attention at Prime Time and Beyond," *Beyond the Numbers* 7, no. 14 (September 2018), United States Bureau of Labor Statistics, https://www.bls.gov/opub /btn/volume-7/television-capturing-americas-attention.htm.

65 Jackson, *Crabgrass Frontier*, 282.

66 This language is characteristic of white evangelicals in particular, but it is still common in churches across many denominations and theological convictions despite the fact that is never appears in the Bible.

67 "Preacher-Graphics," *Church Voice*, May 24, 1962. Note here the theme of alcohol, a regular appeal used in maintaining segregation and lower-caste status for Black people going back to Reconstruction-era politics. See chapter 2 of this work for further detail on that context. For more on alcohol and the ways in which prohibition and temperance efforts had a long life in battles over white supremacy and individualized moral purity, see Greenwood, *Bittersweet Legacy*, 78–110. On the battles over liquor by the drink in Mecklenburg County, waged with Baptists, including FBC's Allen Bailey, at the forefront of resistance to liberalized alcohol service, see Charles Clifton McShane, "Class, Christ, and Cocktails: The Clash of Business Boosterism and Southern Baptism in Charlotte, North Carolina, 1965–1980" (Master's thesis, University of North Carolina at Charlotte, 2011); and Chuck McShane, "How Charlotte Got Liquored Up," *Charlotte Magazine*, October 24, 2017, https://tinyurl.com/cs9vy7yv. Jesse Curtis also raises the issue of individualized sin as a response by evangelicals to social issues in his insightful introduction to *Myth of Colorblind Christians*, 1–10.

68 Interview with David Reule.

69 Mostly but not completely. The remarkable story of Dorothy Counts and her attempts to desegregate Harding High School in 1957 attracted global attention.

70 One key organizer of protests in Charlotte was Dr. Reginald Hawkins, a dentist and Presbyterian minister. "We shall not be pacified with gradualism; we shall not

be satisfied with tokenism," he said. His public speeches and actions got results for the movement in Charlotte. Hawkins is not adequately remembered locally. On the marches he organized that led to the desegregation of many public facilities in Charlotte, see "Smith Students March in Protest," *Charlotte News*, May 21, 1963; "Charlotte Negroes March in First Protest since August," *Charlotte Observer*, May 21, 1963. Importantly, the march referenced in these articles took place on the anniversary of the Mecklenburg Declaration of Independence, a legendary—and perhaps fabulist!—document signed May 20, 1775, a full year before the national Declaration of Independence, declaring colonists' freedom from British rule. On Hawkins, also see "The Militant Dentist," a profile by Charlotte journalist Emiene Wright, *Creative Loafing Charlotte*, February 6, 2013, available at https://tinyurl.com/5st9seba.

71 Charles Jones, Charlotte resident and local leader of the student movement in the 1960s, told the story of a group of students dressed in their Sunday best showing up at one of the "First Church" sanctuaries downtown, though he would not say of which denomination. A deacon greeted the students at the door and asked them their business. "We came to church this morning," Jones said. The deacon, blocking the door with his body, asked, "And who invited you?" Jones responded, "Jesus Christ did, but I guess he ain't here." And he and the students left.

72 *Church Voice*, April 21, 1960. The question of whether Kennedy, or any Catholic, could serve as president was a common question in Protestant circles around the country. The issue was typically framed as one of allegiance, asking whether a Catholic's ultimate allegiance would be to the state or to the church.

73 *Church Voice*, February 21, 1963.

74 *Church Voice*, December 5, 1963.

75 *Church Voice*, July 18, 1963.

76 From "Rejoice," an unpublished paper written by FBC member Nancy Kistler and provided to the author from Ms. Kistler's private collection. Quotes from p. 8 and p. 6, respectively.

77 Dupont, *Mississippi Praying*, 113. Dupont's account of the ministry of Douglas Hudgins, pastor of First Baptist Church Jackson, Mississippi, is quite helpful for understanding the theo-politics of segregation inside white churches at the time and especially for influential SBC pastors like his contemporary Carl Bates. Though Bates and Hudgins were different in many ways, there are moments when their writings and public statements are nearly verbatim. This is especially true around the consumption of alcohol, always a convenient strategy for Southern Baptists hoping to distract from their complicity in white supremacy. See Dupont's work on Hudgins in *Mississippi Praying*, 105–20.

78 Interview with Bill Leonard, June 24, 2021. King's famous letter was written as a response to an open letter from white clergymen in Birmingham to King. They asked King to be patient and not to be divisive. King's response remains one of the most important essays in American letters.

79 Luther King Jr., *A Testament of Hope*, 299.

80 Jennings, *The Christian Imagination*, 233. For a broader context of this idea in Jennings, see *The Christian Imagination*, 207–49; and Willie James Jennings, "To Be a Christian Intellectual," *Fuller*, 4. Available online at https://tinyurl.com/m8usy2hz and in W. Benjamin Boswell, *Confronting Whiteness: A Spiritual Journey of Reflection, Conversation, and Transformation* (Nashville: Upper Room Books, 2022), 199–203.

81 Principality, in Christian theology, is a power or order that stands opposed to God. On whiteness as a principality, see Jennings, "To Be a Christian Intellectual."

CHAPTER EIGHT

1 State statute is North Carolina GS 160A Article 22. The criteria were initially very strict and were gradually loosened to allow cities to more easily take control of neighborhoods. See chapter 3.

2 "Lonely," *Charlotte Observer*, February 5, 1964. The *Observer* photo archives have been a rich but unreliable source of photo documentation. The entire year 1964 has been deemed lost. Online newspaper archives can give a glimpse of photos like the one described but not in high enough resolution to reprint here.

3 "First Baptist Considering Move to Brooklyn Site," *Charlotte Observer*, June 29, 1964. The potential move to Brooklyn was also mentioned in *Church Voice*, June 25, 1964, but not in any detail.

4 "First Baptist May Move to Brooklyn," *Charlotte Observer*, February 1, 1965.

5 Willie James Jennings, "Can White People Be Saved?" in *Can "White" People Be Saved? Triangulating Race, Theology, and Mission*, ed. Love L. Sechrest, Johnny Ramirez-Johnson, and Amos Young (Downers Grove, IL: IVP Academic, 2018), 29.

6 *Charlotte Observer*, September 22, 1912.

7 Ps 137.

8 "First Baptist Relocation Plans Nearer to Reality," *Charlotte Observer*, February 12, 1965.

9 "Brooklyn Tract Shoved in First Baptist's Direction," *Charlotte Observer*, February 18, 1965.

10 Mecklenburg County Register of Deeds, Book 2918, 404–6. The 1951 Sanborn appears to show even more lots that would have become, in part, portioned into the current FBC land. The matter is confused by the changes the city made in the street grid when they eliminated much of both 1st and 2nd Streets and curved them into a new street called 2nd, now Martin Luther King Jr. Blvd. The adjustment of the street right-of-way makes specific boundaries unclear.

11 "Brooklyn Church Gets New-Home Cash."

12 The RC's use of lot size as a tool of exclusion was not lost on Black residents as it was happening. See, e.g., "Some Would Remain but Are Forced Out," *Charlotte Observer*, April 18, 1965.

13 For one exploration of the missionary fervor of Manifest Destiny and its fusion with Christian mission, see Enns and Myers, *Healing Haunted Histories*, 132–41.

14 A variety of those planning publications is available through J. Murrey Atkins Library, University of North Caroline at Charlotte. One collection of twentieth-century plans is collected under the title "Living Charlotte: The Postwar Development of a New South City," available online at https://tinyurl.com/bdzm37un.

15 Hilary Ballon and Kenneth T. Jackson, *Robert Moses and the Modern City: The Transformation of New York* (New York: W. W. Norton, 2007), 98–99.

16 "Chamber Asks Bid Rejection," *Charlotte Observer*, April 7, 1965; "Brooklyn—Who Is to Build What?" *Charlotte Observer*, April 8, 1965. The two winning bids from those car dealerships became a minor subplot unto itself. City Council and the RC spoke

publicly against the acceptance of the winning bids by the auto dealers on the grounds that two new potential bidders had been located, one in theory and the other with a bid that arrived twenty minutes late, and that car lots did not fit with the city's plan and purpose in the Urban Renewal program. The Chamber of Commerce weighed in strongly, with one member lamenting, "We're going to all this trouble (to clear the Brooklyn slums) and then we're going to fill it up with used cars and little shacks." The commission pondered going to the state to seek legal changes to help it deny the winning bids. That idea was short-lived, though, and the RC eventually approved the bids. Notably, the attorney for both car dealers was FBC member Bill Poe. In pressing the dealers' claims and disputing the RC's claim to deny based on their desired plans for the site, he asked, "Who is to say which has the greater public interest?" Both the *Charlotte Observer* and the *Charlotte News* contain multiple reports and editorials regarding the discussion, dated beginning March 31, 1965, through April 15, 1965. Charlotte City Council minutes from April 20, 1965 (book 45, 288) show a resolution approving the sale of the lots in question but record no public discussion.

17 "Brooklyn Tract Shoved in First Baptist's Direction."

18 "Church to Discuss Moving," *Church Voice*, February 18, 1965.

19 "First Baptist Feels 'Unity' in Relocation," *Charlotte Observer*, February 22, 1965.

20 "Church to Vote on Proposed Site," *Church Voice*, February 25, 1965; "First Baptist Feels 'Unity' in Relocation." The hymn, which Bates cited as the closing hymn that day, is "Lead On, O King Eternal," lyrics written by Ernest W. Shurtleff in 1887.

21 *Church Voice*, February 25, 1965.

22 *Church Voice*, February 25, 1965.

23 FBC business meeting minutes, February 28, 1965, 147-E, 147-F. I've offered this image and another like it, with Bill Poe and his children (see above, chapter 5), that require some reflection on parenting in white families and the spiritual formation of children racialized as white. I also conducted several hours of interviews with other people raised at FBC who decided to remove their participation in this project. In each of their stories, adults holding significant power demurred when faced with the opportunity to offer significant moral guidance to their children about a key issue. On the surface, the decisions those adults made were acts of trust in their children and in what they would have labeled as the work of the Holy Spirit in and through their children.

But given the racial and political strategies of the day, other influences were operating within the decisions of influential adults. Indeed, one of the primary strategies of whiteness, as Charles Mills has shown, is an "epistemology of ignorance," that is to say, a strategy of not knowing (see chapter 9 for more on this). Perhaps the most direct way of stating that is that the most innocent-appearing method for passing along race-based supremacy without having it challenged is by asking children to remain childish. Rather than instructing them about moral complexity—which opens the possibility of a challenge to white domination—white parents commonly avoid such discussions at all. Such strategy in white households and institutions maintains an image of innocence or the simplistic application of the doctrine of providence. The result of this insistence on innocence is the reproduction of the moral infancy that whiteness relies on to achieve widespread destruction at the hands of innocent and ignorant people. See Mills, *The Racial Contract*. One popular-level volume that offers more perspective on Mills's insights is Crystal M. Fleming, *How to Be Less*

Stupid about Race: On Racism, White Supremacy, and the Racial Divide (Boston: Beacon, 2018).

24 FBC business meeting minutes, February 28, 1965, 147-A. The selection read aloud was Num 13:21–33, which is printed in the back of this book and is analyzed in the text below. The record of the day uses the title "We Are Well Able," which appears to be the title of Bates's sermon for the day. The previous midweek newsletter confirms this. Bates's sermons appear to have been mostly extemporaneous, according to his family, and no known file of those he wrote down exists.

25 FBC business meeting minutes, February 28, 1965, 147-A.

26 "Church Votes to Relocate," *Church Voice*, March 4, 1965.

27 David Day, *Conquest: How Societies Overwhelm Others* (Oxford: Oxford University Press, 2008) is an exploration of the social, political, and geographical strategies by which societies conquer others in ventures to expand their territory. On "Claiming by Naming," see 49–68. See also Pitkanen, *Commentary on Numbers*, 40–50.

28 The occurrence happens in the announcement of a Future Program Committee forum in *Church Voice*, June 25, 1964.

29 See chapter 5.

30 That happened to Moses a lot too.

31 FBC business meeting notes, February 28, 1965, 147H–I. The notes from that day appear to be a direct transcript of the meeting. The section cited does not have a heading indicating it is formally Bates's sermon, but it appears to be that. The notes claim that there is an audio recording, but I am unable to locate it.

32 I have narrated the Numbers 13 text in the way that I believe First Baptist was reading it. However, it is essential to note that postcolonial and womanist scholars have offered other critical readings of the text that deserve careful reflection. In short, those readings highlight the existence and worth of the Canaanites and the other peoples who inhabited Canaan prior to Israel settling there. Those people, such readings remind us, also need justice. Reading texts like Numbers 13 without considering the Canaanites can serve as a justification for settler-colonial regimes as the strategies employed by the Israelites in the text look remarkably like modern-day settler-colonial strategies. For further reflection, see Delores Williams, *Sisters in the Wilderness: The Challenge of Womanist God-Talk* (Maryknoll, NY: Orbis Books, 1993), 143–77; Naim S. Ateek, "A Palestinian Perspective: Biblical Perspectives on the Land," in *Voices from the Margin: Interpreting the Bible in the Third World*, 3rd ed., ed. R. S. Sugirtharajah (Maryknoll, NY: Orbis Books, 2006), 227–41; Pitkanen, *Commentary on Numbers*. Further, it is worth noting that among the theological errors happening in Bates's reading is its flirtation with *supersessionism*, the idea that Christians have superseded the Jews as the heirs to the covenant with the God of Israel. Jennings, *The Christian Imagination*, makes numerous mentions of the faulty doctrine, covering its racial context and relation to Discovery in particular.

33 The following year, Bates would be selected by a local department store as one of Charlotte's ten best-dressed men! See "10 Men Named to Best Dressed List," *Charlotte News*, March 8, 1966.

34 FBC business meeting notes, February 28, 1965, 147H.

35 Jennings, "Can White People Be Saved?," 33.

36 FBC business meeting notes, February 28, 1965, 147H.

37 Jantzen, *God, Race, and History*, 17.

38 See above, chapter 5.

39 *Church Voice*, March 4, 1965.

40 "Welcome Surprises Make Dream a Reality," *Charlotte Observer*, February 2, 1988.

41 "Church's Bid for Brooklyn Tract Accepted," *Charlotte Observer*, June 10, 1965.

42 Interview with Rev. Sandra Caldwell Williams, March 22, 2023.

43 "A Mixed Blessing for Church," *Charlotte Observer*, April 18, 1965.

CHAPTER NINE

1 Original magazine archived at SBHLA. Reprints of the article, produced by the SBC and circulated to churches and likely at various denominational gatherings and conventions, are available at SBHLA in the Sunday School Board, Church Architecture Department collection, box 7, folder 7.1. *Baptist Standard* was published by the Executive Committee of the SBC and "distributed to pastors, educational directors, music directors, full-time denominational workers, Baptist faculty members, chaplains and missionaries of the Southern Baptist Convention," as well as retirees from any of those groups, according to the publisher's statement of the magazine. It had a wide readership among those in convention leadership, from local pastors to high-ranking executives.

2 Ross F. Hidy, *The Story of St. Mark's Square: How the Oldest Lutheran Congregation in California Helped Rebuild San Francisco* (Concord, CA: Lutheran Pioneer Press, 1997), 12–24. Hidy was pastor of St. Mark's during Urban Renewal. Thanks to Charlotte pastor John Cleghorn for sharing the resource with me.

3 See https://tinyurl.com/mrxmnfwy for an overview. Thanks to Drew Phillips for helping me to make this connection.

4 Summary of the Waco/Baylor Renewal project available through Waco History Project at https://tinyurl.com/rzrjwf48; Platt, "Sandtown," *Baylor Line*, spring 2018 edition, available online at https://tinyurl.com/a95mvvpp; additional information from interview with Ashley Thornton; Baptist General Convention of Texas (BGCT) Report of Special Church-State Committee available in archives of BGCT. Thanks to Dr. Alan Lafever for the assistance in locating this report.

5 One white minister who was far ahead of his peers was Rev. Edward Cahill, the minister at the Unitarian Church of Charlotte. In a 1952 sermon at his church, Cahill preached about a series of media stories about a supposed "crime wave" in Charlotte. He sought to undercut the developing narrative of Black pathology and instead placed the blame on an unjust society held in place by white leadership and white interests: "The real [issue] about which we are concerned derives directly from the fact that the city of Charlotte is not a united community. In reality there are two communities—one superior, the other inferior; one first class, the other second class; one with all the gravy, the other with the leftovers. . . . The fundamental laws of decent human relationships have been violated for generations." A printed copy of the sermon, entitled "Crime, Religion, and Human Relations," is in the Kelly M. Alexander Papers, box 29, folder 13. For more on Cahill and his legacy in Charlotte, see Gordon D. Gibson, *Southern Witness: Unitarians and Universalists in the Civil Rights Era* (Boston: Skinner House, 2015), 27–36.

6 Pamela Grundy, *Legacy: Three Centuries of Black History in Charlotte, North Carolina* (Charlotte, NC: Nerve Media Productions, 2022), 70–71; see also chapter 7 in this work, especially footnote 369.

7 Interview with Ashley Hogewood.

8 See "Our Town," *Charlotte News*, April 12, 1963; also, *Covenant Presbyterian Church: The First Fifty Years* (Charlotte, NC: Covenant Presbyterian Church, 1997), 52–53, 193–96.

9 Notes from August 15, 1966, meeting in Avery Hood Papers, MS 399, box 2; "Religious Affiliates Formed to Help Families Relocate," *Charlotte News*, October 6, 1966.

10 Deed located at Mecklenburg County Register of Deeds, book 2918, 404.

11 Charlotte City Council minutes, November 27, 1967, available through Charlotte City website at https://charlottenc.gov/CityClerk/Pages/Minutes.aspx. See also "W. J. Smith's New Job," *Charlotte Observer*, December 1, 1967.

12 See, e.g., "Killing the Goose," *Charlotte Observer*, May 29, 1967; "W. J. Smith Carolinas UCS Vice President," *Charlotte Observer*, May 26, 1967; "Baptist Vote Would Oust Two Churches," *Charlotte Observer*, October 21, 1967.

13 Letter from Smith to Raymond King, December 12, 1967, in Stanford R. Brookshire Papers, box 2, folder 17.

14 I recognize that the narrative jump of several years here is not ideal. Unfortunately, when I attempted to complete the research into some of the key decision-making and processes around the move, the archives at First Baptist had suddenly become inaccessible for the foreseeable future.

15 "Carl Bates Heads Southern Baptists," *Charlotte Observer*, June 3, 1970. Bates's papers from his SBC presidency are available in the collection at SBHLA.

16 The bulletin from this service is in the archive at First Baptist Church.

17 Derrida, *Specters of Marx*, 173.

18 Jennings on the colonization and taming of the Americas: "Taming the wilderness meant much more than clearing the land. It meant that you were willing to place your bodies in the unfolding drama of destroying the Native inhabitants. Participating in the destruction of Indigenous peoples was one of the primary ways immigrants signaled to the world and to themselves that they were part of the American landscape, the formation of a White nation in contrast to the 'Indians!' Yet taming the wilderness was also an analogy for stripping away their immigrant past—that is, those cultural artifacts that signaled indebtedness to the old country, the old cultural ways, and the primitive mentalities of lower classes of the Old World." From "Can White People Be Saved?," 37.

19 Guy Carswell was one of twelve men who helped to found Myers Park Baptist in 1943.

20 Interview with Nancy Kistler, September 24, 2020; Interview with Joe McKeever, January 25, 2022; "First Baptist Church Opens New Sanctuary," *Charlotte Observer*, February 8, 1988; "Church Gets $100,000 for Bell Tower," *Charlotte Observer*, March 2, 1972.

21 "Baptists Dedicate New Church," *Charlotte Observer*, August 28, 1972.

22 Bates letter, 2. Cited above in chapter 7.

23 "Baptists Dedicate New Church."

24 Hymn also called "To Him Who Hallows All Our Days," text by John Leonidas Rosser. Hymn #499 in the 1956 Baptist Hymnal.

25 In Southern Baptist tradition, as with some other Protestant groups, a building or some other place of sacred significance is "dedicated" rather than "consecrated." Such a dedication would focus primarily around spoken words and prayers but typically does not include symbolic or sacramental actions. A litany is generally a reading from a script with multiple parts, usually in responsive form between a single speaker and the rest of the group.

26 Ps 127:1 KJV.

27 All quotes from the program for the opening worship service at FBC, August 27, 1972. Available in archives of First Baptist Church.

28 "First Church, Charlotte, Dedicates New Facilities Near Downtown Area," *Biblical Recorder*, September 2, 1972.

29 Hope's statement from that day continued, "If any 'lesson from life' can be extracted from our experience it is simply that our people with unwavering faith attempted great things for God and found that God, as He does in all of life, abundantly answered. And just as He answered the 'Impossible Dream' of our church, He as forcefully and decisively is the answer to our individual life's dream, hope and aspiration. And that's the truth." The sentence from Warren regarding "attempt great things for God" is directly quoted in his 1957 presidential address to the Southern Baptist Convention, "Now Therefore Perform." The text of Warren's address is available at SBHLA in the 1957 *Annual of the Southern Baptist Convention*, 70–74. Quoted text from p. 72.

CHAPTER TEN

1 Interview with Regina and Tiffany North, January 28, 2022. In all direct quotations from interviews, I have done my best to render people's speech exactly as they spoke. When unavoidable, I have edited as lightly as possible for clarity.

2 Regina North is a direct descendant of Abram's brother Jacob. Abram and Annie North appear to have no direct descendants still living, based on all the data I could gather.

3 Interview with Regina and Tiffany North, January 28, 2022.

4 Interview with Brandi North Williams, February 22, 2022.

5 Interview with Brandi North Williams, April 19, 2023.

6 Among her various roles, Brandi does brilliant work with the national nonprofit Hip Hop Caucus. Read more about her at https://hiphopcaucus.org/team/brandi-williams/.

7 Derrida, *Specters of Marx*, 26.

8 On blockbusting, see Rothstein, *Color of Law*, 95–100; Lipsitz, *How Racism Takes Place*, 103–4; Cashin, *White Space, Black Hood*, 15–16; Taylor, *Race for Profit*, 48–49.

9 See "Housing Letter Well Distributed," *Charlotte Observer*, November 7, 1965; "Real Estate Man 'Proud of Role' in Negro Housing," *Charlotte Observer*, November 5, 1965; Byrum Brevard Brookshire obituary, *Charlotte Observer*, May 5, 2006.

10 Taylor cites a 1963 *Saturday Evening Post* article on blockbusting where one speculator stated that "if anybody who is well established in this business doesn't earn $100,000 a year, they are loafing." Taylor comments, "Blockbusting thrived for two reasons: redlining and the artificial barriers to Blacks' housing mobility and the growth of a Black population desperate for living space." See Taylor, *Race for Profit*, 48.

11 Fullilove, *Root Shock*. Fullilove is a psychologist and public health professional. This very important study examines Urban Renewal projects and their aftermath using the metaphor of "root shock," where a flourishing and mature plant struggles to thrive after being transplanted. Fullilove's work takes into account, in a clear and compelling way, both the structural issues that made rebuilding spaces like Brooklyn impossible and the psychological and cultural costs that prevented such rebuilding.

12 Hazeline had no children.

13 "First of Brooklyn Homeowners Sells," *Charlotte Observer*, October 7, 1961.

14 A note on these figures: I used municipal assessments on the Mecklenburg County Tax Collector's website. I ran all purchase numbers through the US Bureau of Labor Statistics Inflation Calculator. I chose to use tax-assessed values in an attempt to keep things as comparable as possible across decades. When Hazeline North Anderson was forced to sell her Brooklyn home, she had to do so at the assessed price given by the county, in a moment where market valuations were at zero because of the Urban Renewal project. However, the tax assessor's values in 2023 tend to underestimate the market price of a property. Based on other land sales within a few blocks of First Baptist, the market value of FBC's current land in 2023 is likely in the vicinity of $80 million, an 1800 percent appreciation over the price they paid, a figure that suggests nearly $1 million in possible losses for the Norths. The 2023 market value of the Oaklawn home is hard to estimate. Gentrification has led to wide price swings in housing there, and the age and size of that house probably give it a relatively low value. A comparably sized lot to that one might sell at a market price of $150,000 in late 2023. That makes the situation slightly different but still leaves a wide, wide gap. It is worth noting that Hazeline had no children and that there seem to be no direct descendants of Abram and Annie North alive. A number of great-nieces and -nephews are still in Charlotte, however.

15 I'm using this language, rather than the more common *privilege*, due to the influence of Olúfẹ́mi O. Táíwò, *Reconsidering Reparations* (New York: Oxford University Press, 2022). Pointing to how advantage accumulates over time is important for understanding how racial privilege works. The issue is not a single point in time, or even a single generation, but the way that advantages build in a manner similar to wealth-building in an interest-bearing account.

16 Mills, *Racial Contract*, 42, 47; see also Shannon Sullivan, *Revealing Whiteness: The Unconscious Habits of Racial Privilege* (Bloomington: Indiana University Press, 2006), 143–66; Lipsitz, *How Racism Takes Place*, 54–56.

17 Lipsitz, *How Racism Takes Place*, 55.

18 See Mills, *The Racial Contract*, 45. See also the chart above, noting that Hazeline North's home stagnated in value until a rush in new investment and white residents beginning around 2020. One common illustration of the devaluing of Black space, on an individual level, is Black homeowners who are having homes appraised. In repeated experiments around the country, a Black family's home is appraised in its normal appearance and then appraised again after being staged with different décor and photographs to look like it is occupied by a white family. The appraisal of the supposed white family's home inevitably comes back significantly higher than the appraisal of the Black family's home. See, e.g., "Home Appraisal with a Black Owner: $472,000. With a White Owner: $750,000," *New York Times*, August 18, 2022.

19 The phrase is from James Baldwin, *The Fire Next Time* (New York: Vintage, 1993), 3.

20 Interview with Regina and Tiffany North, January 28, 2022.
21 Gordon, *Ghostly Matters*, xvi.
22 Gordon, *Ghostly Matters*, 17.
23 National groups like NCOBRA, and scholars like Darity and Mullen, generally reserve the term *reparations* specifically for a national program of "acknowledgement, redress, and closure" encompassing the fullness of American political, economic, and social life. I am generally avoiding the language of *reparations* while suggesting reparative efforts from institutions other than the federal government. Smaller efforts are certainly like reparations, but they fall short of a national scheme in their ability to repair and to create long-term change across an entire culture. Small-scale efforts at penance are nevertheless important—perhaps essential—in the way they open imaginative space for creating an alternative world.
24 Interview with Brandi North Williams, February 22, 2022.
25 In *The Brothers Karamazov*, a wishful young woman who is scared of loving people in real life seeks the counsel of Father Zosima. He chastises her to engage in active love. "Love in action is a harsh and dreadful thing, compared to love in dreams," he says. This was a favorite story of Dorothy Day.
26 William A. Darity Jr. and A. Kirsten Mullen, *From Here to Equality: Reparations for Black Americans in the 21st Century* (Chapel Hill: University of North Carolina Press, 2020), 3. Quoted in Táíwò, *Reconsidering Reparations*, 124–25.
27 Robin D. G. Kelley has some powerful statements along these lines in an interview with George Yancy regarding the Tulsa Race Massacre and class issues raised by the persistence of rhetoric about "Black Wall Streets." See George Yancy, "Robin D. G. Kelley: The Tulsa Race Massacre Went Way Beyond 'Black Wall Street,'" *Truthout*, June 1, 2021. https://tinyurl.com/mt4389m8.
28 Táíwò, *Reconsidering Reparations*, 126.
29 Táíwò, *Reconsidering Reparations*, 126. The internal quote is Táíwò's citation of Adolph Reed and Merlin Chowkwanyun, "Race, Class, Crisis: The Discourse of Racial Disparity and Its Analytical Discontents," *Socialist Register* 48 (2012): 165.
30 FBC-West is the congregation formed by the Black members who left Beulah Baptist in 1867–68 to form an independent congregation. See chapter 2.
31 Interview with Janet Garner-Mullins, October 1, 2021.
32 Curtis, *Myth of Colorblind Christians*, 4.
33 I know that not all of my readers are Christian or religious at all. Nevertheless, rituals of song and text are familiar to all. The simplest example is the recitation of a pledge to a flag or the singing of a national anthem. Both are acts of civil religion that do similar kinds of work the Bible texts and hymns do, namely, inculcating people into a culture, a set of beliefs, or a way of life.
34 Augustine's famous dictum says, "Who sings, prays twice."
35 On "watershed discipleship," see the writing and teaching of Ched Myers, including "A Watershed Moment," *Sojourners*, May 2014, 20–24. Other writings available at https://chedmyers.org.
36 We'll consider gentrification and the situation in 2023 in chapter 12.
37 One of the few stories I encountered in my research that took space and place as a part of a full accounting of how white Christians might attend to our debts was the story of Lake Street Church and Second Baptist Church in Evanston, Illinois. Like Charlotte's First Baptist and First Baptist-West, and indeed like so many other

congregations around the country, those two Illinois congregations split when Black members departed to form Second Baptist so as to have their own institution where they would have authority and full membership. Since about 2019, Lake Street Church has been working on how to make reparations as part of the City of Evanston's plan for a municipal reparations program. Under the leadership of Rev. Dr. Michael Woolf, the congregation has worked to consider how their physical plant—building, land, etc.—needed to be part of their actions of repentance. Woolf's stance was controversial inside the congregation at first, but his membership came to recognize how their physical space as both practical resource and symbolic marker was part of their accumulated advantage, an advantage that Second Baptist did not have on account of the way white supremacy worked in their history. Lake Street's work, which is ongoing, now includes utilizing some of their resources under the leadership and direction of Second Baptist while forging a relationship that might heal their divisions without allowing a liberal congregation the satisfaction of soothing their—perhaps misplaced—guilt by simply giving their assets away. Interview with Michael Woolf, January 31, 2023. See also "What Reparations Is Costing My Church," *Sojourners*, February 23, 2022, available online at https://tinyurl.com/4ykww4nn.

38 Derrida begins *Specters of Marx* in this way: "Someone, you or me, comes forward and says: '*I would like to learn to live finally*,'" xvi. Italics are original to the text.

39 That's a fancy word that means "habitually silent."

40 Táíwò, *Reconsidering Reparations*, 7.

41 Robin D. G. Kelley points out that Black reparations movements have often had multiple goals and that often they were not primarily about money: "The demand for reparations was about social justice, reconciliation, reconstructing the internal life of Black America, and eliminating institutional racism. This is why reparations proposals from Black radical movements focus less on individual payments than on securing funds to build autonomous Black institutions, improving community life, and in some cases establishing a homeland that will develop African Americans to develop a political economy geared more toward collective needs than toward accumulation." See Robin D. G. Kelley, *Freedom Dreams: The Black Radical Imagination*, revised ed. (Boston: Beacon, 2022), 114.

CHAPTER ELEVEN

1 Baldwin, *The Fire Next Time*, 5–6.

2 Uptown Farmers' Market is a separate organization from First Baptist Church. The market uses church space at a very, very low cost, and many of the market volunteers are church members, but the two organizations are distinct entities.

3 Interview with Jan Johnson, Gloria Medlock, and Marvette Monroe, December 5, 2022.

4 Interview with Johnson, Medlock, and Monroe, December 5, 2022.

5 Enns and Myers, *Healing Haunted Histories*, 214.

6 Enns and Myers, *Healing Haunted Histories*, 214–23; Tuck and Yang, "Decolonization," 9–28. Enns and Myers have a taxonomy of ten of these moves, some of them common among all settlers, some of them corresponding to the political and theological predilections of those who use them (e.g., conservative or liberal moves to innocence). I have selected to explore the three moves to innocence ubiquitous

among all settlers, or in this case, specifically in white Christians, for their salience in the written and verbal record I have encountered in the course of this study.

7   Enns and Myers call this "exoneration by conscientization." See *Healing Haunted Histories*, 220.

8   Matt Jantzen's helpful analysis of the conceptions and historical uses of the doctrine of providence is important. It looks carefully at race and history in statements on providence and how the doctrine has been used to justify European colonization and the establishment of systems of white supremacy. See *God, Race, and History*, 11–31.

9   Stanford R. Brookshire Papers, MS 41, box 2 of 6, folder 2:6.

10 Local press still regularly consults McColl and speculates about his ongoing influence, as in Jim Morrill, "Who's in Charge in Charlotte?", *Charlotte Magazine*, January 22, 2023, available online at https://tinyurl.com/phx7y99t.

11 North Carolina National Bank. Under McColl's guidance, NCNB worked loopholes in laws that curtailed interstate banking practices. NCNB began buying banks across multiple states, eventually becoming NationsBank and after that Bank of America, one of the largest financial conglomerates in the world.

12 Interview with Hugh McColl, January 16, 2020.

13 See Enns and Myers, *Healing Haunted Histories*, 215–16, for their discussion on personal dissociation.

14 Interview with David Reule, September 23, 2020.

15 Enns and Myers, *Healing Haunted Histories*, 216.

16 Welch's pastorate lasted from 2018 to 2022. I am quite grateful for him and his openness to me. Without his generosity in time and access to the archives at First Baptist, this project likely would never have gotten started, much less reached any completion.

17 Interview with Welch, March 3, 2021. He appears to mean *grievous*, not "grieving." As a matter of record, the church did not grieve over the loss of Brooklyn. They scarcely knew it was happening and even now barely know it happened.

18 Welch's thinking changed a bit as we worked together, as seen later in this chapter. I include these statements here not only as documentation of our work but also for the way that they echoed the sentiments of many of his congregants.

19 Tuck and Yang say that such moves "are strategies or positionings that attempt to relieve the settler of feelings of guilt or responsibility without giving up land or power or privilege, without having to change much at all." See "Decolonization," 10.

20 If the answer is no, it's awful hard to preach the resurrection.

21 Toni Morrison, cited in Gordon, *Ghostly Matters*, 184.

22 Frances Fielden Eppley, *The First Baptist Church of Charlotte: Its Heritage* (Charlotte, NC: First Baptist Church of Charlotte, 1981), 106–7.

23 Welch's only prefatory comments to the sermon were, "As I've thought and prayed, I think the most significant and important thing that I could say this morning is to take your Bibles and turn to the book of John. What we need is not a word necessarily from me, not a word from a pastor. A word from a politician. But what we need is a word from God. From the word of God." Then he commenced to read the morning's Scripture. I was struck by the similarity between his strategy and the strategy of C. C. Warren and the Southern Baptist Convention when faced with addressing *Brown v. Board* and the legacy of white supremacy in segregation.

24 Welch sermon at First Baptist Church of Charlotte, January 10, 2021. Available at https://www.youtube.com/watch?v=JZ-11mRnOA4.

25 Mills, *The Racial Contract*, 18. *Epistemology* is a fancy word meaning something like "strategy for knowing." Epistemological inquiry might include questions like: How do we know what we know? How do we know what we do not know? What purpose does our knowing or not-knowing serve? Mills's work cited here is deeply important and approachable. Readers still looking for a more popular-level text might consult Crystal Fleming, *How to Be Less Stupid about Race*.

26 Mills, *The Racial Contract*, 3.

27 Mills, *The Racial Contract*, 18.

28 Jesse Curtis casts such moves not as white evangelicalism but as *evangelical whiteness*. He says, "Through this inversion, whiteness becomes as much religious as racial as it takes on theological, institutional, and temporal inflections." See Curtis, *Myth of Colorblind Christians*, 6–7.

29 Mills, *The Racial Contract*, 93.

30 Mills, *The Racial Contract*, 93.

31 Enns and Myers identify this move as being bound up in "ideologies of superiority," which function "to justify conquest and to absolve us of transgression" (*Healing Haunted Histories*, 217). I am building from their category but identifying it in close relation to "willful ignorance" in this case.

32 Interview with David Reule, September 23, 2020.

33 Mills, *The Racial Contract*, 18 (emphasis mine).

34 "Haunting is a frightening experience. It always registers the harm inflicted or the loss sustained by a social violence done in the past or in the present. But haunting, unlike trauma, is distinctive for producing something-to-be-done." Gordon, *Ghostly Matters*, xvi.

35 Gordon, *Ghostly Matters*, 183.

36 Interview with Johnson, Medlock, and Monroe, December 5, 2022.

37 Lyles is the first Black woman to be mayor of Charlotte. She comes from a family with deep roots in Charlotte over multiple generations.

38 Interview with Robert Welch, June 10, 2021.

39 "Specters or ghosts appear when the trouble they represent and symptomize is no longer being contained or repressed or blocked from view. The ghost, as I understand it, is not the invisible or some ineffable excess. . . . Haunting and the appearance of specters or ghosts is one way . . . we are notified that what's been concealed is very much alive and present." Gordon, *Ghostly Matters*, xvi.

40 Interview with FBC History group, August 25, 2021.

41 Gordon, *Ghostly Matters*, 98.

42 Enns and Myers, *Healing Haunted Histories*, 215–16.

43 Malcolm X: "The white liberal differs from the white conservative only in one way: the liberal is more deceitful than the conservative. The liberal is more hypocritical than the conservative. Both want power but the white liberal is the one who has perfected the art of posing as the Negro's friend and benefactor; and by winning the friendship, allegiance, and support of the Negro, the white liberal is able to use the Negro as a pawn or tool in this political 'football game' that is constantly raging between the white liberals and white conservatives." See "God's Judgment of White America," available online at https://tinyurl.com/mrywb653.

44 Gordon, *Ghostly Matters*, 166.

45 Jennings, "Can White People Be Saved?," 34.

46 Jennings, "Can White People Be Saved?," 34.

47 Gordon, *Ghostly Matters*, 134. Gordon here is reflecting on Luisa Valenzuela's novel *He Who Searches*.

48 Ched Myers, *Who Will Roll Away the Stone? Discipleship Queries for First World Christians* (Maryknoll, NY: Orbis Books, 1994), 77. Myers is referring here to Num 14:27, in the episode that immediately follows Numbers 13, discussed above in chapter 6. In the paragraphs that follow, I am deeply informed by Myers's reflections on Mark 9 in *Who Will Roll Away the Stone?*, 76–108.

49 Enns and Myers, *Healing Haunted Histories*, 220.

50 Interview with Johnson, Medlock, and Monroe, December 5, 2022.

51 Hartman, *Scenes of Subjection*, 26.

52 Hartman, *Scenes of Subjection*, 29.

53 Hartman, *Scenes of Subjection*, 31.

54 This is common language in much of Myers's work. See, e.g., *Who Will Roll Away the Stone?*, 76–108.

CHAPTER TWELVE

1 W. E. B. Du Bois, *Darkwater: Voices from within the Veil* (New York: Harcourt, Brace and Howe, 1920), 30.

2 Theologian Willie Jennings helpfully frames how such a view is part of the racialized project of modernity, which removes the considerations of space and place as key characters inside the story of a people. See Jennings's talk "Why the Body is the Land and the Land is the Body: Thoughts and Conversation," April 4, 2023, available at https://tinyurl.com/5xfwjz7h.

3 The conclusion to Toni Morrison's novel *Beloved* includes the refrain "This is not a story to pass on." See Toni Morrison, *Beloved* (New York: Plume, 1997), 275.

4 Hartman, *Scenes of Subjection*, xxix.

5 A few articles from the building's history include "Baptist Church Formed in Glenwood Section," *Charlotte Observer*, December 1, 1925; "Church Plans New Building," *Charlotte Observer*, April 16, 1930; "Enderly Park Baptist Opens Today," *Charlotte Observer*, June 12, 1938; "News Notes," *Biblical Recorder*, August 17, 1938; "Groundbreaking Tomorrow for New Church," *Charlotte Observer*, August 6, 1977.

6 Ferrell's case led to the unusual move of Charlotte-Mecklenburg police officer Randall Kerrick being charged with voluntary manslaughter. Many news accounts from the time are available, including "Funeral for Man Shot by CMPD," *Charlotte Observer*, September 28, 2013.

7 Gordon, *Ghostly Matters*, 16.

8 Curtis, *Myth of Colorblind Christians*, 6–7. White evangelicals were, in the period of his study, and still are, deeply invested in whiteness. In that sense, Curtis says, "White evangelicalism can be understood as a religio-racial identity . . . a means of identification with the racial hierarchy rather than resistance to it" (7).

9 Ps 118:22; Matt 21:42.

10 Gordon, *Ghostly Matters*, 22.

11 Readers in northern or western US cities with high costs of living might think that price tag sounds like a deal! Here in the South, it seems outrageous, especially given the enormous appreciation in a short period of time.

12 A group of neighbors across several neighborhoods worked for years on this, and West Side Community Land Trust was our proud accomplishment. In early 2023, eight years later, the organization has 10 single-family houses ready for sale to low-income homeowners and another 120 units being constructed for low-income seniors. Learn more about West Side CLT at http://westsideclt.org. See also Greg Lacour, "Inside the West Side Community Land Trust's Fight Against Gentrification," *Charlotte Magazine*, March 27, 2018, https://tinyurl.com/mphz252w.

13 I find most of the writing and discourse around gentrification to be frustrating. It too easily shows recency bias and often focuses on the aesthetic aspects that take place in the last five years of a fifty-year project. Gentrification is the current iteration of cycles that feature decades of disinvestment followed by rapid reinvestment and its resultant displacement. Several of the works cited within this book offer more theoretical depth than discussions about certain types of businesses or individualized accounts of consumer choices without consideration of the systemic nature of the issue, including Lipsitz, *How Racism Takes Place*, and Cashin, *White Space, Black Hood*. One important practitioner in areas of spatial justice is Roberto Bedoya. See his "Spatial Justice: Rasquachification, Race, and the City," Creative Time Reports, September 15, 2014, https://tinyurl.com/zrt74xrr; and "Placemaking and the Politics of Belonging and Dis-Belonging," *GIA Reader* 24, no. 1 (Winter 2013), https://tinyurl.com/49mbkb69.

14 Myers, *Who Will Roll Away the Stone?*, 77.

15 Lest it concern some readers, I do mean *generally*, and not *without exception*. I am speaking not in the sense of "race essentialism," where racial identity is a fixed category dealing with skin color, but in the sense Baldwin means when he says that "white is just a metaphor for power, and that is simply a way of describing Chase Manhattan Bank." I would, however, challenge white readers who think they are one of the exceptions to dig deeper. I think that, too, but that does not make it true.

16 Mills, *The Racial Contract*, 11. Italics are original to the text.

17 Mills, *The Racial Contract*, 12.

18 Mills, *The Racial Contract*, 133.

19 Larry Kent Graham, *Moral Injury: Restoring Wounded Souls* (Nashville: Abingdon Press, 2017), 24, cited in Chanequa Walker-Barnes, *I Bring the Voices of My People: A Womanist Vision for Racial Reconciliation* (Grand Rapids, MI: Eerdmans, 2019), 126. See also Enns and Myers, *Healing Haunted Histories*, 230–32. The idea of moral injury was first identified by theorists thinking about war and its intractable moral conflicts, where soldiers have to make choices that violate their deepest moral restrictions against killing.

20 Walker-Barnes, *I Bring the Voices*, 126. I have quoted from Walker-Barnes several times here. Her book *I Bring the Voices* is an important contribution to antiracist literature, and the chapter from which I am drawing, "The Unbearable Whiteness of Being," is essential reading for white people engaged in antiracism work. It has deeply informed my reflections.

21 Walker-Barnes identifies four ways in which white enculturation harms white people, the outworking of moral injury in both our inner and social lives. She names those

injuries as conformity, trust in authority, selective sight, and egoethnocentrism. See her analysis in *I Bring the Voices*, 136–55.

22 See Walker-Barnes, *I Bring the Voices*, 127.

23 Interview with Chanequa Walker-Barnes, September 21, 2021.

24 Interview with Chanequa Walker-Barnes, September 21, 2021.

25 Walker-Barnes appealed to this idea in our interview, citing her teacher Peter Storey. She mentions the same idea in the Foreword to this book.

26 Derrida: "At bottom, the specter is the future, it is always to come, it presents itself only as that which could come or come back." *Specters of Marx*, 48.

27 The quote is from Sigmund Freud, cited in Myers, *Who Will Roll Away the Stone?*, 77.

28 Myers, *Who Will Roll Away the Stone?*, 100.

29 Myers's reading of the silencing spirit is especially influential to me here. See *Binding the Strong Man*, 253–56.

30 Myers, *Who Will Roll Away the Stone?*, 101.

31 Myers, *Who Will Roll Away the Stone?*, 101.

32 The Housing Choice Voucher (HCV) system, sometimes known as Section 8, provides rental subsidies into the private rental market. Tenants pay a portion of their income, and local housing authorities pay the balance of a fair market rent to a private landlord. The system has some advantages, including robust requirements on landlords to maintain properties at relatively high levels. Nevertheless, it is rife with inequalities. In some localities, including mine, landlords can legally discriminate based on the source of a potential tenant's income, making it easy to opt out of the system altogether. HCVs are woefully underfunded. In Charlotte, the waiting list for a voucher is years long, despite pressing needs. And the system is a classic representation of neoliberal "public-private" partnerships, which try to resolve the problems created by capitalism through a slightly modified capitalism. The results of neoliberal projects like HCVs are abundantly clear: they don't work.

33 For further resources on community land trusts, see the website of Grounded Solutions Network, the national network of CLTs, at https://groundedsolutions.org/.

34 Gordon, *Ghostly Matters*, 203.

35 "The Fence: Alexander Beams, Symbol Comes Down," *Charlotte News*, January 7, 1969.

36 Of interest to this work, James H. Carson, enslaver of Annie Carson North; Samuel Smith; Smith's father, Benjamin Rush Smith; and his brother Benjamin Rush Smith are all buried in the Elmwood section.

Bibliography

MANUSCRIPT COLLECTIONS

David M. Rubenstein Rare Book and Manuscript Library, Duke University
  North Carolina Mutual Life Insurance Company Archives
  Carlyle Marney Papers
J. Murrey Atkins Library, University of North Carolina at Charlotte
  Fred Alexander Papers
  Kelly Alexander Sr. Papers
  Brooklyn Oral History Project
  Stanford R. Brookshire Papers
  Charlotte Redevelopment Commission Collection
  Avery Hood Papers
Library of Congress, Washington, DC
  NAACP Collection
The Louis Round Wilson Special Collections Library, University of North Carolina at
  Chapel Hill
  North Carolina Collection
Manuscripts and Rare Book Department, J. Y. Joyner Library, East Carolina University,
  Greenville, NC
Robinson-Spangler Carolina Room, Charlotte Mecklenburg Library, Charlotte, NC
Sanborn Insurance Maps of Charlotte
Special Collections Room, Johnson C. Smith University, Charlotte, NC
Special Collections and Archives, Wake Forest University
  North Carolina Baptist Collection
Wofford College, Spartanburg, SC
  South Carolina United Methodist Collection

CHURCH AND DENOMINATIONAL ARCHIVAL COLLECTIONS

Baptist General Convention of Texas, Waco, TX
Clinton Chapel AME Zion Church, Charlotte, NC
Dilworth United Methodist Church, Charlotte, NC
First Baptist Church, Charlotte, NC
First Baptist Church-West, Charlotte, NC

First Presbyterian Church, Charlotte, NC
First United Methodist Church, Charlotte, NC
Friendship Missionary Baptist Church, Charlotte, NC
Myers Park Baptist Church, Charlotte, NC
Myers Park United Methodist Church, Charlotte, NC
St. John's Baptist Church, Charlotte, NC
Southern Baptist Historical Library and Archive, Nashville, TN
    Baptist Jubilee Advance Collection
    Carl Bates Papers
    Home Mission Board, Metropolitan Missions Records
    Race Relations and Southern Baptists
    Sunday School Board, Church Architecture Department
    C. C. Warren Papers
    1956 Proceedings of the Southern Baptist Convention
    1957 Proceedings of the Southern Baptist Convention

GOVERNMENT RECORDS

"Brooklyn Area Blight Study," published by Charlotte-Mecklenburg Planning Commission, 1958
City Clerk's Office, Charlotte, NC
    Charlotte City Council Minutes
    Charlotte City Council Resolutions
HHM and Associates, Historic Furnishings Report, Martin Luther King Jr. Birth Home, Martin Luther King Jr. National Historical Park, Atlanta, GA, Volume I: Historical Data, January 2021
Mecklenburg County Register of Deeds
United States Bureau of the Census
    Seventh Census (1850), Steele Creek, Mecklenburg County; St. Bartholomew's Parish, Colleton County, SC Schedule 2
    Eighth Census (1860), Steele Creek, Mecklenburg County
    Ninth Census (1870), Charlotte City Ward 1; Charlotte City Ward 3
    Tenth Census (1880), Charlotte City Ward 1
    Twelfth Census (1900), Charlotte City Ward 2
    Thirteenth Census (1910), Charlotte, NC, Ward 2
United States Civil War Soldier Records and Profiles, 1861–1865
United States Register of Civil, Military, and Naval Service, 1863–1959, vol. 2

NEWSPAPERS, MAGAZINES, AND DIRECTORIES

Baylor Line (Waco, TX)
Biblical Recorder (NC)
Charleston (SC) *Daily Courier*
Charleston (SC) *Mercury*

Charlotte City Directory
Charlotte Democrat
Charlotte Evening Chronicle
Charlotte Magazine
Charlotte News
Charlotte Observer
Christian Century
Creative Loafing Charlotte
Greenville (SC) *Enterprise*
Keowee (SC) *Courier*
Los Angeles Times
New York Times
News of Orange County (NC)
Sojourners
Star of Zion (Charlotte, NC)
Washington Post

INTERVIEWS

Rod Alexander Jr., May 4, 2021
Ebbie Bailey, October 8, 2021
Richard Campbell, September 24, 2020
First Baptist Church History Group, August 25, 2021
Rev. Janet Garner-Mullins, January 5, 2022
Ashley Hogewood, December 10, 2020
Joan Hope, April 6, 2023
Helen Kirk, May 27, 2021
Nancy Kistler, October 29, 2020
Jan Johnson, December 5, 2022
Rev. Dr. Bill Leonard, June 24, 2021
Rev. Joe McKeever, January 25, 2022
Gloria Medlock, December 5, 2022
Marvette Monroe, December 5, 2022
Regina North, January 28, 2022
Tiffany North, January 28, 2022
Brenda Porter-Dewitt, March 22, 2023
Ken Poe, February 4, 2021
Rick Poe, December 7, 2022
David Reule, September 24, 2020
Ashley Thornton, February 1, 2023
Dr. Chanequa Walker-Barnes, September 21, 2021
Rev. Robert Welch, March 3, 2021; June 10, 2021
Rev. Sandra Caldwell Williams, March 22, 2023
Brandi North Williams, February 22, 2022
Rev. Dr. Michael Woolf, January 31, 2023

SELF-PUBLISHED CHURCH HISTORY BOOKS

I have given these a separate category because they tend to be written by members of churches about their own institutions and often lack the scholarly rigor expected of other historical works. Further, they are often difficult to locate outside of the libraries of the churches that published them. When available elsewhere, I have noted this in a brief annotation.

Book of Memories: In Celebration, 73rd Anniversary of the Friendship Baptist Church. Friendship Baptist Church, 1963.
> Obtained from private collection of Brenda Porter-Dewitt, by consent of Friendship Missionary Baptist Church.

Covenant Presbyterian Church: The First Fifty Years. Covenant Presbyterian Church, 1997.
> Obtained from collection of Covenant Presbyterian Church.

Crowe, John Marvin. *Biography of a Thriving Church: A History of First Baptist Church, Charlotte, NC, 1832–1952.* First Baptist Church, 1952.
> In collection at First Baptist Charlotte and at J. Murrey Atkins Library, University of North Carolina at Charlotte. Available online through Library Service Center, Duke University, https://tinyurl.com/2p9vjtjb.

Ellis, Marion Arthur. *By a Dream Possessed: Myers Park Baptist Church.* Myers Park Baptist Church, 1997.
> Obtained from collection at Myers Park Baptist Church.

Eppley, Frances Fielden. *The First Baptist Church of Charlotte: Its Heritage.* First Baptist Church, 1981.
> In collection at First Baptist Church and at J. Murrey Atkins Library, University of North Carolina at Charlotte.

First Baptist Church: A Century of Christian Witnessing: 1867–1967. First Baptist Church-West, 1967.
> This volume is written about the church now known as First Baptist Church-West. Available through Joyner Library, East Carolina University, and accessible online at https://tinyurl.com/mrxwvxmm.

The First Baptist Church in the City of Charlotte, North Carolina: January, 1937: A Handbook of the Church, Its People and Work. First Baptist Church, 1937.
> In collection at First Baptist Church and at J. Murrey Atkins Library, University of North Carolina at Charlotte.

Hidy, Ross F. *The Story of St. Mark's Square: How the Oldest Lutheran Congregation in California Helped Rebuild San Francisco.* Concord, CA: Lutheran Pioneer Press, 1997.

One Hundred Years of Working for Christ: The Centennial History of Friendship Missionary Baptist Church, 1890–1990. Friendship Missionary Baptist Church, 1990.
> Obtained from collection at Friendship Missionary Baptist Church.

Stickell, Lois. *200 Years in the Heart of Charlotte: A History of First Presbyterian Church.* First Presbyterian Church of Charlotte, 2021.
> Obtained from collection at First Presbyterian Church.

BOOKS AND ARTICLES

Akhmatova, Anna. *My Half Century: Selected Prose.* Edited by Ronald Meyer. Ann Arbor, MI: Ardis Publishers, 1992.

Ateek, Naim S. "A Palestinian Perspective: Biblical Perspectives on the Land." In *Voices from the Margin: Interpreting the Bible in the Third World*. 3rd ed., edited by R. S. Sugirtharajah. Maryknoll, NY: Orbis Books, 2006.

Baldwin, Davarian L. *In the Shadow of the Ivory Tower: How Universities Are Plundering Our Cities*. New York: Bold Type, 2021.

Baldwin, James. *The Cross of Redemption: Uncollected Writings*. Edited by Randall Kenan. New York: Vintage, 2010.

———. *The Fire Next Time*. New York: Vintage, 1993.

Ballon, Hilary, and Kenneth T. Jackson. *Robert Moses and the Modern City: The Transformation of New York*. New York: W. W. Norton, 2007.

Bantum, Brian. *The Death of Race: Building a New Christianity in a Racial World*. Minneapolis: Fortress, 2016.

Baptist, Edward E. *The Half Has Never Been Told: Slavery and the Making of American Capitalism*. New York: Basic Books, 2014.

Baradaran, Mehrsa. *The Color of Money: Black Banking and the Racial Wealth Gap*. Cambridge, MA: Belknap, 2017.

Barber II, Rev. Dr. William J., with Jonathan Wilson-Hartgrove. *The Third Reconstruction: How a Moral Movement Is Overcoming the Politics of Division and Fear*. Boston: Beacon, 2016.

Beckert, Sven. *Empire of Cotton: A Global History*. New York: Vintage, 2014.

Bedoya, Roberto. "Spatial Justice: Rasquachification, Race, and the City." Creative Time Reports, September 15, 2014. https://tinyurl.com/zrt74xrr.

Boswell, W. Benjamin. *Confronting Whiteness: A Spiritual Journey of Reflection, Conversation, and Transformation*. Nashville: Upper Room Books, 2022.

Brueggemann, Walter. *The Land: Place as Gift, Promise, and Challenge in Biblical Faith*. 2nd ed. Minneapolis: Fortress, 2002.

Brunson, James E., III. *Black Baseball: A Comprehensive Record of the Teams, Players, Managers, Owners, and Umpires*. Jefferson, NC: McFarland, 2019.

Cash, W. J. "Close View of a Calvinist Lhasa." *American Mercury*, April 1933.

Cashin, Sheryll. *White Space, Black Hood: Opportunity Hoarding and Segregation in the Age of Inequality*. Boston: Beacon, 2021.

Charles, Mark, and Soong-Chan Rah. *Unsettling Truths: The Ongoing, Dehumanizing Legacy of the Doctrine of Discovery*. Downers Grove, IL: InterVarsity, 2019.

Coffin, Alex. *Brookshire and Belk: Businessmen in City Hall*. Charlotte: University of North Carolina Press, 1985.

Coates, Ta-Nehisi. *We Were Eight Years in Power: An American Tragedy*. New York: One World, 2017.

Cone, James. *The Spirituals and the Blues: An Interpretation*. Maryknoll, NY: Orbis Books, 1992.

Crow, Jeffrey, and Robert Durden. *Maverick Republican in the Old North State: A Political Biography of Daniel L. Russell*. Baton Rouge: Louisiana State University Press, 1977.

Crummy, Ione. "The Subversion of Gleaning in Balzac's *Les Paysans* and in Millet's *Les Glaneuses*." *Neohelicon* XXVI (1999): 9–18.

Curtis, Jesse. *The Myth of Colorblind Christians: Evangelicals and White Supremacy in the Civil Rights Era*. New York: New York University Press, 2021.

Darity, William A., Jr., and A. Kirsten Mullen. *From Here to Equality: Reparations for Black Americans in the 21st Century*. Chapel Hill: University of North Carolina Press, 2020.

Davis, Ellen F. *Scripture, Culture, and Agriculture: An Agrarian Reading of the Bible*. New York: Cambridge University Press, 2009.

Day, David. *Conquest: How Societies Overwhelm Others*. Oxford: Oxford University Press, 2008.

Derrida, Jacques. *Specters of Marx*. New York: Routledge Classics, 1994.

Diamond, Andrew J. *Chicago on the Make: Power and Inequality in a Modern City*. Oakland: University of California Press, 2017.

Du Bois, W. E. B. *Darkwater: Voices from within the Veil*. New York: Harcourt, Brace and Howe, 1920.

Dupont, Carolyn Renee. *Mississippi Praying: Southern White Evangelicals and the Civil Rights Movement, 1945–1975*. New York: New York University Press, 2013.

Enns, Elaine, and Ched Myers. *Healing Haunted Histories: A Settler Discipleship of Decolonization*. Eugene, OR: Cascade Books, 2021.

Fleming, Crystal M. *How to Be Less Stupid about Race: On Racism, White Supremacy, and the Racial Divide*. Boston: Beacon, 2018.

Fratello, Bradley. "France Embraces Millet: The Intertwined Fates of *The Gleaners* and *The Angelus*." *Art Bulletin* 85, no. 4 (December 2003): 685–701.

Foner, Eric. *Reconstruction: America's Unfinished Revolution, 1863–1877*. Updated ed. New York: Harper Perennial, 2014.

Fullilove, Mindy. *Root Shock: How Tearing Up City Neighborhoods Hurts America, and What We Can Do about It*. New York: New Village, 2004.

Gaillard, Frye. *The Dream Long Deferred: The Landmark Struggle for Desegregation in Charlotte, NC*. 3rd ed. Columbia, SC: University of South Carolina Press, 2006.

Gelfand, Mark I. *A Nation of Cities: The Federal Government and Urban America, 1933–1965*. New York: Oxford University Press, 1975.

Gibson, Gordon D. *Southern Witness: Unitarians and Universalists in the Civil Rights Era*. Boston: Skinner House, 2015.

Gilmore, Glenda Elizabeth. *Gender and Jim Crow: Women and the Politics of White Supremacy in North Carolina 1896–1920*. Chapel Hill: University of North Carolina Press, 1996.

Gilmore, Ruth Wilson. *Abolition Geography: Essays towards Liberation*. New York: Verso, 2022.

Graff, Michael, and Nick Ochsner. *The Vote Collectors: The True Story of the Scamsters, Politicians, and Preachers behind the Nation's Greatest Electoral Fraud*. Chapel Hill: University of North Carolina Press, 2021.

Graham, Larry Kent. *Moral Injury: Restoring Wounded Souls*. Nashville: Abingdon, 2017.

Greenwood, Janette Thomas. *Bittersweet Legacy: The Black and White "Better Classes" in Charlotte, 1850–1910*. Chapel Hill: University of North Carolina Press, 1994.

Greer, Scott. *Urban Renewal and American Cities: The Dilemma of Democratic Intervention*. Indianapolis: Bobbs-Merrill, 1965.

Grundy, Pamela. *Legacy: Three Centuries of Black History in Charlotte, North Carolina*. Charlotte, NC: Nerve Media Productions, 2022.

Gordon, Avery. *Ghostly Matters: Haunting and the Sociological Imagination*. Minneapolis: University of Minnesota Press, 2008.

Gutierrez, Gustavo. *We Drink from Our Own Wells: The Spiritual Journey of a People*. 20th anniversary ed. Maryknoll, NY: Orbis Books, 2003.

Hanchett, Thomas W. *Sorting Out the New South City: Race, Class, and Urban Development in Charlotte, 1875–1975.* 2nd ed. Chapel Hill: University of North Carolina Press, 2020.

———. "US Tax Policy and the Shopping Center Boom of the 1950s and 1960s." *American Historical Review* 101 (October 1996): 1082–110.

Hartman, Saidiya. *Scenes of Subjection: Terror, Slavery, and Self-Making in Nineteenth-Century America.* Revised ed. New York: W. W. Norton, 2022.

———. "Venus in Two Acts." *Small Axe* 12, no. 2 (June 2008): 1–14.

Herzog, William R., II. *Parables as Subversive Speech: Jesus as Pedagogue of the Oppressed.* Louisville, KY: Westminster/John Knox, 1994.

Hirsch, Arnold R. *Making the Second Ghetto: Race and Housing in Chicago, 1940–1960.* Chicago: University of Chicago Press, 1998.

Hood, Walter, and Grace Mitchell Tada, eds. *Black Landscapes Matter.* Charlottesville: University of Virginia Press, 2020.

Hunt, James L. "Fusion of Republicans and Populists." In *The Encyclopedia of North Carolina*, edited by William S. Powell. Chapel Hill: University of North Carolina Press, 2006.

Jackson, Kenneth T. *Crabgrass Frontier: The Suburbanization of the United States.* New York: Oxford University Press, 1985.

———. "Race, Ethnicity, and Real Estate Appraisal: The Home Owners Loan Corporation and the Federal Housing Administration." *Journal of Urban History* 6, no. 4 (August 1980): 419–52.

Jacobs, Jane. *The Death and Life of Great American Cities.* New York: Vintage, 1992.

Jantzen, Matt R. *God, Race, and History: Liberating Providence.* Lanham, MD: Lexington Books, 2021.

Jennings, Willie James. *Acts. Belief: A Theological Commentary on the Bible.* Louisville, KY: Westminster John Knox, 2017.

———. *After Whiteness: An Education in Belonging.* Grand Rapids, MI: Eerdmans, 2020.

———. "Can White People Be Saved?: Reflections on the Relationship of Missions and Whiteness." In *Can "White" People Be Saved? Triangulating Race, Theology, and Mission*, edited by Love L. Sechrest, Johnny Ramirez-Johnson, and Amos Young. Downers Grove, IL: IVP Academic, 2018.

———. *The Christian Imagination: Theology and the Origins of Race.* New Haven, CT: Yale University Press, 2010.

———. "To Be a Christian Intellectual." *Fuller Magazine* 4 (2015), https://tinyurl .com/m8usy2hz.

Kelley, Robin D. G. *Freedom Dreams: The Black Radical Imagination.* Revised ed. Boston: Beacon, 2022.

Kendi, Ibram X. *How to Be an Antiracist.* New York: One World, 2019.

———. *Stamped from the Beginning: The Definitive History of Racist Ideas in America.* New York: Nation Books, 2016.

King, Martin Luther., Jr. *A Testament of Hope: The Essential Writings and Speeches of Martin Luther King, Jr.* Edited by James M. Washington. New York: HarperCollins, 1986.

Kistler, Nancy. "Rejoice." Unpublished paper, 1999. Used by permission.

Korver-Glenn, Elizabeth. *Race Brokers: Housing Markets and Segregation in 21st Century Urban America.* Oxford: Oxford University Press, 2021.

Krantz-Kent, Rachel. "Television, Capturing America's Attention at Prime Time and Beyond." *Beyond the Numbers* 7, no. 14 (September 2018). United States Bureau of Labor Statistics, https://www.bls.gov/opub/btn/volume-7/television-capturing-americas-attention.htm.

Kruse, Kevin M. *White Flight: Atlanta and the Making of Modern Conservatism.* Princeton, NJ: Princeton University Press, 2005.

Kwon, Duke L., and Gregory Thompson. *Reparations: A Christian Call for Repentance and Repair.* Grand Rapids, MI: Brazos, 2021.

Lacour, Greg. "Inside the West Side Community Land Trust's Fight against Gentrification." *Charlotte Magazine,* March 27, 2018. https://tinyurl.com/mphz252w.

Lassiter, Matthew D. *The Silent Majority: Suburban Politics in the Sunbelt South.* Princeton, NJ: Princeton University Press, 2006.

Leonard, Bill J. *God's Last and Only Hope: The Fragmentation of the Southern Baptist Convention.* Grand Rapids, MI: Eerdmans, 1990.

Lipsitz, George. *How Racism Takes Place.* Philadelphia: Temple University Press, 2011.

Love, Rose Leary. *Plum Thickets and Field Daisies.* Charlotte-Mecklenburg Library. Accessed May 15, 2023. https://tinyurl.com/2p9a3enc.

Madden, David, and Peter Marcuse. *In Defense of Housing.* New York: Verso, 2016.

Marsh, Charles. *God's Long Summer: Stories of Faith and Civil Rights.* Princeton, NJ: Princeton University Press, 1997.

McClintock Fulkerson, Mary, and Marcia W. Mount Shoop. *A Body Broken, a Body Betrayed: Race, Memory, and Eucharist in White-Dominant Churches.* Eugene, OR: Cascade Books, 2015.

McKinney, Gordon D. *Zeb Vance: North Carolina's Civil War Governor and Gilded Age Political Leader.* Chapel Hill: University of North Carolina Press, 2013.

McKittrick, Katherine. *Demonic Grounds: Black Women and the Cartographies of Struggle.* Minneapolis: University of Minnesota Press, 2006.

———. "Mathematics Black Life." *Black Scholar* 44, no. 2 (Summer 2014): 16–28.

———. "On Plantations, Prisons, and a Black Sense of Place." *Social and Cultural Geography* 12, no. 8 (December 2011): 947–63.

McShane, Charles Clifton. "Class, Christ and Cocktails: The Clash of Business Boosterism and Southern Baptism in Charlotte, North Carolina, 1965–1980." Master's thesis, University of North Carolina at Charlotte, 2011.

McShane, Chuck. "How Charlotte Got Liquored Up." *Charlotte Magazine,* October 24, 2017. https://tinyurl.com/cs9vy7yv.

Mills, Charles W. *The Racial Contract.* Ithaca, NY: Cornell University Press, 1997.

Milgrom, Jacob. *Numbers. The JPS Torah Commentary.* Philadelphia: Jewish Publication Society, 2003.

Morrison, Toni. *Beloved.* New York: Plume, 1997.

———. "Five Years of Terror: A Conversation with Miriam Horn." *US News and World Report,* October 19, 1987.

———. "Unspeakable Things Unspoken: The Afro-American Presence in American Literature." *Michigan Quarterly Review* 28, no. 1 (Winter 1989): 1–34.

Murphy, Alexandra R., Richard Rand, Brian T. Allen, James Ganz, and Alexis Goodin. *Jean-Francois Millet: Drawn Into the Light. An Exhibition Catalogue.* Williamstown, MA: Clark Art Institute, 1999.

Myers, Ched. *Binding the Strong Man: A Political Reading of Mark's Story of Jesus.* Maryknoll, NY: Orbis Books, 1988.

———. *Who Will Roll Away the Stone? Discipleship Queries for First World Christians.* Maryknoll, NY: Orbis Books, 1994.

Myles, Robert J., ed. *Class Struggle in the New Testament.* Lanham, MD: Lexington Books, 2019.

Pitkanen, Pekka. *A Commentary on Numbers: Narrative, Ritual, and Colonialism.* London: Routledge, 2018.

Rothman, Joshua D. *The Ledger and the Chain: How Domestic Slave Traders Shaped America.* New York: Basic Books, 2021.

Rothstein, Richard. *The Color of Law: The Forgotten History of How Our Government Segregated America.* New York: Liveright Publishing, 2017.

Ruttenberg, Danya. *On Repentance and Repair: Making Amends in an Unapologetic World.* Boston: Beacon, 2022.

Satter, Beryl. *Family Properties: Race, Real Estate, and the Exploitation of Black Urban America.* New York: Metropolitan Books, 2009.

Semuels, Alana. "Segregation Had to Be 'Invented.'" *Atlantic,* February 17, 2017.

Sugirtharajah, R. S., ed. *Voices from the Margin: Interpreting the Bible in the Third World.* 3rd ed. Maryknoll, NY: Orbis Books, 2006.

Sullivan, Shannon. *Revealing Whiteness: The Unconscious Habits of Racial Privilege.* Bloomington: Indiana University, 2006.

Táíwò, Olúfẹ́mi O. *Reconsidering Reparations.* New York: Oxford University Press, 2022.

Taylor, Keeanga-Yamahtta. *Race for Profit: How Banks and the Real Estate Industry Undermined Black Homeownership.* Chapel Hill: University of North Carolina Press, 2019.

Tinker, George. *Missionary Conquest: The Gospel and Native American Cultural Genocide.* Minneapolis: Fortress, 1993.

Tisby, Jemar. *The Color of Compromise: The Truth about the American Church's Complicity in Racism.* Grand Rapids, MI: Zondervan, 2019.

Trelease, Allen W. "Reconstruction." In *The Encyclopedia of North Carolina,* edited by William S. Powell. Chapel Hill: University of North Carolina Press, 2006.

Tuck, Eve, and C. Ree. "A Glossary of Haunting." In *Handbook of Autoethnography,* edited by Stacy Holman Jones, Tony E. Adams, and Carolyn Ellis, 639–58. Philadelphia: Routledge, 2018.

Tuck, Eve, and K. Wayne Yang. "Decolonization Is Not a Metaphor." *Decolonization* 1, no. 1 (2012): 1–40.

Ture, Norman B. *Accelerated Depreciation in the United States, 1954–1960.* New York: National Bureau of Economic Research, 1967.

Walker-Barnes, Chanequa. *I Bring the Voices of My People: A Womanist Vision for Racial Reconciliation.* Grand Rapids, MI: Eerdmans, 2019.

Weare, Walter B. *Black Business in the New South: A Social History of the North Carolina Mutual Life Insurance Company.* Urbana: University of Illinois Press, 1973.

Wild, Mark. "Liberal Protestants and Urban Renewal." *Religion and American Culture: A Journal of Interpretation* 25, no. 1 (Winter 2015): 110–46.

———. *Renewal: Liberal Protestants and the American City after World War II.* Chicago: University of Chicago Press, 2019.

Williams, Delores. *Sisters in the Wilderness: The Challenge of Womanist God-Talk.* Maryknoll, NY: Orbis Books, 1993.

Winter, Gibson. *The Suburban Captivity of the Churches: An Analysis of Protestant Responsibility in the Expanding Metropolis*. New York: Doubleday, 1961.

Yancy, George. "Robin D. G. Kelley: The Tulsa Race Massacre Went Way Beyond 'Black Wall Street.'" *Truthout*, June 1, 2021. https://tinyurl.com/mt4389m8.

Younger, George D. *The Church and Urban Renewal*. New York: J. B. Lippincott, 1965.

Zucchino, David. *Wilmington's Lie: The Murderous Coup of 1898 and the Rise of White Supremacy*. New York: Atlantic Monthly, 2020.

Index of Subjects and Names

Alexander, Fred, 86–87
Alexander, Kelly, 61, 75–76

Bailey, Allen, 55, 68, 111, 119, 176
Baptist General Convention of Texas, 144
baseball, 20, 25
Bates, Carl E.
  pastoral leadership of, 65, 77–78,
    105–12, 117–26, 130–39, 148,
    151–54, 168–70, 182
  personal history, 70–72
Baylor University, 71, 144
Beulah Baptist Church, 21–24, 27–29, 121
blockbusting, 159, 197
Boulware, Henry, 35
Broach, Claude, 145
Brooklyn neighborhood. *See also* Second
  Ward
  Black life in, 1–14, 46, 51–52, 59
  current development and status,
    195–96
  early development of, 38–41
  memory of at First Baptist, 174,
    179–84
  Urban Renewal, 73–80, 87, 90, 92, 96,
    99, 102–6, 112–14, 127–32, 137–41,
    146, 149–50, 154, 159, 161–69
Brookshire, B. Brevard, 159
Brookshire, Stanford R.
  chamber of commerce president,
    74–75
  mayoralty of, 85–89, 99–101, 115, 133,
    145, 151, 159
Brown v. Board of Education, 64

Campbell, Ivy, 4
Campbell, Richard, 4
Catawba people, 18, 137, 166, 203
Charlotte Chamber of Commerce,
  73–74, 85
Charlotte City Council, 73–74, 81,
  102, 148
Charlotte Redevelopment Commission
  initial commission, 61–63
  second commission, 11–13, 73–83,
    86–89, 92, 98–99, 106, 115, 128–33,
    139–40, 147–48, 176
Citizens' Committee on Urban Renewal,
  86–102
Clinton Chapel AME Zion Church, 26,
  31–33, 46, 159, 196
Community Land Trusts, 198–99,
  204–5
Covenant Presbyterian Church,
  146–47, 176
Cunningham, J. C., 32

Democratic Party, 25, 32–38
Dilworth Methodist Church, 97, 99
Dilworth neighborhood, 90, 97, 102,
  145–46
Dilworth Rotary Club, 90–92, 96, 98
Dilworth–Wilmore Association, 87–88,
  97, 100
Doctrine of Discovery, 84, 108, 130,
  138–39

Enderly Park neighborhood, 111,
  195–97, 204

Federal Housing Administration (FHA), 44–496, 56, 104
First Baptist Church. *See also* Beulah Baptist Church; Tryon Street Baptist Church
  cultural and theological resources within, 168–70
  current status, 193–7, 207
  discussion of moves, 101, 104–13, 115–48
  early development, 21–24, 36–37
  growth under C. C. Warren, 53–56, 63, 68–69
  memory of Brooklyn at, 173–75, 180–87
  placement in cityscape, 1–15
  possible repair and repentance, 160–65
  under pastor Carl Bates, 70–71, 76–77
First Baptist Church—West, 24, 113
First Union National Bank, 13, 54–55, 129–33, 138
First Ward neighborhood, 102, 113, 145
Friendship Baptist Church
  Brooklyn location, 51–53
  displacement, 78–81
  relocation of, 113–16, 131, 139–40
Fusion Movement, 33–38
Future Program Committee
  appointment, 68
  early planning, 72, 76–78
  final planning, 127–29, 131, 134
  recommendations, 105–10

Garner-Mullins, Janet, 167
Gleaners, The, 47–49
gleaning, 47–49
Grace AME Zion Church, 40
Great Depression, 42, 60, 111, 123
Greenville neighborhood, 8–10, 89, 102, 145
Grier, Arthur S., 86–87

Harrell, William, 143–44
hauntings, 5–8, 13, 49–50, 129, 136, 149–50, 157, 164, 174–75, 182, 186–90, 193–207

Hildebrandt, Richard E., 95–102, 145, 163–65, 182, 188
Hope, C. C., 53–55, 68, 77, 105–7, 117–24, 127–30, 134–36, 140, 148–49, 154, 176
Homeowner's Loan Corporation, 43–46, 56, 82
Housing Act of 1949, 57
Housing Act of 1954, 85

Johnson C. Smith University, 155–59
Johnson, Jan, 173–74, 179, 184–85

Kennedy, Francis Milton, 17–18
Kerry, Coleman, Jr., 51–53, 79–81, 113–15, 140–41
King, Martin Luther, Jr., 49, 93, 126
King, Raymond E., 8–10, 163, 170
Kinney, Lee, 82–83, 162

Marney, Carlyle, 95, 100–101, 182, 188
McClernon, Robert, 93–95
McColl, Hugh, 176–77
McNeill, Medd F., 88–102, 165, 188
Mecklenburg Baptist Association, 118, 146–48
Millet, Jean-Francois, 47–49
Monroe, Marvette, 185
moral injury, 200–201
Mullins, E. Y., 37
Myers Park Baptist Church, 88, 92–95, 100–101, 165
Myers Park neighborhood, 103–4, 111, 121
Myers Street Graded School, 38–39

National Association for the Advancement of Colored People (NAACP), 60–61, 75, 85, 93, 132
NC Mutual Insurance Co., 38–39, 58
New Deal, 42–43, 60, 82–83
North, Abram, 15–26, 31–42, 46–49, 154–58, 161, 163, 179, 185, 196–97, 206–7
North, Annice Carson, 25–6, 31–42, 46–49, 149, 154–55, 161–63, 179, 196, 206–7

North Carolina General Assembly, 62–63, 73
North, Regina, 155–58, 163–64
North, Tiffany, 155–56
Northwest Expressway, 140–58

Obenshain, Wiley, 131

Palmer's Alley, 62, 73
Pinewood Cemetery, 42, 47, 206–7
Poe, Bill, 55, 68, 102–4, 110–12, 117–24, 134, 144, 150, 154, 163, 176
providence (doctrine of), 107–9, 120–26, 139, 141, 152, 175, 179

Reconstruction, 1, 18–19, 26–29
redlining, 44–45, 82, 197
Religious Affiliates, 146–47
Renewalists, 94–95
Republican Party, 25, 32–35
Reule, David, 177, 183
Rouzer, Elmer, 93

Sawyer, Vernon, 72–73, 78–83, 88, 113–15, 128, 133, 139, 145, 196
Schaller, Lyle, 93–934
Schenk, John, 26
Second Presbyterian Church, 78
Second Ward neighborhood, 31–38, 113, 128, 147, 159, 181, 196, 207. *See also* Brooklyn
Shaw, Victor, 61
silencing spirit, 5–15, 91, 136, 171–72, 189–92, 194, 200–206
Sixteenth Street Baptist Church, 115
Smith, Benjamin Rush, 27, 42
Smith, Samuel P., 15, 20–24, 27, 29
Smith, W. J., 12–13, 55, 68, 107, 117, 129, 148, 176–77
Southern Baptist Convention, 54, 63–72, 90, 100, 121, 143–44, 148, 196–97
Southern Baptist Theological Seminary, 170
Springs, Bessie North, 39, 40, 157
St. John's Baptist Church, 145

St. Louis University, 144
St. Mark's Lutheran Church (Charlotte), 78
St. Mark's Lutheran Church (San Francisco), 144
Strawn, Zeb, 87–88, 99–100
suburbanization, 56–57, 77, 104, 109, 114, 117–26, 154, 173

Third Ward neighborhood, 20, 26, 31, 36, 96, 102, 113, 145, 167
Tillman, Benjamin, 35
Trinity Presbyterian Church, 9
Tryon Street, 23, 25, 27, 29, 35–36, 41, 104, 121, 132
Tryon Street Baptist Church, 27–28

Uptown Farmers' Market, 173–74, 183–85, 190
Urban Redevelopment Administration, 58–59, 62, 72–73, 85–88
urban renewal
    in Charlotte, 7–9, 11–17, 42, 55–63, 72–76, 80–102, 144–54
    financial legacy of, 159–67
    and gentrification, 195–202
    theology of, 167–72
    around United States, 132–33, 143–44

Vance, Zebulon, 23

Warren, Casper Carl, 54–57, 63–72, 107, 110, 125, 148, 154, 182
Washington Heights neighborhood, 40, 158
Waters, Martin, 74, 82
Weddington, J. H., 34
Welch, Robert, 178–81, 185–86, 190
West Side Community Land Trust, 198–99, 204–5
Western Addition, San Francisco, 144
Williams, Brandi North, 156–57, 165, 189
Wilmington, North Carolina, 36
Wilmore Presbyterian Church, 97, 100, 165
Wright, Reynard, 1–10, 196